MANAGING RELATIONSHIPS IN A CORPORATE BANK

Chris Farrance
MBA FCIM MCIM

The Royal Bank of Scotland

The Applied Diploma in Corporate Banking was developed in association with The Royal Bank of Scotland.

Financial World Publishing
IFS House
4–9 Burgate Lane
Canterbury
Kent
CT1 2XJ
United Kingdom

T   01227 812012
F   01227 479641
E   editorial@ifslearning.com
W   www.ifslearning.com

Financial World Publications are published by The Chartered Institute of Bankers, a non-profit making registered educational charity.

Typeset by John Smith

Printed by Ashford Colour Press Ltd.

© Chartered Institute of Bankers 2002

ISBN 0-85297-683-6

CONTENTS

		Page
1	The Importance of Managing Relationships	1
2	CRM and Technology	17
3	Business, Marketing and Portfolio Planning	27
4	Best Business Practice	51
5	Delivering Corporate Capabilities	59
6	Viewing the Organization	73
7	Portfolio Planning	87
8	Key Account Planning	103
9	Building Referral Networks and Cold Calling	113
10	Industry and Customer Profiling	123
11	Organizational Buyer Behaviour and the Decision-Making Unit	139
12	Relationship Building Activity and Communications Strategy	151
13	Creating a Professional Image	165
14	Presentation Skills	187
15	Presenting Customer-Focused Solutions	199
16	Working in Teams	225
17	Managing and Motivating Teams and Team Members	245
18	Recruitment, Training and Performance Management	257
19	The Way Forward	279
	Appendix	283
	Bibliography	291
	Index	295

1

THE IMPORTANCE OF
MANAGING RELATIONSHIPS

1.1 Overview

In this chapter we explore the drivers and economics of CRM, the relationship component and the quest for competitive advantage and differentiation. We also take a look at services marketing.

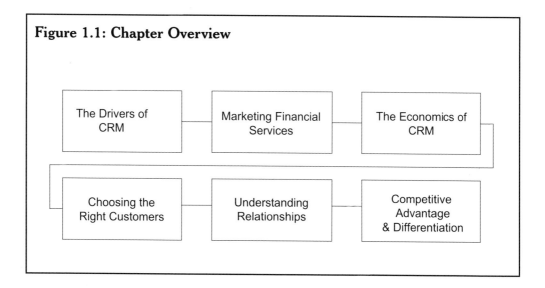

Figure 1.1: Chapter Overview

- The Drivers of CRM
- Marketing Financial Services
- The Economics of CRM
- Choosing the Right Customers
- Understanding Relationships
- Competitive Advantage & Differentiation

1.2 The Drivers of CRM

The Marketplace

Global warming seems to be adding another level of variability – or richness if you prefer – to climatic conditions the world over. So it is with the markets in which today's companies operate. There is no steady state, but increasing flux, more high winds, storms and floods with few English or even Indian summers. In short, more unpredictable risk than potential reward.

Sometimes, as a result of this, companies take on a siege mentality, batten down the hatches and become insular. The customer sometimes gets lost but as Peter Drucker reminds us:

> 'There is only one valid definition of business purpose: to create a customer. It is the customer who determines what a business is. What the business thinks it produces is not of the first importance – especially not to the future of the business and its success. What the customer thinks he is buying and considers 'value' is decisive – it determines what a business is, what it produces and whether it will prosper.'

Among the broader environmental issues that banks and their customers face in these times are:

- rising stakeholder expectations (such as customers, staff, shareholders and the community);

- industry consolidation both inside and outside of banking;

- the shift of power from bank to customer as a result of easier access to information and knowledge;

- increasing competition as traditional markets, margins and business models come under threat from increasing transparency (the ability of the customer to see how you make your profit);

- the changing profile of earnings towards fee income as corporate customers borrow less and disintermediate the banks;

- the management of risk in an increasingly volatile marketplace;

- the risks and costs of staying on the technology curve;

- the trend towards networking and partnering by both banks and customers to deliver products and services underpinned by technology: eg outsourcing, just-in-time delivery, multi-partner service delivery;

- developing staff to operate in an environment of increasingly extensive regulation.

These challenges place a premium on clear thinking and leadership within all companies. It also places a premium on the ability to continuously refine, re-define and re-invent – to develop an organizational flexibility that is capable of continuous change and improvement. Not the least it places a premium on those who are at the point of interface between bank and customer – the relationship managers.

Banks have, therefore, been forced to re-evaluate the way they do business.

Figure 1.2: Banks: A Change of Style

- Old
  - ➤ emphasis on traditional banking skills
  - ➤ authority determined by grade and function
  - ➤ hierarchical & functionally based structures
  - ➤ multiple interfaces, several points of relationship management
  - ➤ primary measurement and management by channel and/or product

- New
  - ➤ marketing led, emphasis on relationship management & branding skills
  - ➤ differential pricing based on value of customer to organization
  - ➤ delegation of decision making to front line
  - ➤ flexible team-based organizational structures
  - ➤ multiple customer interfaces, single point of customer relationship management
  - ➤ primary profit measurement and management by customer and customer segment

Banks: A Change of Style
Source KPMG Report 1997

The Strategic Imperative

Successful banks today are those that have a very clear understanding of what they are, what they can do and those customers they want to attract and serve. Gone are the days when companies can afford to be all things to all men. This concept of strategic intent is an important one because it provides the benchmark against which all activities should be assessed. It's important to remember that this focus needs to be sufficiently flexible to respond to changing market conditions and customer needs, not to mention severe national and international external shocks such as changes of government, exchange rate movements, the oil crises and the attack on the World Trade Centre on September 11.

Increasingly companies today are focusing around the trilogy of customer intimacy, product leadership and operational excellence.

Classically companies are encouraged to focus on one of these three areas as a source of competitive advantage. The risk in not doing so, as Michael Porter describes it, is to be 'stuck in the middle'. Customer intimacy goes straight to the heart of CRM. In corporate banking product leadership (or at least parity) is a prerequisite and all banks continually look to reduce their fixed infrastructure and variable operating costs.

An important point is that banks are able to exercise choice about the markets and customers they serve and the product array that supports this activity. Some banks have

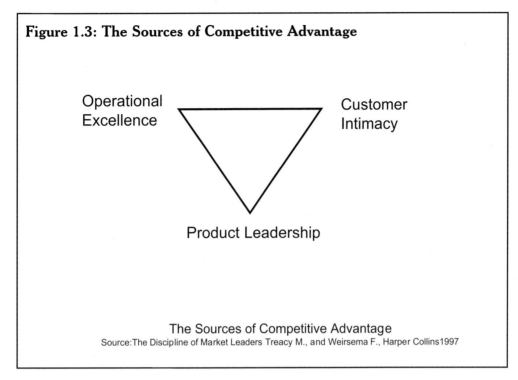

Figure 1.3: The Sources of Competitive Advantage

Operational Excellence

Customer Intimacy

Product Leadership

The Sources of Competitive Advantage
Source:The Discipline of Market Leaders Treacy M., and Weirsema F., Harper Collins1997

decided that there are areas of business they will not compete in, be it corporate, investment or global banking. In doing so, they will have been guided by shareholder and economic value principles. These decisions are particularly difficult for established players shaped by history and tradition. New entrants such as First Direct and the Internet banks do not have this cultural baggage or the typically high fixed costs of universal banks and are, therefore, able to cherry pick the markets and customers they target.

1.3 Marketing Financial Services

The marketing of services has always been regarded as more difficult than, for example, cars, electrical goods or the vast array of products commonly seen today on supermarket shelves. This is because they have a number of characteristics that make them different:

Intangibility:

A service cannot be seen, touched or displayed. A customer may purchase a service but typically has nothing physical to display as a result of that purchase, eg a forward exchange contract.

Inseparability:

Delivery and consumption of the service occur at the same time whereas tangible goods have a cycle of production, delivery and consumption, eg a meal at a restaurant.

Heterogeneity:

Many service providers face the difficulty of maintaining consistency in delivery. Typically this is because people are involved and programming complete consistency needs robots. There is of course a continuum here from, say, McDonalds at one end to a barrister at the other.

Perishability:

It is not possible to store services. Additionally since the 'manufacturing' capacity is the staff, matching resource levels to meet variable customer demand levels is an additional challenge, eg public transport during the rush hour.

Table 1.1 Distinguishing Services

Distinguishing services
1. Services are transient – they are 'consumed' then and there. They have no lasting material being and may leave only memories or promises.
2. Services are mainly represented by people – they cannot be separated from the person of the provider, whose personal characteristics are 'on show' to the consumer and indeed form an important part of consumer perception.
3. Services are only finally selected face to face with the consumer and at the time of consumption. They are perishable – generally you cannot have a production run and store services against future demand.
4. Services are, therefore, essentially a series of 'one off' production runs. It is difficult to achieve standardization or exercise the same controls over production you would with a product, for example, through quality controls.
5. This production/consumption process goes on, for the most part, unsupervised and depends on the individual reactions of the provider for success.
6. The process is also open to influence from the consumer, not just in some indirect way, as through research or even the exercise of choice, but directly since they participate in and help make the final product. Indeed, in some cases – as, for example, in a restaurant or bar, the customer may actually be the key ingredient in success; it is they rather than the food or drink, who are the attraction to others.
7. As a result of the previous six points, it is the culture in which these acts are performed which mostly conditions perceptions of service and this culture is internal and external. It is about the way we work and the way we manage.

Irons K., *Managing Services Companies, Strategies for Success*, Economic Intelligence Unit, 1994

Financial services marketing has another overlay of features such as risk, complexity and information levels. The term 'confusion marketing' comes to mind, with many suppliers still cloaking their product offerings in a fog of detail and legal jargon. This creates a perception of power in the hands of the supplier that is increasingly being undermined as access to information and product comparability improves. In any market, exercising this supplier power is dangerous, in the corporate market where the balance of power may in fact lie with the customer, the risks are self-evident.

Note that one of the key success factors for successful delivery in a services company is culture, and we shall return to this later.

1.4 The Economics of CRM

In essence the marketing and sales activities of companies have two main objectives. These are to attract or recruit new customers and to retain existing customers – more specifically those that are of value to the organization. If we consider a company's activities in this way, then some interesting economics emerge. The conventional wisdom is that it is fifteen times more expensive to recruit a new customer than to sell to an existing customer – so there is a strong economic argument for retaining existing customers.

A number of other benefits accrue:

- Existing customers are typically more responsive to the offers you make to them – they have in a sense already bought the brand;

- Existing customers give you a warm prospect base for cross-selling and up-selling your products;

- There is a strong positive correlation between the number of products a customer holds and levels of satisfaction and loyalty;

- The more products a customer has, the less likely they are to defect to a competitor;

- The longer a customer is with you the more likely they are to provide you with information – this helps to target product offers better;

- There is over time an opportunity – by understanding how the customer prefers to buy from you – to re-shape your delivery costs, particularly if you can migrate your customers to lower cost channels;

- If customers stay with you, all things being equal they are more likely to recommend you – thus reducing recruitment costs;

- Studies point to a correlation between customer retention and staff retention – the outcome is improved staff morale;

- Companies that understand the economics of retention typically invest in early warning processes and defined recovery processes for defecting customers;

- Newly recruited customers may be serially dissatisfied with banks in general and therefore increase servicing costs.

The challenge then is to position yourself as the preferred supplier for your customers. One of the difficulties with financial products is predicting when customers might need them. Being a preferred supplier means your company is top of the list and you get a chance to pitch for the new business.

Frequently, pressures to deliver short-term results to satisfy the financial markets and shareholders, are blamed for a 'pile it high, sell it cheap mentality'. Many mortgage providers overtly buy volume with short-run highly discounted offers. This retention focus tends to take companies away from the corporate totem pole of market share and towards a philosophy of improving 'share of wallet'. This means getting more of the aggregate total that the customer spends in a particular category of goods and services. As result, levels of customer retention may well be a better indicator of company performance than bottom-line performance.

At its heart is a different philosophy about the way you do business, which can be summarized as follows:

Table 1.2 Transactional v Relationship Banking

Transactional Banking	Relationship Banking
Single-sale focus	Customer-retention focus
Product-feature focus	Product-benefit focus
Short timescale	Long timescale
Little customer service	High customer service
Driven contact	Contact levels agreed with customers
Quality comes from production	Quality comes from people
Transaction source of profit	Lifetime revenue
One-way product knowledge	Two way interpersonal skills
Sufficiency of product	Trust
Marketing = selling	Marketing = harnessing the corporate capabilities for the benefit of the customer

It might seem that these two broad streams of activity are mutually exclusive, but as we shall see later some customers will want only transactional relationship. The issue is not what you do but how you do it – any transactional activity must sit within an overarching strategy that puts the customer first.

1.5 Choosing the Right Customers

So, companies cannot be all things to all men – they have to focus their capabilities on those customers that they wish to serve.

These questions are, of course, rhetorical although some companies may have as an objective market share as opposed to the quality and relative profitability of existing business. This is described as 'growing the top line', whereas a focus on profitability is described as 'growing the bottom line' From a purely commercial perspective, the criteria for the customers they wish to serve are pretty straightforward – those who are profitable now together with those who have the potential to be profitable in the future.

Many companies have therefore harnessed the tools of database analysis to sort their customers by levels of profitability. This is based on both today's profitability – as a defensive move to protect current income levels – and the income streams that may come in the future. Here the concept of 'lifetime value' surfaces. This predicts a revenue stream based on the predicted buying behaviour of the customer – this can be valued at today's prices by using discounted cashflow techniques. Again database analyses can shape the thinking here and these hypotheses can be matched to the actual behaviour over time.

This then leads to the concept of portfolio management – segregating customers by levels of relative profitability as a basis for directing the marketing, sales and overall resource commitment of the organization, bearing in mind that by their very nature resources are both costly and finite. Portfolio management can be applied to customers, markets, industry sector, geographical coverage, and so on.

Applying Pareto's rule to customer profitability would suggest that 80% of the income comes from 20% of the customers. In banking the relationship is often more stark than that – say

---

Figure 1.4: Who are the Right Customers?

Who are the 'right' customers?

- Is it satisfaction?
- Is it usage frequency?
- Is it multiple product holding?
- Is it new business?
- Is it the switchers?
- Is it the high borrowers?
- Is it those who generate the highest gross income?

95% of the profit coming from 5% of the customers – these would be your Tier 1 customers.

It is frequently said that the past is no reliable guide to the future. So, in today's competitive environment, the concept of lifetime value might be somewhat idealistic and it would be dangerous to rely on it totally. Nonetheless it does offer a basis on which to think about customer profitability and underpins the need to focus on customer retention. Clearly the longer profitable customers stay with you, the greater the aggregate profitability.

This approach will be developed later. For the moment though, a word of warning. Some of the language used to describe these customer segments is often not attractive and is demeaning to clients – it should be avoided.

The focus on profitability inevitably leads to a discussion about what to do with customers who are unprofitable. By its very nature this is a sensitive issue. Firstly, you avoid recruiting them! Then you consider with varying levels of pro-activity migrating them to lower-cost delivery channels or as a last resort pricing them away or making the terms and conditions under which you will do business so onerous that they go of their own accord. These activities are an integral part of a CRM strategy.

1.6 Understanding Relationships

Let us look for a moment at what we mean by relationships in the context of CRM.

Talk about relationships and indeed loyalty is quite emotive – probably even more so in financial services where there is a palpable sense of incongruity. Clearly the notion of a close personal relationship in a personal context is not what we are talking about. But we are talking about something that over time and with increasing trust can move beyond just simple buying and selling.

It all lies in the eyes of the beholder – the customer and companies would do well to remember this. You do not own the relationship with the customer, the customer does. Do customers want a relationship with their bank or do they just want them to do their job properly? At its most basic the likelihood is that there may be a pattern of purchases over time, some repeat, some new. But there is a more fundamental issue here. Is continued buying over time really an indicator of loyalty and a deeper relationship or is it just a pattern of behaviour and no more than that?

In all probability if asked customers might perceive themselves to be somewhere along a continuum from no relationship to a perceived deep relationship and no loyalty to rock steady loyalty with differing levels of warmth. Some will be content to position their relationship manager as an 'order-taker' and use self-service as much as possible.

This is more akin to a transaction-based model. Some may feel that the relationship goes beyond the purely functional to a higher order of trust and empathy. This might be shown as follows:

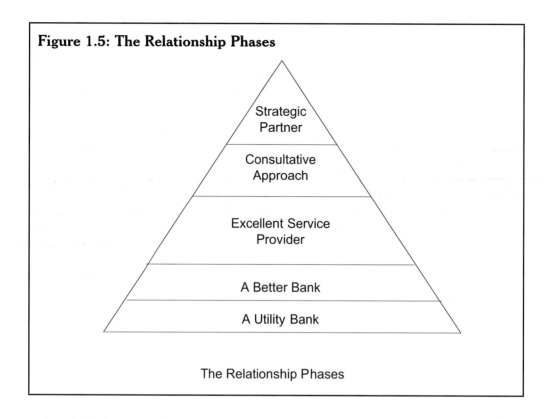

Figure 1.5: The Relationship Phases

The Relationship Phases

Among the critical success factors of relationship quality are delivering superior high value, understanding the WIIFM factor (What's In It For Me) and trust and confidence. The latter help to reduce risk and uncertainty. Customers will think, for example, that the relationship manager is on their side, not just an employee of the company. This can put stress on the relationship manager – we shall look at this again in a later chapter.

Remember, any investment of resource in getting closer to the customers is worthwhile only if the customer is responsive and today or tomorrow's value justifies it. It has to be recognized that quite simply customers may be unwilling to interact in a way the bank is prepared to respond to. For those customers who are responsive and appropriately profitable, the goal is an interactive long-term participative relationship. Remember too that the customer has a need to stay competitive and profitable also.

Relationship management has an internal dimension also because most banks have specialists in the corporate banking arena to support the relationship managers. Customers will expect their relationship manager to be able to mobilize the whole resources of the bank if necessary to help to solve their problems.

1.7 Competitive Advantage and Differentiation

At the heart of any marketing strategy is the challenge of making customers want to buy from you. This powerful and compelling reason to buy is called competitive advantage – why customers come to you rather than go to your competitors. The aim of any company is to be the automatic choice for that product or service category but, failing that, to be on the mental list of potential suppliers the customer will have. If the relationship is good, then your expectation would be that the customer would come to you before going to anyone else.

Creating this advantage once is not enough. To be successful companies must do this on a rolling basis. If this happens – and for as long as it continues to happen – it is called a sustainable competitive advantage. In practice it is rather like the Tour de France where a breakout rider is gradually hauled back into the ranks by the peleton. There are business risks if heavy investment is made in an area that is not valued or quickly overtaken by further developments – think of the recent technology, telecommunications and dot.com bubble and the huge sums paid for 3G licences.

In a mature, well-supplied and highly competitive market such as corporate banking, sustainable competitive advantage is difficult. But in all cases the starting point for an understanding of competitive advantage must be an understanding of customers' needs compared with what your competitors are currently offering and what you understand their business development strategies to be.

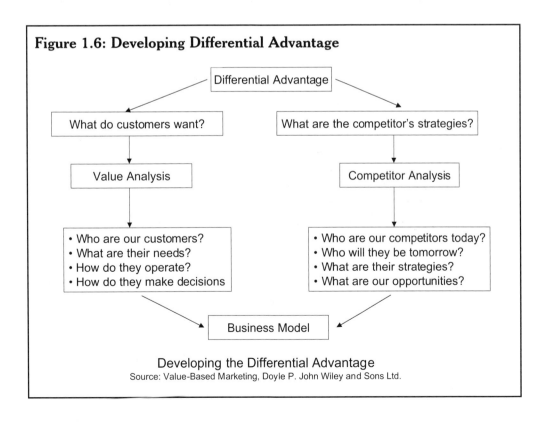

Figure 1.6: Developing Differential Advantage

Developing the Differential Advantage
Source: Value-Based Marketing, Doyle P. John Wiley and Sons Ltd.

The strength of companies that have a competitive advantage of this nature is that – all things being equal – they will be able to charge a price premium for this perceived added value they offer. Note that the orthodox view is that competing on price alone is rarely a sustainable strategy because it can be easily matched in the short term by competitors and often just results in lower margins across the industry – free current account banking was a classic example. Pricing benefits usually accrue to new entrants, niche operators or new start-ups such as First Direct that do not have the high fixed cost base that afflict existing banks.

Rarely is competitive advantage likely to be one single element of a product or service – more often it is a cocktail of attributes. In a service industry such as banking, the good news for relationship managers is that increasingly it is people who make the difference – hence the emphasis on developing relationship managers!

Table 1.3 Advantages within the Organization

Advantages within the Organization

Economies of scope – Internal synergies – Flexibility – Speed of response

---

Functional Advantages

Production	**R&D**	**Marketing**
• Process technology	• Product technology	• New product development
• Production efficiency	• Patents	• Brand
• Scale economies		• Pricing
• Experience		• Salesforce
• Product quality		• Customer knowledge
		• Service range
		• Customer access channels

Advantages from External Relationships

Customer Loyalty – Access to Financial Resources – Intermediaries – Extended Networks

---

Adapted from *Sources of Competitive Advantage The Marketing Book* Michael J Baker Butterworth Heineman 1997

The key issue is the one of understanding from a customer's perspective what he or she values – 'the value proposition' as it is called. This value can come from a range of rational and emotional factors. Rational factors for a mid-market corporate, for example, might range from speed in extending facilities to ease of parking, the emotional that the relationship manager remembered the football team he/she supported.

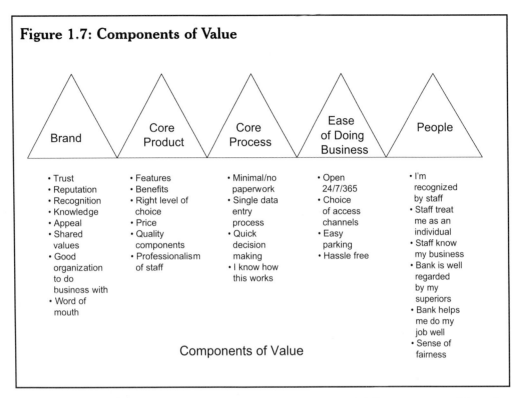

Figure 1.7: Components of Value

Brand	Core Product	Core Process	Ease of Doing Business	People
• Trust • Reputation • Recognition • Knowledge • Appeal • Shared values • Good organization to do business with • Word of mouth	• Features • Benefits • Right level of choice • Price • Quality components • Professionalism of staff	• Minimal/no paperwork • Single data entry process • Quick decision making • I know how this works	• Open 24/7/365 • Choice of access channels • Easy parking • Hassle free	• I'm recognized by staff • Staff treat me as an individual • Staff know my business • Bank is well regarded by my superiors • Bank helps me do my job well • Sense of fairness

Components of Value

The company's brand is often seen as a critical component of differentiation and has also the capability to meet a number of rational and emotional needs. Successful brands are significant assets and usually the result of sustained investment over time. This is exemplified in the goodwill that is paid over and above the value of the tangible assets by acquiring companies.

A common mistake is to think of this customer buying process from an organization's perspective – that is to say looking out from inside the company rather into the company from the customer's perspective and in terms of product features rather than benefits that will satisfy the customer's needs. We shall return to this in a later chapter. Being capable of seeing things from the customer's perspective is a hallmark of successful relationship managers. Remember also that there will be explicit and inexplicit costs to the customer – the latter would include the time it takes them to complete the buying process, the ease or otherwise of doing business with you and perceptions of risk and uncertainty.

The purpose of this activity is to be able to charge a price premium for your product or service. Without any form of differentiation your product becomes what is called a 'commodity' with no differentiating features. As such you will be able to recover no more than the prevailing price in the marketplace.

A number of points are worth mentioning here.

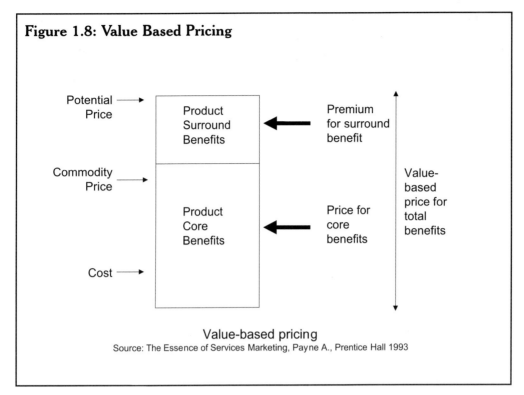

Figure 1.8: Value Based Pricing

Value-based pricing

Source: The Essence of Services Marketing, Payne A., Prentice Hall 1993

Firstly one of the potential outcomes of commodity pricing is a price war, which is generally to be avoided unless you are the lowest cost producer and can weather the storm.

Secondly, because you are the lowest cost producer does not mean that you have to charge the lowest prices – you can just profit from the higher margins.

Thirdly, there need not be any rational relationship between cost and price, the issue is what the consumer is prepared to pay based on his or her perception of value – the pricing of aspirational brands and ticket touts are examples.

Lastly, it is very difficult using conventional market research to get a handle on what customers are prepared to pay, so a good deal of judgement is necessary.

Fully understanding your competitor's offering is a key input into defining your own competitive positioning and the source of your competitive advantage. Many companies do this by a process known as benchmarking – comparing the quality of your total market, offering the brand attributes, the product, the processes and the service bundle including your people with the best in the market. Note that best in the market extends beyond best in the industry. Customers draw on a whole range of experiences in assessing the performance of their bank so that it is imperative to take a wider perspective than just the industry.

Some companies have mixed views about benchmarking – how can you be the best if you are just copying the competitors? There is some validity in this but it is rather like the comedian's line 'It's the way that I tell 'em'. The challenge is to take the best of breed from a range of diverse sources and blend them together in a way that optimizes the capabilities of your organization to form a unique and differential advantage.

2
CRM AND TECHNOLOGY

2.1 Overview

Here we take a look at the history of CRM and its development from a number of standalone systems to an integrated enterprise-wide application.

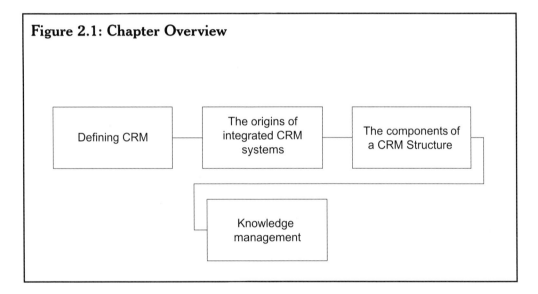

Figure 2.1: Chapter Overview

2.2 Defining CRM

Definitions abound and they are usually shaped by the nature of the supplier who is trying to sell to your company! Such suppliers may be offering IT software, database analysis tools, call centre management, sales force automation and a whole host of other services. We shall look at these components in more detail later.

For the time being let us settle on a definition of CRM along the following lines:

'CRM is the bringing together of every part of business that touches the customer – marketing, sales, customer service, all channels such as branches, the telephone, Internet and your bank brand – through the integration of people, processes and technology. It links customers, your work colleagues and the third parties you yourself deal with'.

At the heart of this is the customer and companies adopting this approach talk about being customer-focused or customer-centric. The phrase 'The Customer is King' comes to mind and although for many companies this still remains just rhetoric the implications are clear for the way you do business. It remains a strong imperative in today's highly competitive marketplace. No longer is Henry Ford's maxim that 'you can have any colour as long as it's black' sufficient.

In this context the phrase 'markets of one' is often used. In practice this may or may not be achievable given the size and nature of your customer base but the core concept of understanding your customers better and their potential needs is an important message. At this stage, judgement is suspended on whether there is in fact a 'relationship' with the customer and no assumptions are made about loyalty.

Note that within the definition the benefits the customer seeks can be delivered in whole by your organization or in partnership with other suppliers. Supplier management is becoming an increasingly important part of doing business today.

Failure to deliver the expected benefits of CRM is high – somewhere in the region of 50% to 70%. Various reasons are given for this including:

- failing to view it as a strategy that impacts on the whole organization;

- no clear strategic direction and leadership;

- poor change management practices;

- going for a 'big bang' approach rather than pacing the change to meet the situation of the company;

- poor project management so there are cost and time overruns;

- a poor understanding and alignment of the core processes that deliver the end benefits to customers;

- technology failing to deliver the claimed benefits;

- poor coordination between IT functions and marketing in defining the outputs required;

- the lack of effective benefit measurement;

- sales forces undermining the system;

- failure to change reward systems to match new performance measures.

The technical challenge should not be understated. The biggest technical difficulty is integrating the different legacy systems and technologies to build a single view of the customer across the organization. Most business systems have grown without sharing knowledge of a customer. Put simply there would be separate records for each of the product areas.

2.3 The Origins of Integrated CRM Systems

Integrated CRM systems have their origin in the combination and coordination of databases driving direct mail activity, call centre management and sales force automation.

Usually there is a sequential history to the building of a CRM system with some or all of the following components:

Marketing Automation

This covers customer personalization, profiling, telemarketing, e-mail marketing, and campaign managements. These activities are designed to get the right mix of the company's products and services in front of the chosen customers at the right time. They involve understanding what customers do and want, matching that knowledge with product and service information, presenting opportunities to customers and measuring success. This ability to measure the efficacy of direct marketing activity, in particular direct mail, has been a source of major competitive advantage for some companies.

Sales Automation

Sales involve the direct transferring of products and services to customers. It covers both making sure the customer receives the correct product and the activities of people within the organization who are responsible for selling – say in branches or call centres. Activities in the sales category might be client or campaign management, sales-call management and contact management.

Sales Force Automation

This includes territory planning, account and lead management systems. Collaborative tools that enable all parties to the transaction to interact with one another fall into this category, as well as systems that put sales peoples directly in touch with customers at the point of sale. Frequently this involves laptop applications with the ability to upload and download information.

Service and Service Fulfilment

This area encompasses the ability of the company to serve customers it already has. Initiatives here might be in the area of e-mail response management, telephony capabilities such as automatic call distribution, computer-telephony integration, queue/workflow management, interactive voice response and predictive dialling.

Customer Self-service

Some companies may consider CRM more specifically as electronic systems or capabilities that can be triggered by the customer. These would include Web self-service, search, interactive chat, e-mail, voice over IP, browser and application sharing, conferencing, and 'call me' capabilities. This is more accurately described as e-CRM, which utilizes Internet access via PC and wireless devices such as mobile phones and PDAs.

E-commerce

Electronic commerce, or E-commerce as it is often called, is not new. For over twenty years, companies have used some form of electronic commerce to conduct their business. For our purposes E-commerce is defined as:

> *'the automation of commercial transactions using computer and communication technologies'.*

Commercial refers to the external perspective of dealing with customers or suppliers as opposed to the internal perspective of your own systems and processes. This would include business-to-business (B2B) and business-to-consumer (B2C) applications.

Clearly awareness and usage has accelerated with the advent of the World Wide Web. Business-to-business usage has been the most prevalent as you might expect with the use of fax, mail and electronic data interchange. Supply chain management such as just in time (JIT) delivery has underpinned this activity as has the ability to transcend time and distance boundaries to trade on a global basis.

Businesses have had to restructure to remain competitive.

Banks face the prospect of being disintermediated as savvy corporate customers go straight to the markets or deal among themselves. Corporates, for example, also have the opportunity to cut banks out when dealing with long-term trading partners by aggregating and netting out liabilities so that only a single payment is made. This is not all doom and gloom, however, as there still remains a strong imperative for intermediaries, although the rules of the game have certainly changed.

Despite the rapidly increasing usage of the Web few personal consumers actually use this as a way of buying, still preferring the more traditional methods. Nonetheless they have become increasingly adept at using it as a product information source to find the most competitive suppliers:

- 5% of unique visitors to sites ultimately become customers;

- 1.6% of visits result in purchases;

- Two-thirds of shoppers who get as far as putting items in a virtual shopping basket abandon the process before checking out.

Source: *'Global Electronic Commerce: theory and case studies'*, Westland J.C., Massachusetts Institute of Technology, 1999.

2.4 The Components of a CRM Architecture

Today, CRM architecture consists of a number of components with a range of functional capabilities and attributes. Some we have already touched on such as value propositions, some are explained here and some, such as the issues of service quality and relationship management, will be dealt with later. From a technology point of view what follows can only be viewed as simplistic but the objective is to give some sense of the whole for the moment.

Legacy Systems

These are labelled P1 to P5 but could be any number depending on how many products there are within the existing or legacy systems, as they are often called. Generally these product files have a silo structure and are on different platforms with different systems and do not speak to other product silos because they are configured to meet the needs of a particular product, such as current accounts as opposed to credit cards, for example.

Middleware

Many systems and central databases are designed to capture and process product rather

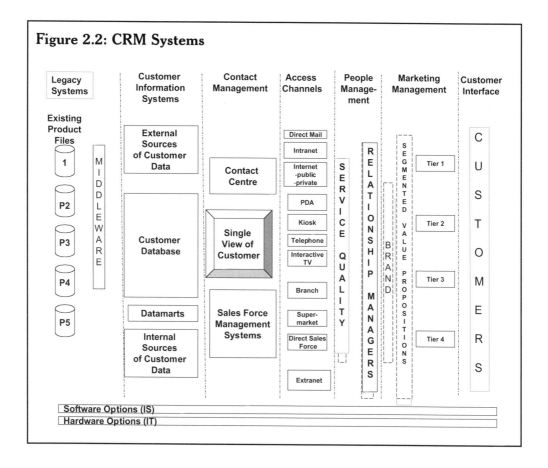

Figure 2.2: CRM Systems

than customer data. To meet the demands of integrating information about customers held on multiple product files many banks have invested heavily in systems to link these together. Frequently this is called middleware because it sits between the legacy systems and staff dealing with customers, for example in the call centre. Often it is referred to as the 'glue' that holds the integrated system together.

Various forms of hardware and software underpin these systems.

Customer Information Systems

External Sources of Customer Data

Many banks take data feeds from external suppliers of customer data – typically these would be Rating Agencies and Credit Reference Agencies.

The Customer Database

This is the heart of the CRM system. The increasing size and scope of organizations makes databases an increasingly important management and competitive tool. The database drives the enriched understanding of customers that is at the heart of a CRM system.

There can be varying levels of automation of databases, which can range from information that is in your head, to written records, to Excel.

Spreadsheets accessible only within an office to centralized computer databases may be real time or may be only periodically refreshed, say, on a monthly basis. The determining issues are volume, cost and utility. Handling the accounts and understanding the value and behaviour of millions of customers as retail banks do demands automation. If, however, the cost outweighs the potential value then low automation is acceptable.

In corporate banking particularly, there is a caveat. Many customers will probably have an expectation that any one who deals with them will know them and be fully aware and up-to-date concerning the detail of their relationship. This can be a challenge and it is in the area of information that is personally held and not shared that problems can arise – particularly if the manager moves on. Information of this nature needs to be shared in a systematic way within the relationship teams if it is not recorded and accessible on the computer.

Typically a database will form the basis of the following activities:

Data aggregation: collecting and maintaining the customer records. The degree of detail should be an outcome of discussion between the business user – in this case the Corporate Banking Division and the IT technicians. This data can be a mix of internal data generated, for example, by account activity and product holdings and usage, and external data such as credit rating agencies.

Customer analysis: the key measures will be size (probably by turnover), risk ratings and customer profitability indices but a wide range of criteria can be used as the basis for statistical analysis to refine customer segmentation. Depending on need, size and complexity, a wide range of statistical analysis and modelling techniques can be used to analyse the customer base among which are cluster analysis, predictive modelling, regression analysis, fuzzy matching and CHAID charts. A common outcome is behavioural scoring which can also provide the basis for product planning and development.

Table 2.1 Database Tools & Activities

Database Tools & Activities
● Data mining
● Decision engines
● Data transformation
● Customer segmentation
● Present-value analysis
● Future/lifetime-value analysis
● Pricing decision engine
● Contact history
● Product usage
● Propensity to buy
● Lead generation
● Sales prompts
● Channel preference
● Behavioural analysis
● Defection alerts

Customer contact intelligence: The database can be used as a proactive tool to drive customer communications and a reactive tool to capture customer-originated contact to provide an on-going contact history. Determining the right level of contact is a function of customer value, the relevance of the communication and what the customer tells you about his or her desired level of interaction.

Campaign management: this is a corollary of the above but is more usually thought of as the process of selecting targets for direct marketing activity which can include direct mail and telemarketing. Recording response data allows the efficacy and profitability of such exercises to be measured and used as the basis for informing further activity. In some cases this may be run on a separate system with bespoke software.

Management information: this can include financial and performance data – such as service quality scores – and can be particularly useful for sharing where third-party suppliers are involved in delivering solutions to customers.

Datamarts

These are specified extracts of data from the main database to meet the needs of specific users who do not need the full detail.

Internal Sources of Data

This is largely self-explanatory but will be not just transactional data based on account activity but also and increasingly 'soft data' from contact staff. This could include complaints. Customer-originated contact is important, particularly if it relates to some form of service failure because this may colour subsequent dealings with the customer.

Contact Management

Contact Centre

This area is an industry in itself with its own hardware and software. Telephone call centres are migrating to contact centres as they become Web-enabled. Advances in telephony and voice recognition play an important part in automating this area. Contact centres, too, may play an important part in supporting other channels, such as branch staff and sales force people.

Single View of Customer

For most if not all organizations this is the pot of gold at the end of the rainbow – a single view of the customer's total relationship, ideally available on a real-time basis, available to all customer contact staff 7/24/365 if necessary. Rarely is this the complete set of data held on the main database but usually an extract appropriate to the business needs of the particular user – often called an 'operational' single view This might also include the customer's contact history. It can be made available in a call centre or distributed to branches and area offices.

Salesforce Management Systems

Often laptop-based, these systems contain a suite of activities aimed at optimizing the focus and activity of sales forces. They cover such areas as prospect selection, sales funnel management, calling programmes, customer records and performance data. Interestingly a high proportion of CRM initiatives fail because the sales force is resistant. Successful salespeople often resent the way in which technology forces them to change a sales process that they have honed and refined over time.

Access Channels

Technology is helping banks to extend the way in which customers can access the bank through kiosks, in-store branches and so on. The use of the description 'access channels' is deliberate – their rationale is to make it easier for customers to do business with you at a time and place of their own choosing. Channel management is a particular challenge for full-service banks that have had to move into the development of Internet access with significant investment and no immediate cost savings. That these self-service channels are cheaper is not in doubt. Many banks are finding, however, that it is the customers they want to stay closest to that use the interpersonal channels, and the lower-value customers that use the face-to-face channels like the branch network.

The Internet aggravates the risk of further disintermediation for the banks. The development of portals and the current debate on account aggregation and the use of 'screen scraping' as it is somewhat inelegantly called pose potential threats as banks struggle to retain their customer base and franchise.

We shall look later at the remaining components of the architecture – people management, service quality and so on.

2.5 Knowledge Management

The technological capabilities we have reviewed in this chapter enable the bank to form strong trusting relationships with its customers This can be extended both to employees and indeed to external partners such as suppliers. This application of information can be described as 'Knowledge Management' and can be used to help banks to make decisions quickly because the underlying technology allows the knowledge to be widely and immediately available. This information is a source of competitive advantage and differentiation.

In the Special Report 'Winning through Knowledge' Part II. Financial World, May 2002, CRM is firmly placed within the realms of Knowledge Management and forms part of the 'relationship capital' of the bank as does an individual's intellectual capital. This it is argued is probably more important than a company's traditional asset base. Bear these issues in mind as we go forward to look at this combination of corporate capabilities as demonstrated by systems and processes and your personal contribution as a relationship manager.

3

BUSINESS, MARKETING AND PORTFOLIO PLANNING

3.1 Overview

From an understanding of the economic imperatives for superior performance we examine the strategic planning process including portfolio models and look at the way in which the marketing mix can be moulded to deliver the required outcome.

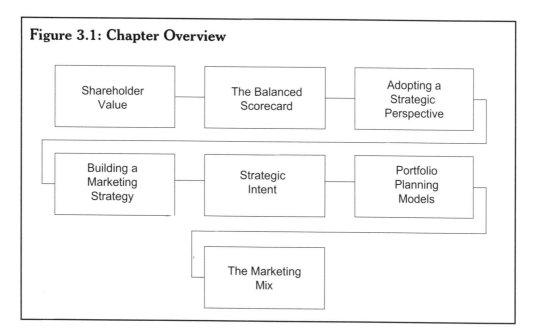

Figure 3.1: Chapter Overview

3.2 Shareholder Value

At the heart of all successful companies is a well-defined business model the core function of which is to deliver sustained economic profit and shareholder value – excluding of course not-for-profit organizations. The original banking model was a very simple one – taking deposits in and then lending these funds on at a margin. This model has clearly become more complex now in terms of its components and increasingly challenging to manage.

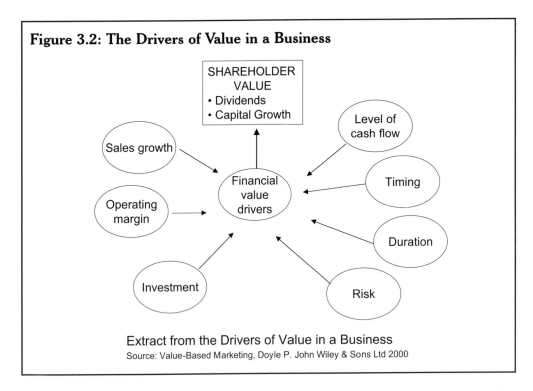

Figure 3.2: The Drivers of Value in a Business

Extract from the Drivers of Value in a Business
Source: Value-Based Marketing, Doyle P. John Wiley & Sons Ltd 2000

Professor Peter Doyle identifies three engines or value drivers of performance that underpin shareholder value (Value-Based Marketing John Wiley & Sons Ltd 2000) – financial, marketing and organizational. We shall look at the last two later.

Fundamental to the lifeblood of a business is the cash flow that is derived from the sales and operating profit margin. These financial value drivers are pertinent at a bank, portfolio and customer level as well as being relevant in terms of the customer' own business. They form a basis on which business performance can be assessed both in terms of internal targets and benchmarking against competitors.

3.3 The Balanced Scorecard

Many companies have an impressive array of Key Performance Indicators (KPIs) covering their business activity. Indeed, the act of deciding what to measure is beneficial insofar that it forces people to clarify what is important in their organizations. Measurement is also about understanding what is happening inside the organization and working out how to generate and sustain improvement.

Increasingly the view is that these indicators should have some overall balance to prevent financial performance, for example, skewing business performance to the detriment of others with a legitimate interest. Such an approach may also help to guard against short-termism – where long-term profitability is sacrificed to short-term needs.

One on the most popular performance measurement frameworks is the Balanced Scorecard (BSC) developed by Kaplan and Norton, which is a framework for translating an organization's vision into a set of performance indicators distributed among four perspectives. In a banking context this might cover:

Table 3.1 The Balanced Scorecard

Customer Perspective	*Financial Perspective*
To achieve the vision how should we look to customers?	If we succeed how do we look to our shareholders?
This perspective examines the ability of the organization to provide quality goods and services to clients achieving high levels of overall customer satisfaction.	This perspective examines the ability of the organization to deliver its own clearly defined long-range shareholder value targets.
Components	**Components**
Customer satisfaction	*Return on capital employed*
Customer retention	*Cost/Income ratio*
Customer acquisition	*Interest margins*
External research rankings, eg Greenwich	*Fee income v interest margin income*
Cross sales ratios	*Fee Income profile*
Key customers profile	*Bad debts and provisions*
Brand image and awareness	*Sector/country exposure*

Internal Business Perspective	*Innovation and Learning Perspective*
To satisfy our customers what management processes must we excel at?	To achieve our vision how must the organization learn and improve?
This perspective examines the internal processes within the organization and their suitability for delivering the customer satisfaction and financial outcomes the organization requires.	This perspective captures the ability of employees and overall organizational alignment to manage the business, adapting creatively to change. Processes will succeed only if adequately skilled and motivated employees are supplied with accurate and timely information.
Components	**Components**
Channel availability & usage profile	*Market innovation*
Key processes alignment	*New product development*
Systems availability	*Employee skills index*
Efficiency improvements	*Training & development strategy*
Out-sourcing	

Through the BSC, an organization monitors its current financial and customer satisfaction performance. In addition it examines its efforts to deliver these external deliverables by internal efforts to improve processes and motivate and educate employees – its ability to learn and improve. This is one of many tools that are holographic, that is to say that they can be used at any level in the organization.

There are a number of other models such as the Business Excellence Model, the Baldrige Award, the Deming Prize, that you may also like to review.

The Devil of Measurement

A word of caution is appropriate about performance measurement in general.

Firstly, there is often a tendency to measure too much – the challenge is to understand not what could be measured but what should be measured. Measurement is extremely powerful – it is often said that people 'march to the measurement' and 'what you measure is what you get'.

Secondly, in exercising power and control, management often uses disappointing performance data in a judgemental way that encourages defensive behaviour and promotes a fear/blame culture. The same information, presented as a basis for discussion to throw up suggestions of where improvement might lie, is far more likely to lead to a positive outcome. This calls for a supportive management style. The challenge arising from this 'human' dimension has been recognized in both the academic and the practitioner community.

Today the nature of this measurement crisis has changed and in many businesses now the problem is excessive measurement. There is a desire to quantify absolutely everything. If the focus is on the customers, there will be proposals to measure customer complaints, satisfaction, loyalty and profitability, returns, rejects and warranty claims – and the list goes on and on. So the current challenge is not necessarily identifying what you could measure, it is identifying what you need to measure so as to concentrate on what is absolutely vital.

3.4 Adopting a Strategic Perspective

The strategic perspective is different from other perspectives because of its longer-term timeframe and potential impact. It can take place at an organizational level but, as we shall see later, there is also an activity called strategic account planning which has the same determining characteristics but works at an individual customer level. There is a view that many Western as opposed to Japanese managers are uncomfortable with strategic planning and that the dynamics of most organizations force fire fighting and tactical activity. There are, however, the equivalent of sprinters, middle-distance runners and marathon runners in thinking terms in all organizations and they should be used according to their innate capabilities.

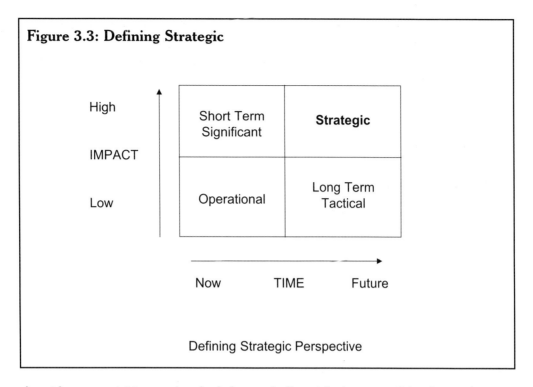

Figure 3.3: Defining Strategic

Defining Strategic Perspective

As with most activities, getting the balance of effort right in terms of the time and energy committed to any planning activity is critical. Many companies now eschew time consuming and highly detailed planning over, say, a five-year timeframe on the basis that the pace of change is such as to render these activities redundant. Nonetheless defining and agreeing at an executive level the key activities and allocating the scarce organizational resources to deliver them and cascading it through the company necessitates some investment in planning.

This strategic planning activity flows through the various levels and functions of the company.

Depending on the history, culture and level of centralization, planning may be top down or bottom up or a combination of both. In banking, this tends to be an iterative process as a dialogue takes place at the various levels to 'reality check' the bank's business objectives – the two-way arrows illustrate this. Note from a terminology point of view, objectives and goals are what you are going to do; strategy is the way you are going to do it.

Corporate planning deals with all the functions of a company such as Finance, HR and Technology. Marketing Planning is a subset of Corporate Planning and Sales Planning a subset of Marketing Planning – think of Russian dolls – one within the other. Our focus is on the Marketing Strategy given that this deals with how a bank realizes the aims of its business model through the satisfaction of customers' needs and has the most direct impact on relationship managers.

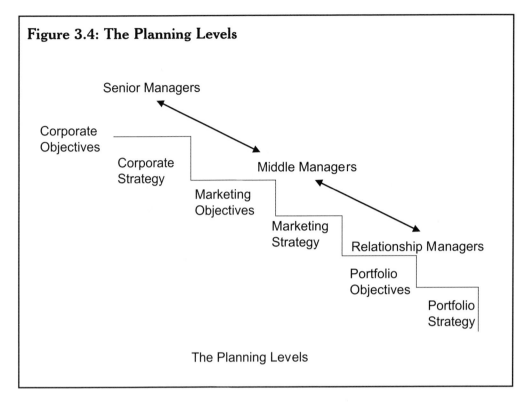

Figure 3.4: The Planning Levels

The Planning Levels

3.5 Building a Marketing Strategy

Building a marketing strategy has a number of key components that are summarized below. Although this is presented as a series of sequential steps, it is iterative, ie companies may go forward to one step and then back to previous ones, depending on the data discovery.

LePESTCo

This analysis is often referred to as environmental scanning and, as with many tools and models, has relevance at the macro (company) level but also at the micro (local market) level. An outline of the key factors is shown here which you may wish to populate from your own experience and corporate banking perspective, particularly in the light of recent events.

Situational Analysis

This has two elements – an internal audit and external audit. Fundamentally, there are two questions to be answered – where are we and how did we get here? Internal data will include data such as company structure, financial performance, customer and product profiles, market shares, margins, service quality ratings, and credit quality.

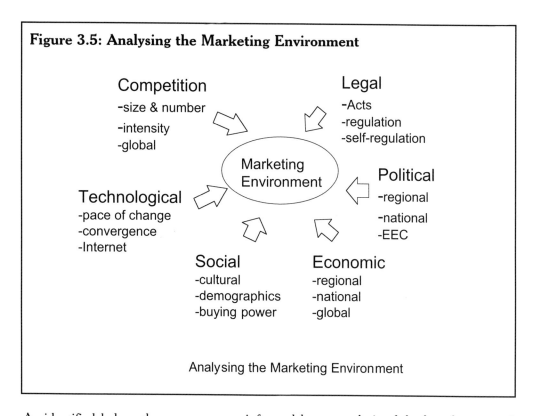

Figure 3.5: Analysing the Marketing Environment

Competition
-size & number
-intensity
-global

Legal
-Acts
-regulation
-self-regulation

Marketing Environment

Technological
-pace of change
-convergence
-Internet

Political
-regional
-national
-EEC

Social
-cultural
-demographics
-buying power

Economic
-regional
-national
-global

Analysing the Marketing Environment

As identified below, these answers are informed by an analysis of the broader external environment using the LePESTCo analysis and in particular the competitive dimensions (using for example Porter's Five Forces Model) to stress test the articulated strategic intent.

One of the roles particularly of marketing is to 'look over the horizon' – to extrapolate current trends and to think creatively about how customers' needs might change. Many companies use scenario planning to help to envision different situations and plan how they might respond to these events. At a marketing planning level, this could be assessing the impact of the enlargement of the EEC or Third World political risk. Similarly, at an account planning level, an example might be how to deal with the risk to income if a larger borrower defected to the competition or anticipating responses to aggressive pricing by a competitor.

Understanding the Competition

In a sense this has an international and national dimension, but also a very local one as you come down to the level of the customer on your patch. In all cases you need to have a good understanding of who your existing and potential rivals might be, how you benchmark against them – the respective strengths and weaknesses and what you can deduce about their strategy from their marketing activity. Understanding their strengths and weaknesses needs to be done at a banking level – credit appetite etc but also done as in the eyes of the customer – for example, perceived brand values, approachability of relationship manager, network coverage etc.

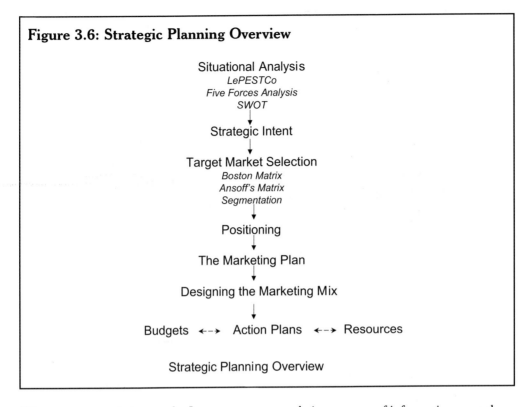

Figure 3.6: Strategic Planning Overview

Situational Analysis
LePESTCo
Five Forces Analysis
SWOT

Strategic Intent

Target Market Selection
Boston Matrix
Ansoff's Matrix
Segmentation

Positioning

The Marketing Plan

Designing the Marketing Mix

Budgets ←-→ Action Plans ←-→ Resources

Strategic Planning Overview

The corporate websites on the Internet are a very obvious source of information – set them up in your 'Favourites' and make a point of visiting them regularly. There are subscription websites that can keep you up-to-date on banking and industry developments. There will be articles in the quality press, press releases, marketing campaigns and interviews with senior people that crop up in magazines such as *Financial World*.

It is often useful to look at job advertisements – even if just to forewarn you that headhunters may be talking to your own staff. Of course, similarly when you are interviewing, candidates will often talk to you about their current role and the organization they work for – as will your own people as they move on to other organizations as long as you keep the networking going.

This information exchange can also take place through day-to-day conversations with customers, vendors and suppliers and at meetings such as conferences, local trade associations and exhibitions. There are also more structured forms of market research such as the work done by Greenwich Associates and NFO Financial Services which we will look at later. The Institute of Financial Services also has a very good information service – see (www.ifsis.org.uk).

This activity needs to be factored into your work schedule – see it as part of your personal development activity at the very least.

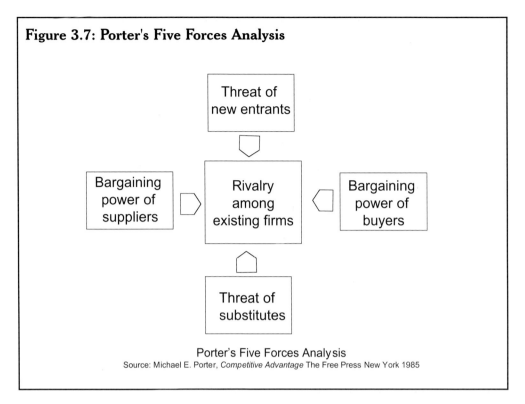

Figure 3.7: Porter's Five Forces Analysis

Porter's Five Forces Analysis
Source: Michael E. Porter, *Competitive Advantage* The Free Press New York 1985

Five Forces Analysis

A useful model for thinking about the competitive landscape is Michael Porter's 'Five Forces Analysis'. History tells us that typically the greatest threat to an established company will come from outside the industry it operates in. Porter's model helps to disaggregate some of these potential sources of competition.

Rivalry among existing firms:

The intensity of the rivalry among existing firms is usually a function of the number of competitors, the level of similarity or commoditization of the products and the overall opportunities for growth. Generally banking is thought of as a mature marketplace with growth coming essentially from existing customers or acquiring customers from other banks. This, particularly in the corporate banking market, means that one of the opportunities for growth lies in attracting business from competitors. This is likely to be more difficult if, say, the major players are pursuing similar credit assessment and pricing policies. A feature of many other markets is new entrants who have 'cherry picked' attractive business by challenging the conventional pricing and service models.

Threat of new entrants:

Banking is a heavily regulated industry with relatively high barriers to entry – such as meeting the necessary prudential capital requirements. Strategic partnerships can, however, mitigate some of these issues – think particularly of the retailers entering the financial services marketplace through their partnerships with existing banks.

Technology can have a major influence here – the way in which on-line service providers can bypass the investment in 'bricks and mortar'. Well-established brands are another barrier to entry, although as we have seen recently – again with the retailers – the strength of these brands can be stretched into other product category areas.

On the other side of the coin, governments are increasingly intervening if industries effectively operative a monopoly, unfairly locking potential competitors out.

Bargaining power of buyers:

Large corporate customers can disintermediate the banks, for example by going straight to the capital markets and investing expertise in their own treasury functions. If multi-banked they can use this strength to argue for more favourable terms. Outside of banking, the car manufactures and food retailers exercise considerable bargaining power in dealing with their suppliers. In many markets, the Internet has had a major impact here in allowing customers to easily search for the best prices.

Threat of substitutes:

Again the threat here is of disintermediation – in theory new products from within an industry are not a problem provided your company could copy them. A particular challenge though is the speed at which technology is converging, resulting in increasingly rapid product obsolescence.

Bargaining power of suppliers:

Banking is interesting because customers can be both suppliers (of liabilities from credit balances) and buyers (of assets from lending). In corporate banking again individual buyers may be hugely influential. Suppliers can be extended to include capital markets and even shareholders who provide risk capital.

SWOT Analysis:

There are many tools and models to help the marketing planning analytical process that also have relevance at an account planning level. A particularly well-known one is the SWOT analysis (Strengths, Weaknesses, Opportunities, Threats). This versatile model can be used at a number of levels, for example, the company as a whole, particular market sectors, product lines, customer segments, and account plans and even competitor analysis.

The challenge in any of the areas being assessed is to minimize the weaknesses and match your strengths to the opportunities. Note that while strengths and weaknesses are internal to the company, opportunities and threats have an external dimension. Completing a

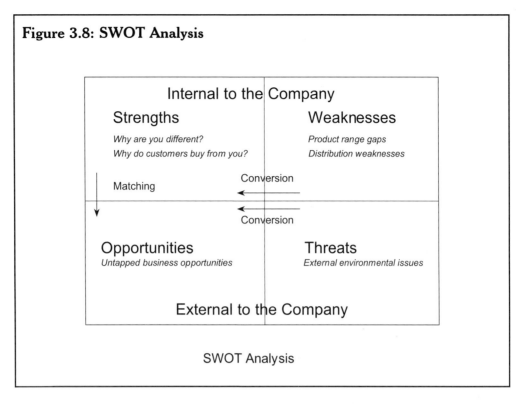

Figure 3.8: SWOT Analysis

SWOT Analysis

SWOT relies on a good level of objectivity, and critiquing the content on a simple 'so what' basis is a useful exercise. If some strengths also feature as weaknesses, then it may be necessary to break them down into sub-issues and then group these accordingly. The challenge is to avoid generalities and think incisively about the components of the boxes.

Let us apply a SWOT, for example, to the travel industry:

Table 3.2 Travel Industry SWOT

Strengths	*Weaknesses*
Fragmentation of industry means multiple opportunities	Cyclical and volatile
	Intense competition
Overseas travel remaining increasingly popular	Fine margins
	Low interest rates dilute earnings on deposits
Low-cost airlines boosting traveller numbers	Vulnerable to movements in exchange rates and fuel costs
Niche products of smaller independents	Changes in distribution and remuneration
	Multiplicity of bonds required
	Travel-related taxes

Opportunities	Threats
Trend of ageing population who hold the most disposable wealth	Price wars
Desire for independence of travellers	Continuing changes in booking behaviour
Bespoked packaging	High technology costs may mean smaller operators cannot achieve economies of scale
'Supermarket' approach in large retail centres	Increasing disaggregation of package tours as travellers use the Web

3.6 Strategic Intent

For most companies the definition or reaffirmation of strategic intent is the start point for business and marketing planning. The essence of any successful strategy, and in particular a CRM strategy, is selecting those customers that you want to serve because they are intrinsically valuable – arising from the actual and potential income they can or will generate – and because the capabilities of your organization can be configured to deliver a superior offering meeting the needs of these customers. These customer needs, and the ability of your organization to satisfy them profitably, is significantly influenced by what is going on in the outside world – or external environment as it is called.

These factors all interlink and tend to have a causal relationship – that is to say what happens to one has an influence on some or all of the others. Successful companies strive for an optimal fit. A particular challenge to companies and in particular banks is to be

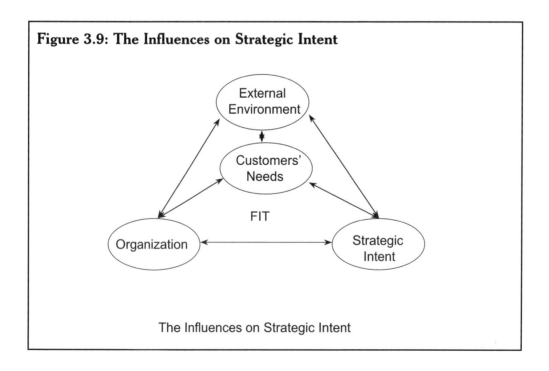

Figure 3.9: The Influences on Strategic Intent

The Influences on Strategic Intent

sufficiently flexible and responsive to be able to stay aligned to their chosen marketplace. The exercising of this choice about what you do with your company's resources is called 'strategic intent', which forms the basis of strategic planning.

Target Market Selection

As we have identified, at the heart of a CRM strategy is choosing those customers you want to serve. In marketing parlance this is called Target Market Selection – the recognition that you will devote your resources to high-value/high-potential customers. You do this in the knowledge that you have a series of attributes that give you a competitive advantage, which results in these customers preferring you rather than the competition.

Underpinning this selection process are a number of analytical tools or Portfolio Planning Models as they are called.

3.7 Portfolio Planning Models

These models have as their focus driving shareholder value. They do so essentially by having a focus on long-term profitability. Many companies, including banks, have found it relatively easier to take costs out of the business to improve productivity – one line of the model below – rather than increase business volumes.

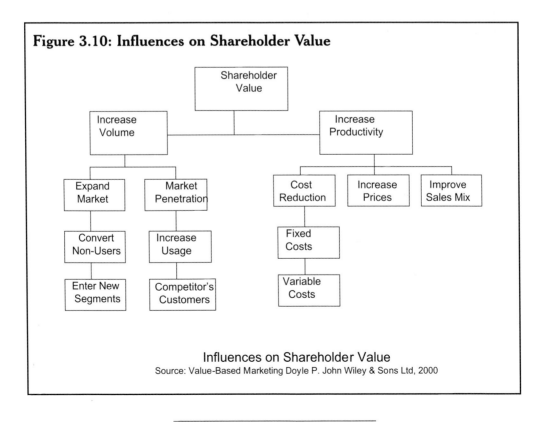

Figure 3.10: Influences on Shareholder Value

Influences on Shareholder Value
Source: Value-Based Marketing Doyle P. John Wiley & Sons Ltd, 2000

Of the many business development portfolio models available here, there are two in particular that should be looked at.

Firstly, though, you will by now have noticed a propensity for many of the models used to be formed of four quadrants! Remember that a model is merely a device for simplifying otherwise complex issues. This simplification is both a strength – making understanding and comprehension easier – and a weakness because taken too literally it can mislead. Some models also show a series of activities in a linear or sequential way – but in practice some steps may be left out and in every case the process will be iterative – ie repeatedly going back to a previous stage or stages.

The Boston Matrix

Designed by the Boston Consulting Group it categorizes the subject matter – products, markets, customers etc in four ways:

Stars

These are high-growth, high-share businesses or products. They often need heavy investment to finance their rapid growth. Eventually their growth will slow down and they will turn into cash cows.

Figure 3.11: The Boston Matrix

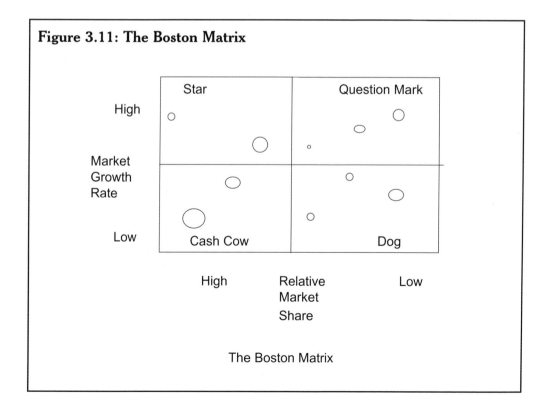

The Boston Matrix

Cash Cows

Cash cows are very profitable, high-share businesses or products but with low predicted growth. Less investment is required to hold market share. Profit is recycled into other areas. Typically this would be low-activity accounts with sizeable non-interest bearing deposits and good quality well-remunerated lending.

Dogs

These are low-growth, low-share products that may or may not be self-sufficient. The challenge is whether to exit or try to build, although there may be few opportunities to grow at a reasonable cost. Statistically the greatest numbers of products fall into this category.

Question Marks (or Problem Children)

These are low-share business units or products in high-growth markets. They require significant investment to hold their share. Management has to decide what to build into stars and what to phase out.

The BCG model can be used to analyse the current status of your product portfolio in the following ways:

1. It will allow you to identify in broad terms those products that are generating core income and those that require further investment.

2. It can also identify those products that on the face of it should be de-listed. Care is necessary here, however, to make sure that the economic contribution is fully understood and the role it may have in the overall portfolio – for example, if the product was not available and customers went elsewhere could this threaten the relationship?

3. It will help to determine how scarce resources should be allocated, particularly the use of the marketing mix (see below).

Ansoff's Matrix

This offers a different perspective on growth opportunities, looking at the two dimensions of market and product development.

These quadrants have different levels of risk associated with them – selling existing products to existing markets has the lowest risk and diversification the highest risk. Any extension of products or markets should be consistent with the company's strategic intent and its core competencies. In today's competitive environment, most organizations recognize that they will have to invest in product and market development often just to stand still.

Figure 3.12: Ansoff's Matrix

	Existing products	New products

Existing markets	Market Penetration
	- cross-selling
	- wins from competitors
	- lower price
	- advertise more
	- increase usage
		Product Development
		- modified or new products
		  to existing markets
		  eg Electronic banking services

New markets	Market Development
	- identifying new markets
	for existing products
	eg Joint ventures
	Geographic expansion
		Diversification
		- start or buy business
		  outside current products
		  and markets
		  eg Portals
		  Third party distribution channels

Ansoff's Matrix

Segmentation

This is the process of dividing customers into groups that are likely to respond in a similar way to the same marketing activity. This analysis can be done against many different factors. In corporate banking, for example, this could be industry (based on the Standard Industry Classification System), geography, turnover, headcount, years trading, buying behaviour, product usage and so on. The following summary of the characteristics of mid-corporates with a turnover up to £100m offers a number of bases (see Figure 3.13).

Segmentation has an external and an internal dimension because it follows that the way you segment your markets externally should be mirrored by your internal organization. In many banks there is an additional dimension here as, given the complexity of some product areas, a single relationship manager cannot be all things to all men. Banks therefore have to decide to what level they want people to be skilled and the level of specialization required. This may add headcount layers but is probably more efficient in cost terms.

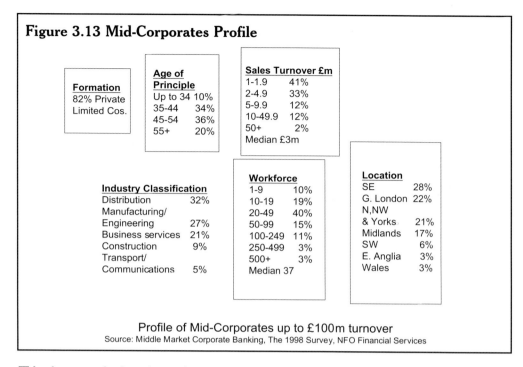

Figure 3.13 Mid-Corporates Profile

Formation
82% Private
Limited Cos.

Age of Principle
Up to 34   10%
35-44   34%
45-54   36%
55+   20%

Sales Turnover £m
1-1.9   41%
2-4.9   33%
5-9.9   12%
10-49.9   12%
50+   2%
Median £3m

Industry Classification
Distribution   32%
Manufacturing/
Engineering   27%
Business services   21%
Construction   9%
Transport/
Communications   5%

Workforce
1-9   10%
10-19   19%
20-49   40%
50-99   15%
100-249   11%
250-499   3%
500+   3%
Median 37

Location
SE   28%
G. London   22%
N,NW
& Yorks   21%
Midlands   17%
SW   6%
E. Anglia   3%
Wales   3%

Profile of Mid-Corporates up to £100m turnover
Source: Middle Market Corporate Banking, The 1998 Survey, NFO Financial Services

Take for example the relationship management structure of an illustrative corporate bank:

Table 3.3 Corporate Market Segmentation

Turnover band	Company characteristics	Bank usage	Relationship manager portfolio size	Level of specialization
£500m+	Corporate & Institutional Multi-nationals FTSE 250	Tier 1 Say 3/5 Tier 2 Say 4/8 Tier 3 Say 10/12	Say 10/15	Industry – Defence, Oil & Chemicals, Shipping etc Products – Derivatives, Treasury, International Cash Management Bespoke solutions
£10m – £500m	Manufacturing, Professional Services, Property, Construction, Retail & Wholesale Say 50-100 employees	Say 2/3	Say 25/35	Still sophisticated product usage with specialists actively supporting relationship managers
£1m – £10m	Sole traders, Owner-managed Businesses, Partnerships and Limited Companies	One major banker	Say 70/100	Largely vanilla products with occasional use of specialists

Clearly this picture will vary from bank to bank and the turnover bands are elastic, not absolutes. Take a look at your own bank to see how the market is segmented, the usage characteristics and where the generalist role moves to the specialist. Size, value and complexity of transactions may also play a part.

The following diagram (Figure 3.14) will give you some idea of the myriad services available – a level of complexity that will be exacerbated as banks bring their corporate and investment banking together:

An absolute necessity is that the segment is intrinsically profitable after allowing for the 'costs to serve' – that is, the appropriate cost of operation for the type of revenue it can generate. A good example here is the low-cost airlines whose lower cost to serve – no frills, rapid turnarounds, on-line booking systems – is damaging the higher fixed-cost and less flexible national carriers.

Positioning

This brings together the competitive advantage we talked about earlier with the choice of target market. The outcome is a pattern of corporate activity that aligns the company to its chosen market or markets. BMW, for example, is positioned in the premium sector of the car market and uses a mix of exclusivity and engineering excellence to underpin this.

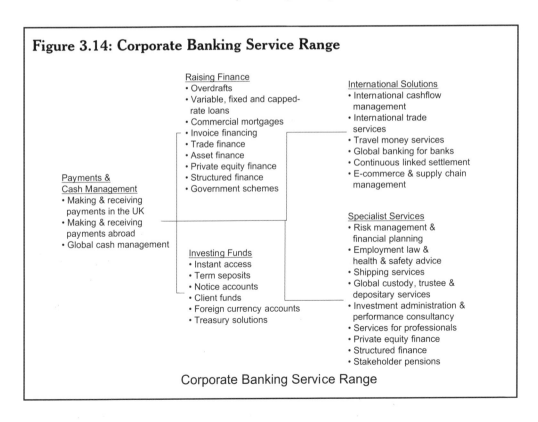

Figure 3.14: Corporate Banking Service Range

Raising Finance
- Overdrafts
- Variable, fixed and capped-rate loans
- Commercial mortgages
- Invoice financing
- Trade finance
- Asset finance
- Private equity finance
- Structured finance
- Government schemes

International Solutions
- International cashflow management
- International trade services
- Travel money services
- Global banking for banks
- Continuous linked settlement
- E-commerce & supply chain management

Payments & Cash Management
- Making & receiving payments in the UK
- Making & receiving payments abroad
- Global cash management

Investing Funds
- Instant access
- Term seposits
- Notice accounts
- Client funds
- Foreign currency accounts
- Treasury solutions

Specialist Services
- Risk management & financial planning
- Employment law & health & safety advice
- Shipping services
- Global custody, trustee & depositary services
- Investment administration & performance consultancy
- Services for professionals
- Private equity finance
- Structured finance
- Stakeholder pensions

Corporate Banking Service Range

The Marketing Plan

The marketing plan is a summary framework bringing together in a single document the data and deliberations that have influenced the marketing strategy and detailing the activities that need to be implemented and executed to carry it out. As with many of the frameworks we have looked at, again it can be used at a macro level – products, customer segments, geographic regions – and a micro level, ie individual customers.

3.8 The Marketing Mix

Once the chosen segments are identified the company must target its marketing effort at those groups and position all elements of the marketing mix to meet their specific needs.

Think of the marketing mix as a set of notes on a piano that can be configured in many different ways to deliver value to customers. In services marketing, People, Processes and Customer Service are added to the more conventional elements of Product, Price, Place and Promotion. The issues of customer service are dealt with separately later.

Particular features of the marketing mix as it applies to corporate banking are:

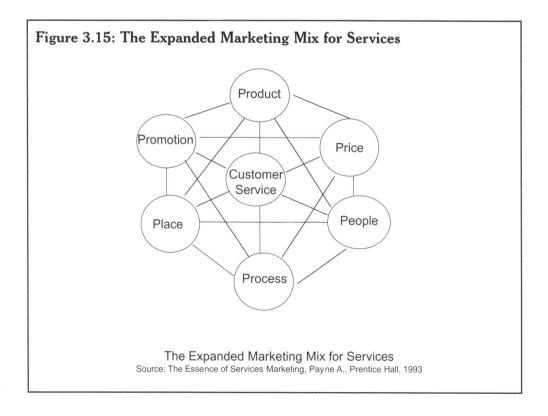

Figure 3.15: The Expanded Marketing Mix for Services

The Expanded Marketing Mix for Services
Source: The Essence of Services Marketing, Payne A., Prentice Hall, 1993

Product

In many cases at the upper end of the corporate market, core product frameworks are structured in a bespoke way to meet customer's needs on a deal-by-deal basis. There may be a high need for flexibility and innovation as product solutions are put together. In most other markets there is a fairly high level of standardization so that the products can be sold 'off the shelf' with some modifications such as price to reflect risk and negotiating power.

A useful concept when thinking about products is the 'Product Life Cycle'. This suggests that there are a number of stages a product goes through from introduction to maturity. The stage a product is at has a significant impact on the way in which the marketing mix is used. Simplistically a product might be premium-priced when new to the market and more competitively priced when the market has matured and is saturated with competitor's offerings. A challenge is to manage the product portfolio so that not all products are in the same place on the curve. Bear in mind that the maturity phase for some products might last tens of years – for example Marmite!

Price

Pricing can be influenced by the bank's competitive positioning, the overall strategic objectives (market share or profitability) and the appetite for credit.

Pricing to reflect the risk in a lending proposition is a challenge in all bank pricing but particularly in corporate banking where large customers are able to command finer rates.

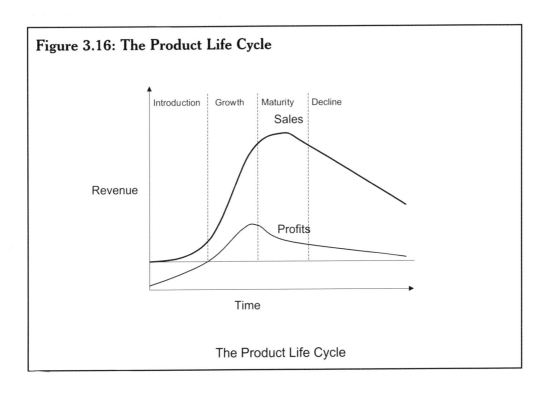

Figure 3.16: The Product Life Cycle

The Product Life Cycle

Understanding what the market will bear requires finely honed competitive intelligence and an understanding of the added value to the customer.

Sensitivity to price will not be uniform across all customers. It can be reduced by a well-developed relationship where there are high levels of customer satisfaction and of course, as we have discussed earlier, by perceptions of value. As such, value can be said to be individualistic, ie it is in the eye of the beholder. In any competitive pricing activity there is a need to have a view as to how the competition may respond.

Table 3.4 The Price of Lending

Cost of funds	Lending margin	Risk premium	Customer perceptions of added value	Price

People

Many banks increasingly view this as a potential source of competitive advantage. Well-established relationships can often withstand the inevitable service disruptions that occur from time to time. The role of people in underpinning the responsiveness, assurance and empathy components of RRATE (see later) are critical.

Process

Process is an important part of the service delivery system as it is frequently transparent to the customer and, indeed, the customer is almost invariably part of the process at some stage. The challenge is, if not to make the process invisible, to make sure it is not at odds with delivering an efficient and effective service to the customer. Indeed research suggests that many companies own up to broken or inadequate processes as the most significant barrier to improving customer relationships. We shall look again at this issue later.

Place

One of the key attributes of being a preferred supplier is being easy to do business with. This is very much to do with accessibility which, in a bricks-and-mortar dominated environment, is where you are but in today's multichannel environment this has been extended to how and when you can be reached – the Martini principle. This discussion often centres on 'distribution channels', ie place, but is better thought of from the customer's perspective as 'access channels'.

Electronic banking has been a feature of corporate banking for some time. It offers benefits to all parties, timeliness, convenience and cost savings. Depending on the nature of the business, many corporates may be multiple users of the bank's access channels. These are frequently under the operational control of different units of the bank that often presents a challenge to delivering a seamless service.

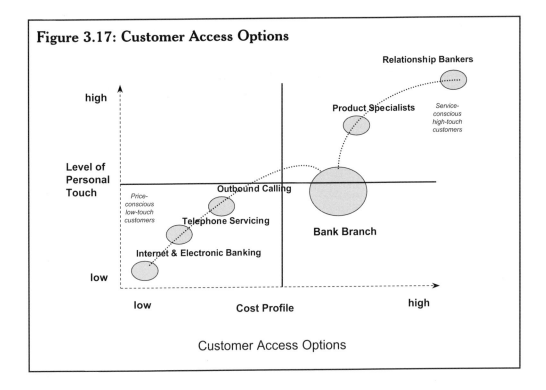

Figure 3.17: Customer Access Options

Customer Access Options

Promotion

A combination of a well-recognized brand and word of mouth feature strongly the corporate marketplace because it is not usual to see the weight of advertising seen in the retail and small business markets. Under this heading we can include PR and sponsorship – the latter may offer opportunities for corporate hospitality.

This activity is coordinated and implemented through action plans, project planning methodologies and budgetary controls of which resource allocation is an important part.

The Four Cs of Marketing

To give a different perspective, in their work on marketing communications, Shultz, Tannenbaum and Lauterborn (1992) proposed the 4Cs instead of the classical 4Ps.

The 4Ps are replaced as:

- *Product becomes Consumer* – as in consumer's needs and wants, the era when whatever you make can be sold is over and you can only sell whatever someone wants to buy.

- *Price becomes Cost* – price is only one aspect of the cost to the customer – perceptions of risk, security and the ancillary costs of time, reconfigured systems etc are all part of the price bundle from the customer's perspective.

- *Place becomes Convenience* – how easy do you make it for the customer to buy from you?

- *Promotion becomes Communication* – a dialogue that engages the customer across multiple channels and communications media, reflecting the *how* and *when* of their contact needs.

4

BEST BUSINESS PRACTICE

4.1 Overview

The definition of risk continues to expand beyond that of just lending as the authorities seek to improve the environment of protection afforded to consumers.

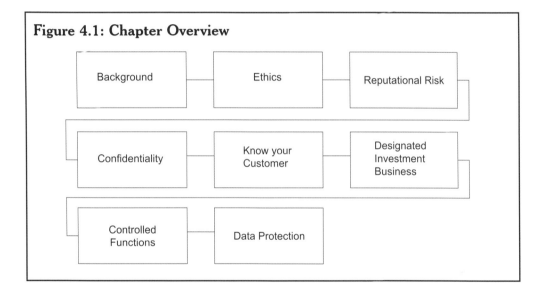

Figure 4.1: Chapter Overview

4.2 Background

The activities of all organizations have come under increasing scrutiny in today's climate of individualism, heightened consumerism, real-time global communications and media scrutiny. Banks have not been immune to these pressures against a backcloth generally of low regard among customers and increasing government and regulatory intervention. This increasingly intrusive environment has extended the definition of risk management that now includes not just credit alone but reputational risk and the increasing scope of compliance. This has imposed significant additional costs, particularly on financial services companies.

Bank regulation largely sits outside the FSA, with the Banking Standards Board responsible for the Banking Code, rather than there being any specific prudential Conduct of Business Rules within the FSA. There is, therefore, a degree of focus on self-regulation on the basis that this has been successful in the past.

Banks have a common law duty to work in an ethical manner appropriate to consumer protection. The Financial Services Authority (FSA), however, identifies a set of business principles that are particularly relevant beyond just their legislative domain as we consider the issue of ethics.

Table 4.1 FSA Business Principles

1 Integrity	A firm must conduct its business with integrity.
2 Skill, care and diligence	A firm must conduct its business with due skill, care and diligence.
3 Management and control	A firm must take reasonable care to organize and control its affairs responsibly and effectively, with adequate risk management systems.
4 Financial prudence	A firm must maintain adequate financial resources.
5 Market conduct	A firm must observe proper standards of market conduct.
6 Customers' interests	A firm must pay due regard to the interests of customers and treat them fairly.
7 Communications with clients	A firm must pay due regard to the information needs of its clients, and communicate information to them in a way that is clear, fair and not misleading.
8 Conflicts of interest	A firm must manage conflicts of interest fairly, both between itself and its customers and between a customer and another client.
9 Customers: relationships of trust	A firm must take reasonable care to ensure the suitability of its advice and discretionary decisions for any customer who is entitled to rely upon its judgement.
10 Clients' assets	A firm must arrange adequate protection for clients' assets when it is responsible for them.
11 Relations with regulators	A firm must deal with its regulators in an open and cooperative way, and must disclose to the FSA appropriately anything relating to the firm of which the FSA would reasonably expect notice.

Source: *FSA Handbook* Release 001 01 December 2001

In exploring the topic of best business practice, we shall consider ethics, reputational risk, confidentiality, money laundering, market abuse and some other aspects of FSA governance. This is by no means a complete picture and you will want to refer to both the internal compliance procedures of your own bank and the FSA's website. You should note that the FSA now also has direct responsibility for areas such as money laundering, that were previously the remit of the Bank of England.

4.3 Ethics

We talked earlier about the characteristics of services such as intangibility, inseparability, and so on. These characteristics mean that at the root of any transaction there has to be a high level of trust between buyer and seller, banker and customer. A fair and open exchange that is not biased in favour of the supplier is essential. To this end the notion of 'confusion marketing' is abhorrent. Nothing is more likely to break down trust than trying to 'pull the wool' over the eyes of the customer, confusing them with acres of small print or locking them into an unfair arrangement.

Ethics is about what is right and what is wrong and has moral and cultural connotations that extend beyond purely legal and regulatory requirements. For example, it may not necessarily be illegal to persuade a customer to buy a potentially risky product where the bank stands to benefit more than the customer, but it certainly may be unethical. This is both a personal and a corporate responsibility.

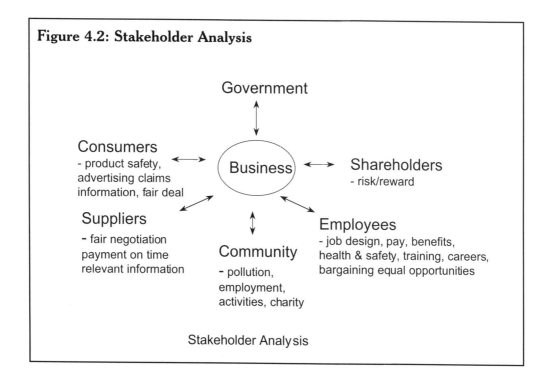

Figure 4.2: Stakeholder Analysis

Stakeholder Analysis

In dealing with organizations, consumers are often adopting wider reference points – or stakeholder analysis as it is called – and thinking not only of the impact to them personally and to their companies but also to the community at large. Companies should think in the same way.

This explicit focus on ethics – as opposed to it being part of written or unwritten codes of conduct, ie ' my word is my bond' – has led to a number of interesting developments. For example, the Co-operative Bank has sought to make its ethical stance a source of competitive differentiation. Barclays Bank has a unit dedicated to researching the views of environmental and ethical organizations such as Friends of the Earth, Greenpeace and Amnesty International. The team, part of the corporate communications department, sends reports to the risk management department to help the bank to make socially responsible credit decisions. Ivory and Sime have a Director of Ethics and Governance.

Ethical investment funds are now well established. Companies can be classified as to the extent of the ethics they practise with companies that invest in countries with oppressive regimes, carry out animal experiments or manufacture alcohol, arms or tobacco being marked down.

4.4 Reputational Risk

Many banks are now acknowledging that this has become an increasingly significant area of risk and are aligning it with operational and credit-risk management. The impact of this risk is the extent to which customers and other significant stakeholders may think or act differently as a result of a particular event and therefore damage revenue and earnings.

For example, both Perrier and Coca Cola historically suffered negative publicity because of product impurities, with a significant impact on their earnings. Similarly Intel was castigated for releasing a chip that was known to miscalculate, albeit statistically infrequently.

On the banking front, Bank of Scotland faced a boycott in 2000 when the bank became identified with antilibertarian views publicly pronounced by one of its American shareholders

Credit Suisse First Boston was involved with a European road show for Taiwan's ministry of finance promoting investment in Taiwan with their minister of finance in attendance. This activity angered the Chinese authorities, which regarded the move as support for Taiwan's independent status. As a result, CSFB were de-listed from several new projects in China.

Barclays Bank's image suffered after media coverage of the bank's decision to close many small local branches and introduce cash machine fees. Announcements were released at the same time disclosing the pay of its senior executives and it also launched an advertising campaign celebrating its size. All of those factors quickly tainted Barclays' reputation.

Loss of trust and loss of public confidence of this nature could be a major factor depending on how these issues look to customers. Banks need to work to maintain levels of trust: reputations are slow to build and quick to fade.

4.5 Confidentiality

Essentially three issues – confidentiality, Chinese walls, and conflicts of interest – can be grouped under this heading that has two broad dimensions. The external dimension – what is said outside the bank – and, increasingly importantly, the internal dimension – what can be said and how information can be handled inside the bank.

Confidentiality

Bankers have always had a duty not to disclose information about a customer to any third party outside the bank without the customer's explicit and usually written authority. This is good banking practice. For personal customers this duty of confidentiality has been extended by the requirements of the Data Protection Act.

Chinese Walls

This describes the process for ensuring that confidentiality is maintained and preventing the inappropriate internal dissemination of customer or price-sensitive information.

In many banks, the helicopter view of a customer's creditworthiness would be at credit committee/board level. The guiding principle is the need to ensure that what takes place is manifestly in the customer's interest. Different legal entities within the bank are not allowed to take advantage of the banking relationship where customer authorization has not been given. Note that in the main information relates to the company's activities but that knowledge, for example, that a director of a client company was selling shares, would also be covered until it was in the public domain.

Conflicts of Interest

The need to consider potential conflicts of interest was already there from a credit risk management perspective – as different specialist areas such as debt finance, derivatives, and asset finance formed views about the creditworthiness of the customer. The need for heightened awareness of the internal perspective comes from the trend towards bringing corporate banking and investment under one roof and big corporate banks of this nature have to be even more careful.

For publicly quoted customers where there are traded investments this potential for conflicts of interest is then extended and the sensitivities are more acute. One area is that of unpublished price-sensitive information – a topic of recent debate has been the way in which market and company analysts may be selective about the information they release to support their recommendations. Another area is that of market abuse – where a company uses confidential information to prefer itself or distort the market at large. Where this information is used at individual and personal level for gain, this becomes insider trading, which the Insider Dealing Criminal Justice Act regulates.

As an aside, there is also a requirement to record hospitality received from customers.

4.5 Know Your Customer

Prevention of money laundering is the key issue here and a number of recent events have heightened the focus in this area to crack down on particularly on money laundering.

New anti-money laundering guidelines have been brought into force designed to alert employees to suspicious transactions. For example, banks in London handled $1.3bn of transactions on behalf of the family and friends of the late General Abacha during his rule in Nigeria. The FSA reported that it had found 'significant weaknesses' in anti-money laundering controls at 15 banks. As a result new training has been put in place designed to alert employees to suspicious transactions but also to avoid alerting customers that enquires may be under way.

Account-opening routines have been tightened up and specified documentation must be made available to establish the bona fides of the persons involved – this includes company directors. If these tougher 'know your customer' criteria are not met the bank may be obliged to decline to open the account. On an on-going basis there is also a responsibility to ensure that mandates are kept up to date.

A related 'know your customer' issue is the need to categorize customers for the purposes of the FSA. Before conducting designated investment business a firm must take reasonable steps to establish whether that customer is a private customer, intermediate customer or market counterparty. These ascribe levels of financial knowledge and sophistication and have an impact on the protection that is available under the provisions of the FSA.

4.6 Designated Investment Business

At a product level, many of the traditional banking products, money transmission, deposit taking, lending, and foreign exchange do not normally require authorization for individuals although they are carried out under the umbrella of various regulations, eg the Banking Acts.

Where the provisions of the FSA do impact is in the conduct of designated investment business, which in a corporate banking context would include products such as shares, bonds and other debentures, money market funds, derivatives and warrants. Sales staff involved with these products need to be accredited and authorized, although in corporate banking they are likely to be relatively few in number. Training and competency is key and the FSA will look for satisfactory evidence in these areas.

4.7 Controlled Functions

Under the more recently introduced FSA regulations, directors of financial companies become personally liable if they fail to ensure that their staff comply with the FSA's regulations and requirements. Accountability falls on a number of control functions such as Compliance Officers and Money Laundering Officers.

4.8 Data Protection

The Data Protection Act 1998 has been introduced to protect individuals' rights to privacy and confidentiality regarding their personal and financial affairs. It relates to personal data, which is defined as any information that 'identifies a living individual'. It includes any information the bank holds about customers, suppliers, prospects and employees. This even includes the collection of business cards that many people in business keep in their briefcase or a Filofax full of names, addresses, e-mail and phone numbers. This is relevant for directors and private individuals as opposed to corporate bodies.

The Act came into force from 31 October 2001 and now covers personal information including paper records. Companies are required to appoint a Data Controller – 'a person (either alone or jointly or in common with other persons) who determines the purposes for which and the manner in which any personal data are, or are to be processed'. Non-compliance may trigger enforcement notices, leading to fines and perhaps claims for compensation for damages and distress from those affected.

5

DELIVERING CORPORATE CAPABILITIES

5.1 Overview

This chapter looks at the many ramifications of the increasing focus of companies on service quality.

Figure 5.1: Chapter Overview

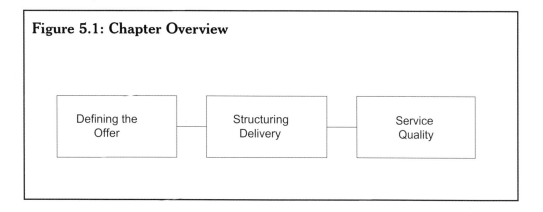

5.2 Defining the Offer

The process of defining target market segments that we identified as an outcome of the planning processes previously, results in the definition of a value proposition for each segment, including the service bundle. These product or service offerings are founded in what it is that the company does best, that it is to say its core capabilities. Note that the service quality requirements are not a 'glaze' that are added as an afterthought but are an integral and engineered part of the overall product offering.

It is also worth noting that the products and services must be the outcome of an informed understanding – which comes from market research and listening closely to your customers – of what their needs are. This will include what they value and what they are prepared to pay for – the combination of functional and emotional benefits that the product comprises.

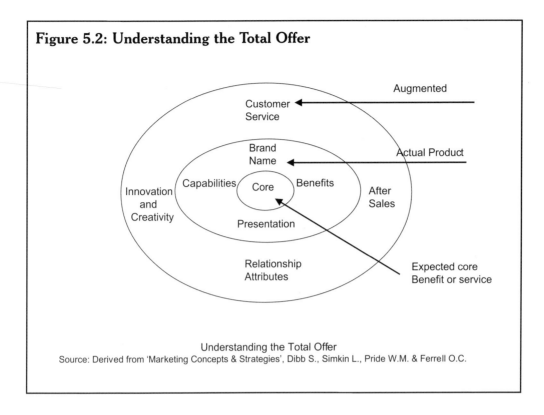

Figure 5.2: Understanding the Total Offer

Understanding the Total Offer
Source: Derived from 'Marketing Concepts & Strategies', Dibb S., Simkin L., Pride W.M. & Ferrell O.C.

Understanding the Total Offer

At a product level it is usual to refer to three layers or concentric rings in product construction, see above.

The core product: the essence of what the buyer is buying that delivers the base required benefit. It is unlikely – other than in the very short-term – that a product that does not deliver at this level will be successful overall.

Expected features: the amalgam of the features and capabilities that includes the presentational elements such as styling, packaging and product name.

The augmented product: the additional services and benefits that surround the core and actual products.

The product offer sits within or alongside a number of other components that represent the total 'customer experience' bundle. These other components comprise its service quality elements, the company brand and – particularly in a corporate banking environment – the way in which the company's culture influences the behaviour of its people as they deliver the product to the marketplace. Expressing this as a matrix and applying it to a cash management offering from an international bank we might get the following:

Table 5.1 A Cash Management Offering Bundle

Product Features	**Service Quality Components**
7/24 availability	World-class customer service
Can transact in 72 of 100+ countries in 12 different languages	Proven record of longevity
Integration with customer's web technology	Experienced industry professionals
Straightthrough processing	Dependable, secure quality processing
Value-added reporting capabilities	A focus on building and maintaining
End-to-end authorization, payment, reporting and supplier financing tool	long-term relationships
Brand Attributes	**Enabling Culture**
Top 5 international bank	Innovative and leading-edge product development
Global reach	Strategy to optimize Internet capabilities
Reputation & market expertise	Positive 'can do' culture
Century of experience	Global perspective
Technological leadership	
Local presence in major financial centres	

5.3 Structuring Delivery

An important part of the way in which corporate capabilities are managed and delivered into the marketplace is the way in which a bank is structured – usually expressed in the form of an organizational chart. This tends to be the result of the historic development of the bank over time as the range of activities has increased, either by organic growth or acquisition.

Much of the thinking about formal organizational structure comes from the classical or scientific management school of thought of the eighteenth and nineteenth centuries. Here

> *'People in organizations are seen as part of a hierarchy, a network of interlinking jobs, defined by detailed job descriptions which specify the task required and the authority and responsibility of the jobholder.'*

Source: *Insight into Management* Lawrence P.A. & Lee R.A. Oxford University Press 1989

A Frenchman, Henri Fayol, developed a number of 'principles of management', among which were:

Unity of command   No member of an organization should receive orders from more than one superior.

Span of control: No supervisor should have more than five subordinates reporting to him or her.

Unity of objective: The objectives of each organizational unit should integrate with and contribute to the achievement of the organizational objectives.

At the shop-floor level, Frederick Winslow Taylor, an American, supplemented these principles as follows:

1. Planning and decision-making should not be left to employees but be passed up the hierarchy to better-qualified and motivated managers.

2. Tasks should be divided into the simplest possible constituent elements and each worker should do as few elements as can be conveniently combined into job.

Much of what happens in large organizations can still be related to these ideas.

There are a number of implications for banks that want to be customer centric:

● There may be a heavy reliance on the informal roles and relationships in the organization to get things done.

● As managers get promoted they may become more distanced from customers.

● Staff will defer to management where they believe they have no authority.

● Staff may be skilled to carry out only the repetitive routine aspects of their job, which may not meet customer's requirements in terms of what they think they should know.

● It becomes increasingly difficult to deliver 'joined up' solutions and service if skills are divided across different parts of the organization.

● Creativity and innovation are a major challenge.

This is clearly a very single-dimensional view of organizational structure – there are of course many alternatives that are shaped by such factors as size, nature of the business and customer needs. You may wish to consider the alternative structures you see among a portfolio of your bank's customers.

5.4 Service Quality

Understanding what customers will pay for

We have identified the important role that service quality (the customer service element from the marketing mix) plays in the total 'customer experience' bundle and this topic merits further closer attention.

Many financial services organizations have focused on service quality as a potential source of competitive advantage and have implemented company-wide programmes to raise the performance bar. Many are finding that being nice to customers is not enough, that it is a journey rather than an end in itself and that customers' expectations continue to rise remorselessly. Indeed, customers' expectations may rise the more favourably disposed they are to a company! Service quality is not without cost, so relative to the customer's expectations and what they are prepared to pay, there must be a point beyond which it is not economic to go.

So, with the economics in mind, service quality can be defined as meeting or exceeding customers' expectations at a price that is acceptable to the customer and at a return that is acceptable to the organization. The challenge is to supply a service commensurate to its cost with a value that the customer recognizes – a contracted mutual value. Note the importance of the customer understanding what is part of the contract or compact – and conversely what is not part of the arrangement – in summary an agreed product or service at an agreed price.

Where the elements are highly engineered or mechanistic such as money transmission then this is quite clear. However, where personal service is a major component then it becomes more problematic. For a relationship manager it is particularly important because the risk is that you end up over servicing an account to an extent that is not justified by the income the customer generates or you set up a pattern of involvement – say dealing with operational issues – that is not part of your core role. Here, customer education is an important part of the exchange process. Generally, transactional service excellence is deemed to be a giver, not a driver, of overall satisfaction levels.

Service Measurement

It has to be remembered that it is the value as perceived by the customer that is important. And, what the customer considers valuable may be different from what the bank considers valuable. In order to be successful banks needs to offer higher perceived value than their competitors. Therefore, it is critical to measure not only how your customers perceive your bank, but also how competitors' customers perceive their banks.

Banks measure customer satisfaction across the corporate market in a number of ways.

- Two major independent surveys are those carried out by Greenwich in the top end of the corporate market and NFO in the mid-market, which may give market share data as well as generic product usage and satisfaction at a bank level – some of this information is shown later.

- Internal, regular and statistically-based cross-sections of the customer base, the findings from which may be attributable to team level.

Banks are also harnessing the capability of the Internet to solicit timely feedback on a one-to-one basis. This is important because relationships can be measured only in terms of the impact of one individual on another. Successful relationship banking is about an open one-to-one exchange. This one-to-one dialogue can be enhanced in a number of ways:

- Structured annual reviews which deal with all aspects of the relationship;

- allowing customers into the bank behind the scenes to see how it works;

- customer panels drawn together to research particular issues;

- research workshops to beta test new product/process developments;

- 360 degree staff appraisal feedback;

- allowing customers to be involved in staff selection and promotion;

- developing case studies and stories with customers that exemplify excellent service.

The idea is not to compromise the bank in the running of its own business but to improve openness and transparency.

Service Quality Gaps

As a bank engineers its service quality it needs to pay attention to the risks of performance gaps emerging in the definition and execution of service standards. These frequently arise from the differing perceptions and expectations of customers, managers and those staff that are actually involved in delivering the service – either directly face-to-face – or as a supporting or back-office function to those that deal directly with customers.

Gaps may emerge because of misunderstanding, misinterpretation and mismanagement. They may also emerge because activities are not aligned or focused in a way that puts the customer first – many companies find it difficult to be customer-centric in all their activities. Process control through the use of a quality model such as ISO 9000 provides a framework to ensure that all the processes required to be delivered are identified and aligned.

This can be simply illustrated by research where customers are asked independently to prioritize a number of key factors.

In the context of service quality, a frequently referred to model for helping to identify the gaps between the perceived service quality that customers receive and their expectations was developed by Parasuraman, Zeithaml and Berry in the 1980s. Their research identified five key gaps:

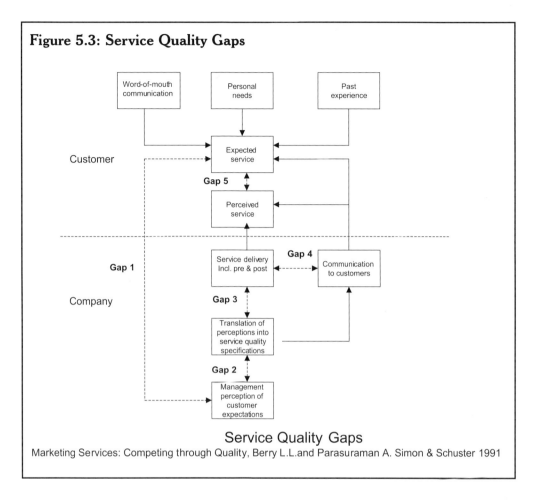

Figure 5.3: Service Quality Gaps

Service Quality Gaps

Marketing Services: Competing through Quality, Berry L.L.and Parasuraman A. Simon & Schuster 1991

Gap 1

This exists because there is a difference between the levels of service that the customer expects to receive and management's interpretation of the customer's expectations.

Market research, feedback from frontline staff and customer complaints are useful indicators here. It is often illustrative to walk back into an organization from the outside and backward engineer a process. An example might be the size and scope of activity of a bank. Bank executives might see this as a service strength, a middle-sized UK corporate might see this as a disadvantage because bigger could equal more impersonal.

Gap 2

This may result from management being unsuccessful in translating the customer's requirements of service quality into service quality standards for the bank and the staff to follow.

For example, managers might think that customers want to see a manager when there is a complaint, customers may prefer for the complaint to dealt with quickly and with the minimum of fuss.

Gap 3

This exists because the actual service delivery, before or after the event, has failed to meet the defined standards.

As we have identified, it is not possible to ensure exactly the same quality of delivery for services as for manufactured products because of the people element. It is possible to go some way – franchises such as McDonald's are interesting example, where attempts are made, usually successfully, to iron out variability in performance.

Gap 4

This arises if the levels of service are not properly communicated or understood by the customer.

Often marketing agencies will put their top people in front of potential clients when pitching for business. If the business is won, they may then disappear into the background. Setting the levels of involvement at the outset is a key requirement.

External to the Bank

Gap 5

This exists if the customer's perception of the service that is being provided falls short of what was hoped for.

An example here might be a relationship manager failing to adequately provide information on a particular service that the customer had alluded to at the last meeting.

In reality some gaps are inevitable – the challenge is not to make them transparent to customers. There is also a risk if managing and minimizing these gaps is not addressed that this may result in internal turf wars and also tension and stress within employees. Most staff want to give good service and will be in their own way as critical of the bank and its management as the customers. The risk is that this tension – and perhaps cynicism – is communicated to customers either explicitly or implicitly through the way staff behave.

Factors influencing Service Quality

Earlier work by Berry looked at understanding the factors that influenced service quality. These five factors (which can be recalled by the initials RRATE) were:

Systems Related

Reliability: the ability to perform the desired service, dependably, accurately and consistently.

For a relationship manager this would mean calling back at an agreed time, producing reports when promised and ensuring accuracy and confidentiality at all times.

People Related

Responsiveness: willingness or readiness of relationship managers to provide timely, prompt service at a time that meets the customer's needs.

For a relationship manager this would mean responding to any urgency communicated by the customer, making decisions promptly, respecting internal deadlines they may have and moving quickly to complete transactions and documentation.

Assurance: the ability to engender trust and confidence through the relationship manager's skill, knowledge and personal qualities.

For a relationship manager this would mean good interpersonal skills, being confident and appropriately knowledgeable about the bank's products, offering a constructive dialogue at all times and having people with whom we can have a good relationship.

Empathy: a focus on the individual needs of customers. It is often compared to a medical consultant's bedside manner

For a relationship manager this would mean being able to understand the customer's perspective, accurately sensing their emotions, recognizing their needs as well as the bank's and being reasonable in negotiating terms, conditions and documentation.

Physically related

Tangibles: physical evidence such as the appearance of relationship managers, their offices (and cars!) and the collateral marketing and sales materials used with the customer.

Note the predominance of people-related factors – underlining the critical influence the relationship manager has on the customer's overall perceptions of service quality.

The Importance of Empathy and Trust

The RRATE factors can be expressed in the form of a hierarchy that has parallels with Maslow's hierarchy of needs. As the basic needs are met, such as reliability and physiological, so the focus moves to the higher-order areas such as empathy and self-actualization. Indeed, in a relationship banking context these may be explicitly linked – helping customers to realize their personal goals may deepen and improve the relationship. It has been suggested that companies that excel at bolstering the customer's esteem are likely to engender customer delight.

Figure 5.4: Matching Expectations and Perceptions

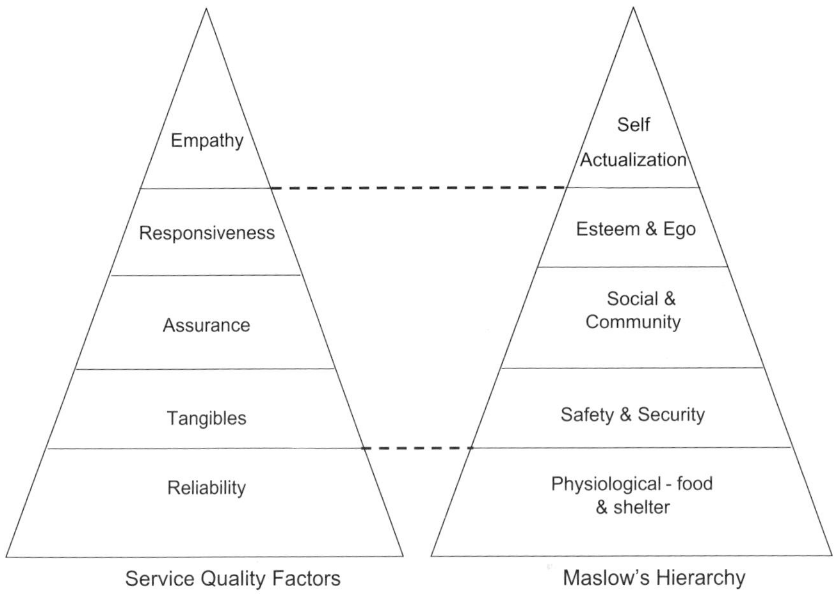
Empathy
Responsiveness
Assurance
Tangibles
Reliability
Self Actualization
Esteem & Ego
Social & Community
Safety & Security
Physiological - food & shelter
Service Quality Factors
Maslow's Hierarchy

Matching Expectations and Perceptions

Underpinning any relationship with staying power is trust. That has to be built on the confidence that what any organization promises is underwritten by a commitment to do just that. We shall come back to this later.

Matching Expectations and Perceptions

What is fundamentally important is to engineer the service delivery to meet customers' requirements. If there is a performance shortfall then clearly this needs to be addressed. However, there is no benefit in adding costly service quality features if the customer does not value them to such an extent that the cost of providing them can be recovered. This demands a two-part questionnaire. Firstly, to define expectations. Secondly, to measure performance against expectations.

For example, in a survey of your bank's treasury capabilities you might ask a battery of questions about the client's expectations of treasury service providers and then the same questions to rate your own service. In this way any delivery gaps can be identified.

Note: in the table the RRATE factor would not be shown in practice although the factors do of course underpin all the questions. Respondents are asked to circle the number that best expresses their expectations of an outstanding treasury department.

Typical questions might include:

Table 5.2 RRATE Questions

Question	RRATE Factor	Rating Not Absolutely Essential						Essential
Being concerned and understanding when there is problem	Empathy	1	2	3	4	5	6	7
Making decisions promptly	Responsiveness	1	2	3	4	5	6	7
Having people with whom we can have an easy relationship	Assurance	1	2	3	4	5	6	7
Doing things right first time	Reliability	1	2	3	4	5	6	7
Understanding our specific needs	Empathy	1	2	3	4	5	6	7

The outcome might then be a chart that would compare expectations with performance in the following way:

Figure 5.5 RRATE

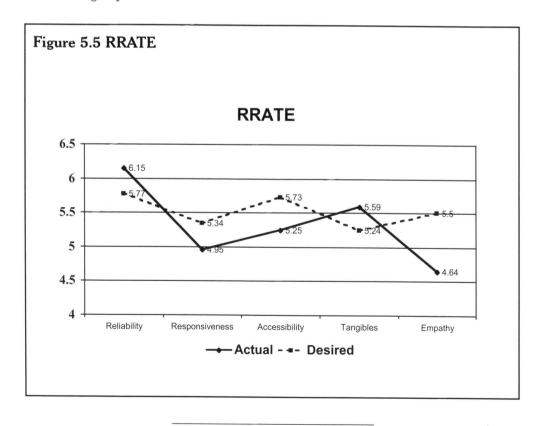

Here, for illustration, expectations about reliability and empathy are not being met, while responsiveness and assurance are being overdelivered. This data can then form the basis of reassessment programmes within the treasury function. This can be done internally also through the use of mystery shopping of the competition (although more typically a feature of the small business and personal retail markets) and audits so that any glaring omissions are identified before the service meets the real customer.

Managing the Tensions

The role of the relationship manager is often described as 'boundary spanning' linking the needs of the customers with the needs of the bank.

Inevitably the pressures relationship managers perceive themselves to be under in the bank influence them. There is a need to feel good about yourself, your bank and the environment you work in. Relationship managers experience less role ambiguity and conflict when they work in an environment that reflects their own values of service.

Current thinking suggests that there is a very strong correlation between staff satisfaction and customer satisfaction and that they may be assumed to be mutually reinforcing. The strands of quality, satisfaction and retention for customers and employees can for the most part be quantitatively linked to profit. Staff retention is an interesting area – it has been suggested that employee tenure is not a measure that will necessarily be valued by customers.

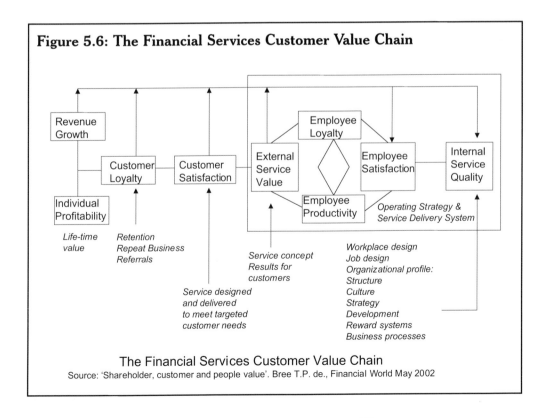

Figure 5.6: The Financial Services Customer Value Chain

The Financial Services Customer Value Chain

Source: 'Shareholder, customer and people value'. Bree T.P. de., Financial World May 2002

However, certainly many customers will claim that being able to deal with the same relationship manager over time is important to them. We shall look again later at the way in which the bank or organization operates impacts on employee satisfaction and motivation.

Customer Satisfaction and Loyalty

Many companies have invested heavily in understanding customer satisfaction and point to recurring surveys given satisfaction levels of 90%+. Unfortunately, research shows that there is no comfort here – satisfied customers are just as likely to defect.

Indeed even customer loyalty and customer retention are not the same. Customers may say they are going to buy from you again but until this happens there is no certainty. NFO (Source: Middle Market Corporate Banking, The 1998 Survey, NFO Financial Services) showed over a one-year period almost two-thirds had been approached by competitor banks – 32% by telephone, 26% by personalized letters, 26% by direct mail and brochures, and 17% by visits. Do your customers tell you when a competitor bank has approached them?

There may be grounds for confidence if you have moved customers to the advocate level on the loyalty ladder, ie to the stage were they are prepared to actively recommend you to others. Some companies believe this is the only real measure of loyalty. Word of mouth has the benefits of lowering advertising costs and getting you like-for-like peer group customers.

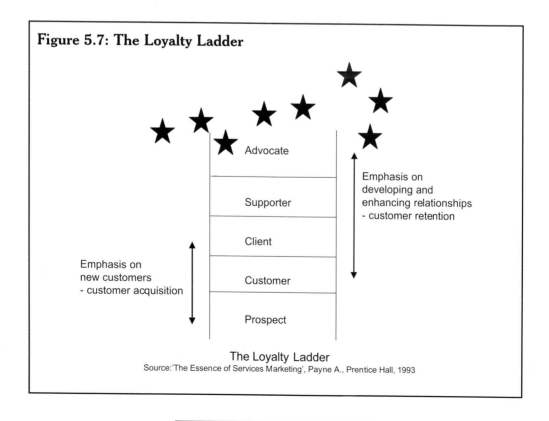

Figure 5.7: The Loyalty Ladder

Advocate

Supporter

Client

Customer

Prospect

Emphasis on new customers - customer acquisition

Emphasis on developing and enhancing relationships - customer retention

The Loyalty Ladder
Source:'The Essence of Services Marketing', Payne A., Prentice Hall, 1993

Xerox found that its 'totally satisfied' customers were six times more likely to repurchase Xerox products during the following eighteen months than its merely satisfied customers. 'Totally satisfied' ranks only two scale points higher than 'merely satisfied' although it earns six times more loyalty.

(Source *Sloan Management Review Fall 1999 Understanding Customer Delight and Outrage* Benjamin Schneider and David E Bowen).

A number of companies have introduced loyalty reward schemes. At one level they can be seen as tactical sales promotion but in some cases – and in the minority – companies are now intelligently using the data on behaviour that, for example, card-based schemes can generate to target relevant offers and increase sales volumes. Note that moving these schemes from a tactical to a strategic tool probably means a significant investment in IT and also reallocating the marketing budget to support segment-focused offers. In a corporate banking context, customers will probably expect this to be reflected in the product pricing although, of course, the thrust of relationship banking is to dilute price sensitivity.

6

VIEWING THE ORGANIZATION

6.1 Overview

Being able to understand and analyse your bank as an organization is as important as being able to understand and analyse your customers. The role of the relationship manager is to provide a bridgehead between these two groups and act as an intermediary to meet the needs of both. Here we look at some techniques for developing that organizational understanding.

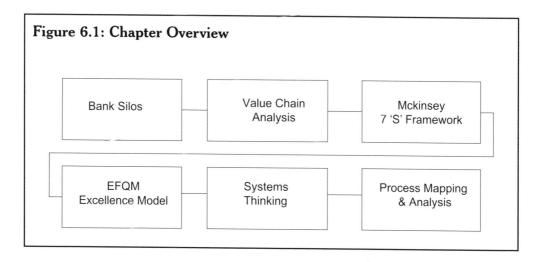

Figure 6.1: Chapter Overview

6.2 Bank Silos

If I asked you to picture your bank as a whole most probably your thoughts would turn to the organizational structure chart – and most probably it would not fit easily on one piece of paper! This, typically, is how organizations divide and manage the myriad roles and accountabilities and particularly in a bank the day-to-day risk management issues.

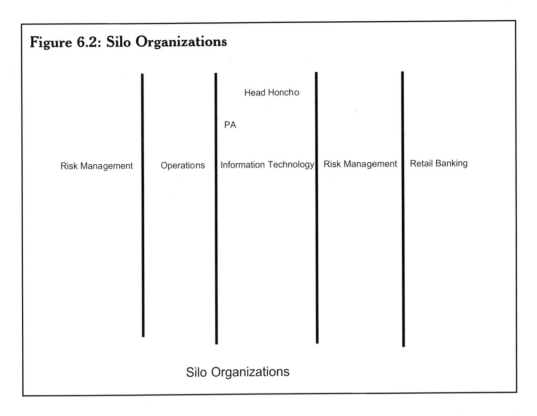

Figure 6.2: Silo Organizations

Head Honcho

PA

Risk Management   Operations   Information Technology   Risk Management   Retail Banking

Silo Organizations

This approach has a number of strengths – clear demarcation lines, functional centres of excellence and a clear understanding of who is the boss. It has a number of weaknesses – it encourages 'silo thinking', makes people status- and authority-conscious and has an internal focus. The risk is that the customer gets lost – in summary, it is not a customer-focused or customer-centric way of doing things. Another risk is that it gives rise to what is described as 'command and control' behaviour – where levels of authority are important, a fear/blame culture exists and individual initiative is stifled out. It is also incomplete – it does not show how the bank interacts with its customers suppliers and partners.

Take now the customer's perspective. The customer expects the relationship manager to be able to harness all the strengths of the organization. This often may mean 'picking and mixing' from various different areas, pulling together cross-functional teams to meet the needs of customers. This cross-functional working is an increasingly common feature of organizational life linking, for example, people from technology, operations and customer-facing areas to improve the way in which customers are served. Product managers work with relationship managers in a similar way.

Aligning company resources to customers' needs is what CRM is all about. It is common to talk about CRM as an 'enterprise-wide' strategy. What does this mean? It means that implementation of the strategy must touch all parts of the company and cannot be just the latest management or marketing fad. CRM needs to be integral part of overall business strategy and demands a response across all the bank's functions.

Most companies who embark on a CRM strategy are finding this is easier said than done. Industry research points to 50% to 70% of companies failing to fully realize the benefits of their CRM strategies. In essence this has to be viewed as a major change management programme, needing integrated working across the whole organization. Inevitably – as we have identified earlier – there is always the potential for conflict between organizational structures, control processes, procedures and operational systems.

The outcome is that there is a need to be able to view the organization in a number of different ways – ways that encourages flexible and adaptive thinking rather than simply a reinforcement of the status quo. To a relationship manager the ability to think in this way will be particularly helpful as you adopt a consultancy problem-solving approach to your customer's needs rather than defining them in terms of the products you have and delivery in terms of organizational fiefdoms.

We shall now look at a number of different ways in which you can scan your bank and a customer's business.

6.3 Value Chain Analysis

If the traditional structure chart is a static, bureaucratic view of the company then another way of thinking holistically, ie seeing things as a whole and from a helicopter view, is by using the concept of a value chain. This derives from a model developed by Michael Porter and suggests that an organization is a series of integrated components, the focus of which is to deliver value through the organization to the customer.

Symbolically the value chain points towards the customer segments and has some parallels with the CRM architecture shown earlier. Clearly it also has some silo and structure connotations but the issue is one of alignment of the parts to deliver the whole in a horizontally integrated way. The challenge is to ensure that each of the hand-off points and boundaries between functions interact seamlessly.

This is a powerful tool for breaking down the silo mentality and developing a true customer focus. It helps in determining areas of competitive advantage but also helps at an operational level for thinking about the alignment and balance of the bank. It triggers a host of questions, such as:

- Can we effectively deliver joined-up solutions to the customer?

- Where are the gaps?

- What improvements can be made?

- Is the approach we take to credit sufficiently responsive to customers?

- Are the business development activities of product specialists and relationship managers as integrated as they could be?

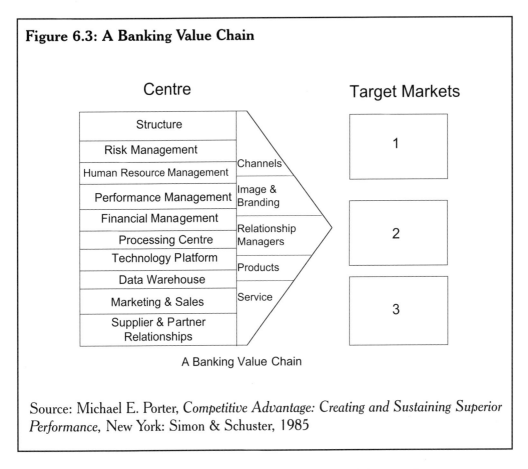

Figure 6.3: A Banking Value Chain

A Banking Value Chain

Source: Michael E. Porter, *Competitive Advantage: Creating and Sustaining Superior Performance*, New York: Simon & Schuster, 1985

● Do we have the right balance between centralization and de-centralization?

6.4 McKinsey 7S Framework

If we now think of organizations as a series of dynamic linkages, we can move from the functionally specific to think in terms of sets of interactive capabilities, competencies and strengths.

One of the models that is helpful in this context is the 7S framework developed by the consultants McKinsey. This framework identifies seven attributes that can be used in concert to define and understand the capability of your bank, or indeed the customers of your bank. These attributes should link together in a way that meets your market's needs by delivering the customer superior value we talked about earlier. It intimates that these factors are continuously interlinked and that any new development at a strategic level – say the adoption of a CRM strategy – or a project level – say the introduction of a new IT system – have an impact in varying degrees in all seven areas. It acknowledges the part that structure plays but puts it alongside all the other factors.

Figure 6.4: The McKinsey 7S Framework

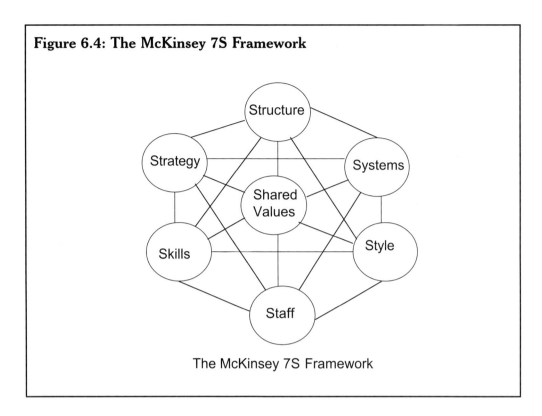

The McKinsey 7S Framework

Dealing with each of the areas in turn:

1. Shared Values

This S is placed at the centre of the framework because it summarizes 'the way we do things around here'. This is often viewed as the glue that holds the company together. It may be a set of written rules – such as mission, vision and values statements together with unspoken but clear cultural and behavioural norms. For example, are you allowed to have fun in the office? Are mistakes seen as learning experiences or is there a fear/blame culture? Are you told what day you can dress down on or is it left to the individual's discretion?

2. Strategy

This is the set of activities that the bank will undertake to achieve the goal of competitive advantage. In large organizations there will be a mix of activities reflecting the needs of the various business units. Often different business units will trade off the same customer base so it is vital to coordinate activities so that customers are not oversolicited and the brand and business prospects damaged.

3. Structure

The orthodox view is that the structure of an organization should follow on from the strategy. Often, though, driven by expediency, organizations will try to implement new strategies on the basis of the old structure as a result, say, of political infighting. Think of the number of mergers that are reported in the press to have been aborted because of personality clashes.

A common feature today is the removal of layers of middle management, moving empowerment to the front line and team working.

4. Style

This is the way in which managers collectively behave with respect to the use of time, attention and symbolic action. These behaviours have a very powerful influence often described as 'walking the talk'. Do managers view their staff as their customers? Are their diaries so crammed with meetings so that their direct reports cannot get to them? Do they cry off from appraisal meetings at the last minute claiming a client or head office meeting? Does the appraisal system capture this behaviour through, say, a 360-degree appraisal process?

5. Staff

These are the people in the organization and the way in which they are supported both by the HR function and the management on a day-to-day basis. 'People are our greatest asset' is an oft-quoted refrain. Does the bank deliver on the rhetoric? Are staff advocates of the bank in the same way you want customers to be? Is there sufficient focus on personal development, including transferable skills? Are incentive schemes appropriately aligned?

6. Skills

This is the collective ability of the organization to deliver the goods through the capabilities of its people. There is a clear link between what the bank wants to do as defined in its strategy and how it delivers the strategy through its people. Inevitably, this is a fluid process with some skills becoming less in demand while others come to the fore. These skills may be functional – such as IT code writing – but they may also be to do with more generic personal attributes such as a positive attitude, enthusiasm and an appetite for creativity and innovation. An important issue is the time it takes to build the required skills levels – think, for example, of nurses and doctors where it takes many years for them to become fully trained.

7. Systems

These are the rules, processes and procedures that typify corporate governance. They should be mutually reinforcing and designed to help rather than to prevent staff from doing the job – in other words a foundation for performance rather than a ceiling. We shall look shortly at the process elements in particular. Some organizations may be highly centralized with very firm control from the centre; other companies may give greater autonomy to the front-line units.

In practical terms, the framework can be used as a guiding tool at the outset of a programme but equally as a diagnostic tool to identify performance gaps on an on-going basis. It therefore has validity as you think about the way your bank goes about its business and your customers also.

6.5 EFQM Excellence Model

Another way of taking an holistic view of the company is to use one of the quality improvement models such the EFQM (see www.efqm.org). Other models you might like to look at include the Malcolm Baldridge model in the USA and the Deming Prize in Japan.

This maps the interrelationships between the enabling areas and the results areas. Performance can be measured in each of these areas using a set of predefined criteria so companies can assess themselves and also be externally accredited so that year-on-year performance can be tracked.

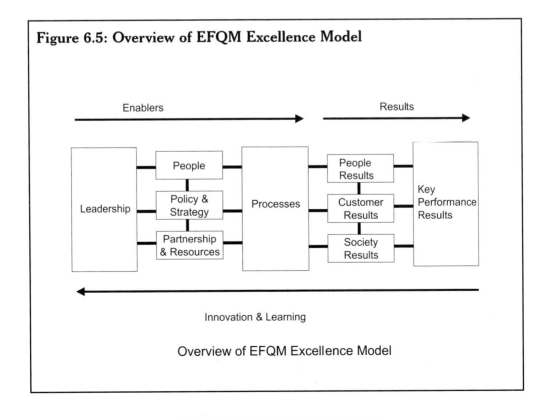

Figure 6.5: Overview of EFQM Excellence Model

Overview of EFQM Excellence Model

Quite often underpinning these models will be accredited quality programmes such as ISO 9000 (see www.iso.ch). ISO 9000 has become an international reference for quality requirements in business-to-business dealings and can be applied to any organization, large or small, whatever its product or service. ISO 9000 focuses on 'quality management' – what the organization does to enhance customer satisfaction by meeting customer requirements and continually improving its performance in this area.

6.6 Systems Thinking

So far we have looked at fairly literal and straightforward models insofar as they bare some relationship to what you are familiar with. The 7S introduces the idea of inter-relationships and a sort of push/pull effect among the factors. If we take this one step further, then this brings us to 'systems thinking'. Remember this is designed to encourage you to think about your bank and your customers 'outside the box' and in a more dynamic way than previously – as part of the development of your consultancy mindset.

Systems thinking is defined as:

> 'a way of thinking about, and a language for describing and understanding, the forces and interrelationships that shape the behaviour of systems.'

For completeness and from the same source:

> 'A system is a perceived whole whose elements 'hang together' because they continually affect each other over time and operate towards a common purpose'.

Source: 'The Fifth Discipline Fieldbook', Senge P.M. et al Nicholas Brealey Publishing 1994

So, systems thinking is the ability to see the organization as a complex whole, in which you understand that everything is connected to everything else but in a much more detailed and free thinking way that the 7S framework. If you do one thing then it has a knock-on effect. It builds on the simplistic interaction identified by the McKinsey framework to allow for more of the complexities inherent in large organizations.

Think of a sailing boat and the interaction of the boat, the people in it, the sea, the wind and then all the areas within these major components – the weather and tidal systems, the capabilities of the sailors and so on.

This systems perspective enables decisions to be made consistent with the company and the customer's long-term best interests and the long-term best interests of the system as a whole. The key is this notion of all of these interrelated parts working with each other and their environment to deliver the total outcome.

How does this help? Well it gets you away from the static, single-dimensional view and ordered functional view of the company. In delivering effective and relevant solutions to

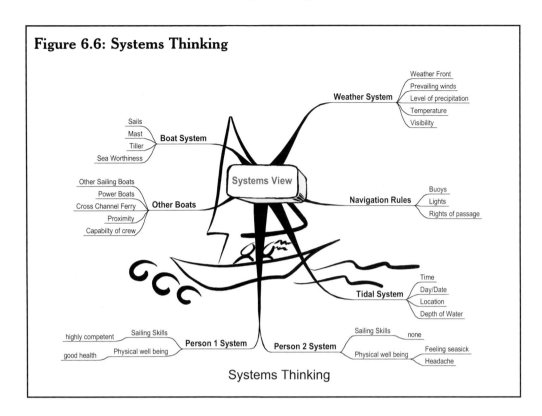

Figure 6.6: Systems Thinking

Systems Thinking

customers and, being able to stay in touch with their changing needs, there is a need to rethink the traditional organization. Relationship managers have a major role to play in this and must not be intimidated just because the bank says 'well, we have always done it this way'. The ability to take an holistic perspective helps to reduce purely factional behaviour. This has a client benefit also, because it helps you look at the way he does business and the challenges he may face that uncovers additional opportunities for your bank to provide the solutions needed.

6.7 Process Mapping and Analysis

With the enquiring mind that systems thinking stimulates, we can now turn to how we understand and capture exactly what an organization does. Most organizations – and banks are no exception – consist of a series of interlinked processes that deliver defined outputs. Note that processes may involve different people but that they should have a shared aim. Note also that process is part of the services marketing mix and the role of process is to link the operations of a bank to the needs of its customers.

Especially in a service industry context, we need to start from an understanding of those processes that have as their main objective the satisfaction of customer needs. Think of processes as a structured way for handling a series of connected tasks. Historically in most organizations the products sold or the ways in which you get your goods and services to market – the distribution channels as they have been called – has determined these processes.

To get this right means looking into the company from the outside to understand where procedures and processes may not be totally aligned to deliver customer satisfaction. It also means having a different perspective of understanding how and what makes large organizations tick. Imagine you were starting with a blank sheet of paper – how might you do things differently?

Think, for example, of the account-opening process, the credit-sanctioning process, the business development process and the portfolio management process that we shall look at later.

It helps to map these and other activities from time to time to see if they are working at optimal efficiency. This might be part of an on-going continuous improvement programme, it may be because there are complaints, and it may be because there is a drive to reduce costs. Indeed the question may well be asked 'Should we be doing that work at all?' The Japanese have a concept of 'muda', which roughly translated means 'every moment of time when nothing of value is happening'. Duplicated activities, unnecessary breaks in the chain or poorly executed handovers often come to light.

There are a number of tools that can be applied to process analysis, among which are:

Pareto Analysis

This is also known as the 80/20 rule and says that a few vital causes are responsible for the majority of the effects. If one of the minor causes is removed then the effect on the total is small. In practical terms this tool helps to focus attention on the key issues and their prioritization. For example, you can use it to analyse the profitability of customers within your portfolio as an input into how your time might be spent.

Fishbone Diagram

This is also known as a cause and effect or Ishikawa diagram. It is used to systematically list and organize the possible causes of a problem where there is no obvious solution. The effect, which may be a target or a problem, is written down as a short summary at the right side of a page. A broad horizontal line pointing at the effect is then drawn. The major factors that contribute to the effect are listed and joined as branches of the main line. Lesser factors emanate from the main branches. In practice a good way to do this analysis is to use Post-it notes that can easily be moved around as the analysis takes place.

Figure 6.7: Pareto's Curve

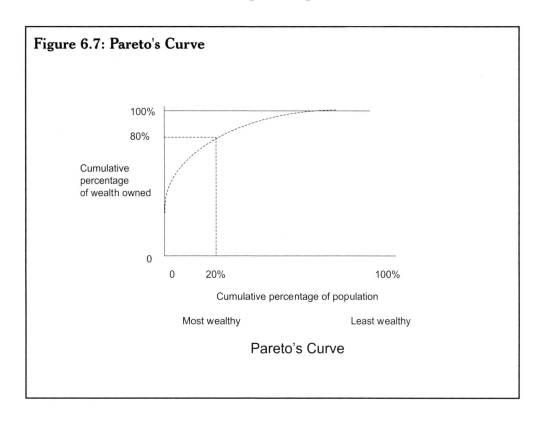

Pareto's Curve

Figure 6.8: Fishbone Diagram

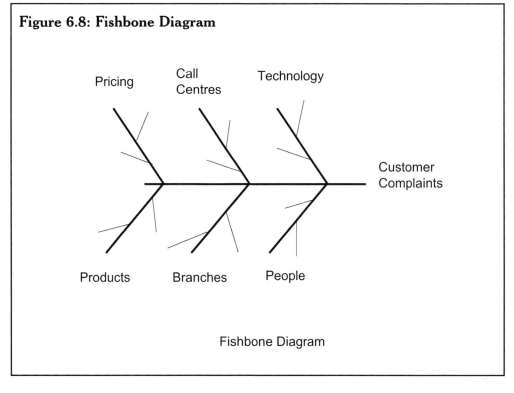

Fishbone Diagram

Blueprinting

As part of the performance improvement process, one of the best-known techniques for process analysis is blueprinting. There are a number of steps:

1. Charting all the components of a service so that it can be seen objectively and clearly (see diagram).

2. Identifying the 'points of failure', for example, those areas which consistently trigger customer complaints.

3. Comparing how it is done now with how it could be done in the future.

4. Defining the critical success factors for the future desired performance and stress testing their feasibility.

5. Designing and implementing the new process together with revised service standards.

Note the dimensions of time, the extent to which the underlying process is transparent to the customer and the points of failure shown on this diagram. This ability to look internally at your own bank and externally at the way the customers go about their business is an added value skill for relationship managers. Many organizations recognize a need for their staff to be 'process literate' in this way.

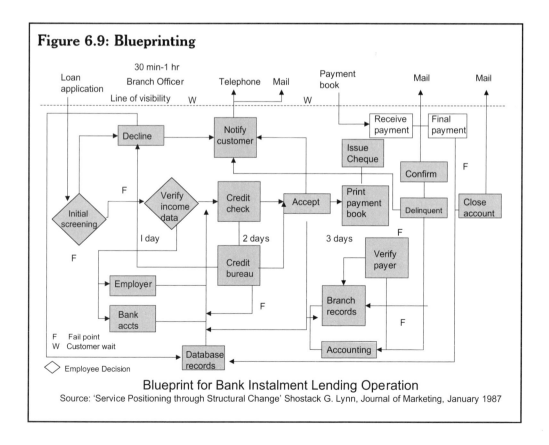

Figure 6.9: Blueprinting

Blueprint for Bank Instalment Lending Operation
Source: 'Service Positioning through Structural Change' Shostack G. Lynn, Journal of Marketing, January 1987

Force Field Analysis

Force field analysis works on the basis that any situation can be analysed as a balance between two sets of forces, one group in support of the status quo, another group against it. The analysis process proceeds in a number of stages:

- Understanding where you are and where you want to get to, say in terms of improving an organizational process;

- Listing the forces for and against change. These can be people, processes, technology, culture, customers' needs and so on. Map them on the diagram below:

- Identify those forces you believe to be the most important. List the actions you could take to reduce the strength of these forces. On the other side – how might you strengthen the proponents of change?

- Identify and apply the resources necessary to help to solve the problem.

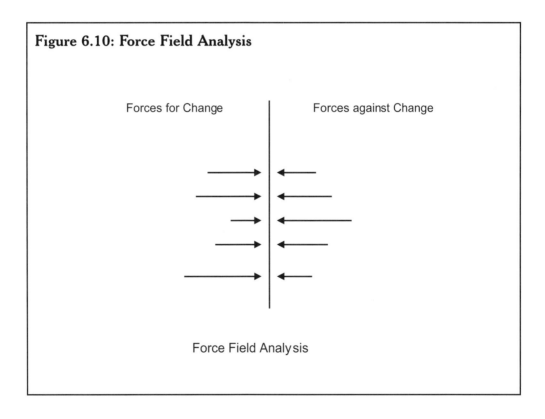

Figure 6.10: Force Field Analysis

Forces for Change Forces against Change

Force Field Analysis

7

PORTFOLIO PLANNING

7.1 Overview

Building on the high level and strategic content of the previous chapters, we now begin to look at some of the more practical issues for relationship managers. In this chapter we look at the following areas:

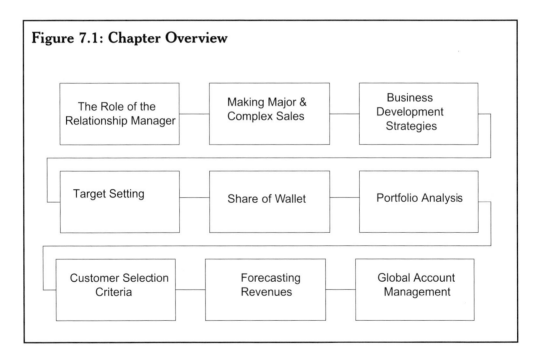

Figure 7.1: Chapter Overview

7.2 The Role of the Relationship Manager

We are going to look now at a number of the key processes and activities that underpin the role of the relationship manager. But before doing so let us get an understanding of his or her responsibilities.

A typical role definition might look like this:

Core Purpose

- Responsible for

  - managing a portfolio of corporate customers;

  - developing and maintaining proactive relationships with new and existing customers to provide them with quality business solutions;

  - maximizing income for the bank through retention, growth and targeted acquisition of clients.

Major Activities and Responsibilities

Customers

- Develop an in-depth understanding of customer and financial needs within the corporate marketplace.

- Tailor customer solutions by utilizing and adapting the full range of bank products and expertise.

Business Development

- Develop and execute a long-term plan of visits to existing and potential customers, building strong relationships with key business influencers to generate new leads.

- Work closely with the corporate development team and other bank business partners to create a marketing strategy for each relationship.

- Use a structured prospecting approach with a view to pursuing new relationships and growing the customer portfolio.

- Build and develop a high profile in the corporate marketplace.

Credit

- Gather and analyse financial information to present sometimes complex properly structured credit applications to be sanctioned, ensuring that ongoing credit processes and information requirements are met.

- Ensure debt-structuring balances customer need with risk.

Income Generation

- Negotiate interest rates, fees and commissions with customers to maximize profitability.

Team Working

- Ensure excellent aftersales care is delivered through close liaison with service providers and product specialists.

- Coach and develop support staff to perform their role and provide excellent customer service.

- Work with the team to maximize business performance.

7.3 Making Major and Complex Sales

The nature of the business – corporate banking – has a significant influence on the way in which a relationship manager goes about customer-related business development.

By definition, not all customer interactions will result in sales. In fact, the first principle of delivering a customer-focused solution is to understand that the pace and nature of the sales process is quite different from more conventional selling. If we assumed that your bank has opted for a customer relationship management strategy then we need to legitimize sales activity in the context of a relationship. This means looking at longer-term value as opposed to short-term wins with no substance. There is nothing inherently wrong in using best sales practice or indeed talking about selling.

The issue is the mindset, culture and style that condition its implementation. Products are solutions to customers' needs not something that has to be offloaded to meet sales targets. Long-term relationships rather than short-term sales are the goal.

Within the field of industrial markets, key account management is an important tool to ensure that relationships with key customers are managed effectively. These may not be directly applicable to banking in their totality but some of the underlying concepts and tools have relevance. Corporate banking has many if not all of the features of what is commonly described as 'Major Sales' – as distinct from highly repetitive low-value transactional selling.

Among these features typically are:

- Infrequent purchases.

- Long selling cycle – multiple calls to realize sales.

- An on-going relationship with customer.

- Meetings that may be to advance to, rather than complete, a sale.

- The seller is often part of the product/solution.

- There is generally a higher risk for the buyer.

- Customer needs are more complex and take longer to develop and understand.

- The purchase is likely to be highly visible and therefore higher risk within the customer's company.

- Success may depend not just on how well you sell but how people within the customer's company sell your offering to their colleagues because there will be many stakeholders involved in the decision, and you may not personally meet all of them.

- Actual and potential costs to the customer are higher.

- Banks are essentially selling professional services, the need for which is often difficult to predict.

- There is a heavy reliance on an in-depth understanding of the customer's business.

- Products are potentially technically complex.

- Sales are usually the result of a group effort (for the relationship manager and the customer).

- The most important discussions and deliberations may go on when the relationship or product manager is not present.

The implication of this is that the traditional and small ticket-selling techniques are not as successful in a major sales environment such as corporate banking – indeed they may work to prevent sales. Let us compare and contrast some of the typical sales activities as they relate to simple sales (as they might occur in other industries) and major sales (as they should occur in corporate banking):

Table 7.1 Comparing Simple & Major Sales

Activity	Simple Sales	Major Sales
Pre-planning	Minimal	Detailed to define account strategy and call objectives
Activity Management	Carefully managed – close attention paid to sales-people's call rates	Not a major driver of performance – needs to be quality not quantity and consistent with account objectives

Meeting Objective	Sale	May be sale but more often action based advancement to sale such as building a more detailed picture of the customer's needs
Opening	Establishing personal rapport Benefit statement Robotic approach	Introduce your self, say why you are there and get permission to ask questions Initially focus on building trust and confidence
Initial Impact	You do not get a second chance to make a first impression	Building a relationship – personal qualities over time that count
Frequency of Meetings	One-off	On-going relationship
Product Features (facts, data)	Slightly positive relationship to call success	No more than neutral impact on call success – focus is on needs and benefits
Product Benefits	Very positive as demonstration of capability	Very positive if matched against customer's explicit needs on a point-by-point basis
Customer Needs – implied, ie statement of problems, difficulties and dissatisfactions	Buying signals Strong predictor of success	Not buying signals or a predictor of success because the customer has to articulate the needs in his/her own words
Customer Needs – explicit, ie needs, wants, desires	Not normally uncovered	Buying signals Strong predictor of success
Solutions	Offered once initial problem identified	Held back until full extent of problems and implications understood
Questions – number	May be high	Depends not on number but type of questions – and the ability to 'stress test' the customer's response

Questions – pre-planning	Rarely carried out	Critical to gaining information, understanding problems and how your products could solve them. Remember – 'Fail to plan, plan to fail'
Probing – use of open questions	Hallmark of a successful call	Not specifically related to success of call
Objections	Seen as buying signals Objections overcome using range of techniques	Seen as barriers Prevent them occurring in the first place by careful planning and anticipation
Negotiations	Typically flat % price reduction offered	Based on understanding of total benefits to customer, of which price is a part. Concede only against a pre-determined range.
Closing	Successful sellers close more often during call and use more types of closes (assumptive, alternative, last chance)	Closing less effective as size of decision increases
Use of Pressure	Successful with small sales – relatively little risk	Irritating to customers – higher degree of personal and professional risk from the customer's perspective and reputational risk for the bank
Measure of Success	Sale completed	May be the completion of a sale but more often commitment to advance – where an event takes place, either in the call or after it, which moves the sale forwards to a decision

Source: Derived from *'Making Major Sales'*, Rackham N., Gower 1990

In addition these sales can generally be classified as complex because they possess one or more of the following elements:

- The buying organization has multiple options

- The selling organization has multiple options

- In both organizations numerous levels of responsibility are involved

- The buying organization's decision-making process is complex, meaning that it is seldom evident to an outsider.

Source: *'The New Strategic Selling'*, Heiman S., and Sanchez D., with Tuleja T., Kogan Page.

Many of the activities we talk about here can form part of a salesforce automation system. These are available separately as 'point' solutions or as part of enterprise-wide CRM systems offered by major suppliers such as Siebel Systems. Rather than buy a ' turnkey' solution – one that covers all your potential needs delivered in one go – some banks have taken the strategic decision to build their own systems, validating the added value of the functionality as they go. You may find from experience of your own bank that the components of an integrated process may exist in a number of forms – mainframe-based, Intranet-based, other PC software such as Excel and also some inevitably paper-based.

7.4 Business Development Strategies

How often have you met high performers who seem to be able to manage their portfolios successfully year after year with little more than the equivalent of a little black book? This is often redolent of a 'deal-making culture' and is not consistent with a relationship

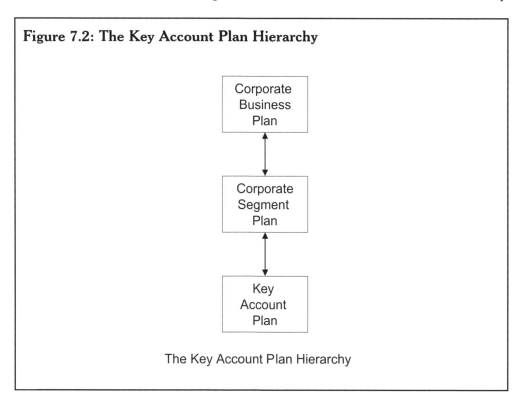

Figure 7.2: The Key Account Plan Hierarchy

The Key Account Plan Hierarchy

management strategy. Unfortunately, although the success is good to have they are not often helpful role models. They can be difficult to manage because there is no baseline against which to assess their performance and if they run at some stage into the relationship manager's equivalent of the wall, it is difficult to know where to go next and what advice as a sales manager or team leader to offer.

This makes the planning process of fundamental importance – starting off by mapping your route rather than just getting in the car and driving off in the hope that you will arrive. This planning activity has a number of layers and it is the key account plan level that we are going to focus on here.

Remember some of the key language here:

Objectives: what you are going to do expressed as goals in an unambiguous way using the SMART acronym:

S **Specific** – the desired result should be specified

M **Measurable** – it must be possible to measure the achievement of the objective against the original target

A **Achievable** – although challenging and stretching, the objective must be capable of being achieved

R **Relevant** – relevant to the needs of the customer, the business and the relationship manager

T **Timescale** – a specific timescale – short-term or long-term – should be set for the objective.

Strategy: how you are going to achieve your objectives. At an account level this would mean:

- Analysing your current position with regard to your business development objectives

- Thinking through a range of possible alternative options

- Determining which combination of these option would best deliver your objectives.

Action Plan: the specific activities to execute your strategy and the planning to achieve it.

We shall be looking in more detail at the key account plan in more detail shortly.

7.5 Target Setting

Targets provide a performance benchmark against which individual and group performance can be measured in relation to the total business development mix that your bank wants to achieve. Although a potentially contentious issue it has a number of benefits – a major one being the motivation of salespeople, which we look at in more detail later.

Targets can be set:

Top down: Senior management decides on the necessary business levels to achieve the required profit/growth/shareholder value that is required by the corporate plan. This is then divided between the areas of the business, and then by region, area, corporate office, and relationship management team and relationship manager.

Bottom up: The individual relationship managers review their own portfolios and plan their activity for the coming year. These figures are then aggregated at the various levels to give a total.

In practice what happens is a mix of the two. A participative process has a number of advantages:

● The relationship manager has a good chance of starting the year with a feeling that the targets are achievable, rather than feeling a sense of 'force majeure'.

● There will be a higher level of commitment and ownership to targets that have been self-determined.

● There is the possibility that relationship managers will set themselves higher targets than they might have been given based on their more detailed understanding of their customers.

Targets may be high-level and broad-brush, eg 'to grow income by 15%', or they may be more detailed such as 'maintain retention at 98% of current portfolio level, introduce six new accounts, achieve a customer satisfaction rating of 85%' and so on. Which approach is taken will depend on how the bank usually goes about this and may also be influenced by the time the relationship manager has been in that role. New managers may need a higher level of specification until they find their feet in their new role.

7.6 Share of Wallet

Most banks now understand that it is quality of earnings that count rather than market share, although of course the two are not mutually exclusive. Most banks also understand that pure volume is insufficient if it is not matched by proportionate profitability. Relationship management seeks to deliver organic growth – by making sure you capture any new business the customer has – and improving up-selling and cross-selling.

Thus the size of a bank's customer base is not nearly as important as its composition. Greenwich Associates research shows the importance of being the lead bank – what they describe as 'the true importance of being truly important'.

Table 7.2 The Importance of being a Lead Bank

Relationship tier	% of revenue earned per tier	Number of banks cited per tier	Percentage of revenue earned per bank
Lead	54	1.9	28
Second Tier	19	2.1	9
Third Tier	13	2.8	5
Fourth Tier	14	7.8	2

Source: *Financial Services without borders, How to Succeed in Professional Financial Services*, Greenwich Associates, John Wiley & Sons, 2001.

This progressive focus and deepening of the customer relationship is often also referred to as 'improving share of wallet' and in particular improving the share of wallet for those customers who are profitable now or have the capability to be so in the future. This suggests, for example, that when prospecting you should focus on those customers who have the ability to deliver high share of wallet as opposed to low. You need think in terms of the difference between true 'relationships' and loosely connected single-product customers.

In its 1993 paper 'Measuring Share of Wallet', The US Business Banking Board suggested that share of wallet can be calculated in two ways – strategic and tactical.

Strategic Share of Wallet: this expresses the relationship between the proportion of all of the customer's financial services expenditure you have at a bank level against the total financial services expenditure of all corporates.

$$\text{Strategic Share of Wallet} = \frac{\text{Bank's share of all Customer's Financial Services Expenditure}}{\text{All Customer's Total Financial Services Expenditure}}$$

It can also be expressed as the percentage of accounts where you have the primary relationship against the base of your market share:

$$\text{Primary Bank Ratio} = \frac{\text{Primary Relationships}}{\text{Share of Customers}}$$

This calculation could also be done against the total of corporate accounts you have as a tracking measure of the penetration of primary relationships versus the rest. This calculation can be further refined if comparative earnings data can be calculated for your products versus the competitors', although clearly there is a good deal more work here and the indicative figures of the more simple calculation may be sufficient.

Clearly a high primary bank ratio is a characteristic of a bank capturing the majority of the customer's revenues, holding 'first choice' position in the customer's mind and indicating a strong relationship position.

Tactical Share of Wallet: This calculates the ratio of customer value captured by the bank versus the total financial services spending by the customer. This gives a proxy for the strength of the relationship and helps to determine a relationship strategy by evaluating the share of revenues captured.

$$\text{Tactical Share of Wallet} = \frac{\text{Bank's share of all Customer's Financial Services Expenditure}}{\text{Individual Customer's Total Financial Services Expenditure}}$$

Traditionally this approach would probably be predicated on holding the current account. Note, however, that the metrics are driven by share of revenues of which the current account may be a part or, indeed, no part where specialist services are involved, particularly at the top end of the corporate market.

To put this approach in perspective the Business Banking Board offer the following quote from a Vice President, Corporate Marketing of an unnamed US Bank:

'In our commercial segment ($5 to $25 million), we derive between five and ten times more income from high share-of-wallet customers. In the middle market ($25-$250 million), the income gap between high share-of-wallet customers and low share-of-wallet relationships is a factor of ten. In the large corporate segment the income difference is a factor of fifteen.'

7.7 Portfolio Analysis

You may recall we identified earlier a number of four-box analytical frameworks such as the Boston Matrix for assessing the relative attractiveness of markets, products or even customer groups. A similar simplified approach – which may, however, provide important insights – can be taken to the accounts in your portfolio.

The value of this approach is that it should get you to think about your portfolio as a whole and not just concentrate on those 'star' customers or those with whom you get on particularly well. As an aside, you should always have a withdrawal strategy that prevents any customer becoming dependent on you personally.

Think here in terms of a portfolio of unit trusts, high-growth, income, special situations and so on.

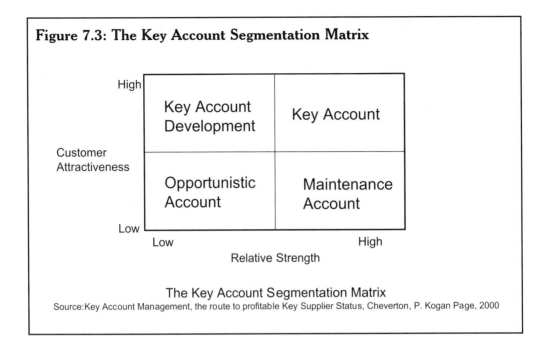

Figure 7.3: The Key Account Segmentation Matrix

The Key Account Segmentation Matrix

Source: Key Account Management, the route to profitable Key Supplier Status, Cheverton, P. Kogan Page, 2000

Key Account Development: remember key customers include not just today's significant customers but also tomorrow's. This segment refers to new customers yet to be identified or perhaps in the sales funnel already. The challenge here is to manage this carefully, giving the right balance of time and attention.

Key Account: the accounts that on an 80/20 basis are providing the bulk of your portfolio income – these will be the focus of your retention activity. Bear in mind that inadequate attention to existing accounts is often a key reason for the competition being successful. Periodically reassess your understanding of the customer needs – treat and view them as new business opportunities to see if this generates a different perspective. Make sure you are front of mind should any opportunities crop up. Make sure that you document the good news and be sure to write to the customer outlining the positive impact your intervention has had.

Heed these words of warning:

> *'The business relationship with an account is never static. It's either getting better or it's decaying. Never delude yourself into believing you have a stable relationship that will continue indefinitely and remain invulnerable to competition. Complacency is the worst of all sins with existing accounts. Face the uncomfortable fact that what you did yesterday is history. What counts with most customers is what you're doing for them today and what you can do for them tomorrow.'*

Source: *Account Strategy for Major Sales,* Rackham N., Gower 1988

Maintenance Account: perhaps those customers who have a mature relationship and are not particularly responsive to marketing activity. Nonetheless they make a useful contribution – in the Boston Matrix these would be the 'Cash Cows'. These may be good customers and loyal personal favourites but the pure economics dictate that there is a need to pull energy and resource back from such customers and avoid time consuming commitments through fewer visits and telephone servicing, for example.

Opportunistic Accounts: these are accounts – and there will be some – that may best respond to a transactional approach – a specific product offer, for example – but where the relationship development opportunities are not strong. Normally they will be considered as and when it fits with your priorities.

You will recognize that an optimal portfolio consists of a balance of new and repeat buyers and that the relative costs of attracting as opposed to retaining customers must be gauged. The degree of resource allocated to each account should be proportional to its propensity to generate sustained profit. It is common to think here in terms of sales efficiency and sales effectiveness:

Sales efficiency: how to get in front of the right customers, for the right amount of time and at the right time for minimum cost.

Sales effectiveness: how to maximize business development and sales potential once you are there.

Often there is a conundrum about what to do with the low-value accounts:

● do you allocate resources in an attempt to make these customers with relatively low or negative lifetime values more profitable?

● do you actively migrate customers with low or negative value away from the bank?

● do you accept their lower contribution and re-prioritize their needs and the levels of service you give them accordingly?

How you treat these accounts will be a combination of macro and micro influences – at a high level your bank's declared strategy on how to handle the low-value accounts. At a relationship manager level it will be affected by the dynamics of your own portfolio and the opportunities within it. Most banks still remain loath to actively manage accounts away although they may do this more often on risk grounds.

7.8 Customer Selection Criteria

Customer attractiveness can be rated on a number of factors such as:

● Size – volume, value, profit opportunity

● Growth potential – value, profit opportunity

- Financial stability – industry and individual risk factors

- Ease of access – geography

- Closeness of existing relationship

- Product usage

- Extent of multi-banking

- Strategic fit – do they see the world in the same way that you do?

- Are they early adopters – do they pick up new ideas and products, or do they wait until the market has tested them first?

- Do they value your offer? Is it relevant to their needs?

- Level of competition – low is attractive

- Their market standing – industry leader, credibility, prestige and so on

Again, your own business circumstances must determine selection and the weighting you give to individual factors. Rating the customers can be carried out intuitively against specific criteria such as those above or alternatively on a statistical basis with a numeric rating of the factors.

You might want to consider this rating from the customer's perspective – how they see your bank and you as a relationship manager. What is the value-added?

7.9 Forecasting Revenues

As we move to the process of identifying key accounts and based on what we have discussed so far, the relationship manager will be forming an overall picture of the likely necessary activity to deliver his or her targets for the next business period. Typically the mix of activity is shown in Figure 7.4.

The next stage is to break this down by customer and product line and we shall look at this later.

7.10 Global Account Management

It is appropriate to acknowledge at this stage the potential complexity to the role that may be added by the need to trade on a global basis. Global trading has accelerated with the increasing abolition of exchange controls, the breakdown of entry barriers to national markets and the relaxation of cross-border capital flows not to mention the instantaneous linkage of foreign markets and 24-hour trading. Banks as always have had to go where their customers are as they expand beyond current geographical barriers and industry boundaries.

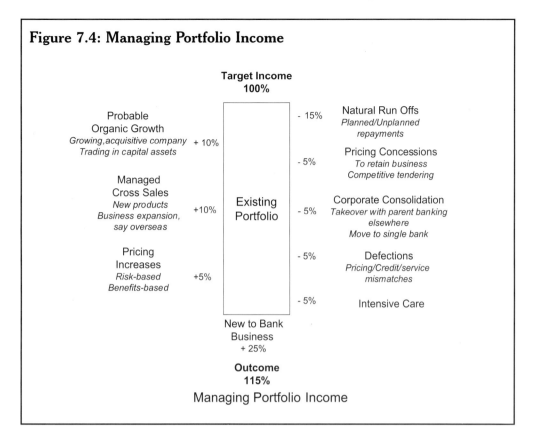

Figure 7.4: Managing Portfolio Income

Target Income
100%

Probable
Organic Growth
Growing,acquisitive company + 10%
Trading in capital assets

Managed
Cross Sales
New products
Business expansion, +10%
say overseas

Pricing
Increases
Risk-based +5%
Benefits-based

Existing
Portfolio

New to Bank
Business
+ 25%

- 15%   Natural Run Offs
Planned/Unplanned
repayments

- 5%   Pricing Concessions
To retain business
Competitive tendering

- 5%   Corporate Consolidation
Takeover with parent banking
elsewhere
Move to single bank

- 5%   Defections
Pricing/Credit/service
mismatches

- 5%   Intensive Care

Outcome
115%
Managing Portfolio Income

Historically multinational banking has had line management authority set up on a national basis with a fair amount of independence but the impact of relationship management has been to increasingly coordinate these activities. Given this and the globalization 'drivers', there are a number of benefits to be gained from global account management including:

● A single point of contact and/or coordinated traffic management so that there is no internal competition;

● The ability to gain additional revenues from the customer's international expansion;

● Efficiency gains that come from economies of scope and scale in servicing customers;

● The leveraging of client knowledge;

● Consistency in service quality and performance leading to reputational benefits and new customers;

● Raising customers' switching costs by increasing interdependence and creating a long-term relationship.

A study reported by David Montgomery and George Yip in Critical Marketing 2001 (Global CRM Challenges) found that in an industrial context for those companies who had instituted global relationship management perceived performance and satisfaction went up by 20%, revenue increased by about 15% – and so did profits.

In this environment, relationship managers may be operating in a framework of perhaps a:

- Global relationship manager who is accountable for the overall customer relationship and is responsible for continually reviewing the client's needs to ensure delivery of the appropriate products and services;

- Regional and local relationship managers working with their clients in the countries of operation who understand the main economic and regulatory characteristics of the local and foreign markets;

- An investment banking advisory relationship manager looking at potential needs from his/her perspective;

- Appropriate product specialists who continue to provide innovative and leading-edge solutions.

Often this places challenges on all aspects of the organization's practices and processes such as the centralization of information, reporting processes, personnel evaluation, compensation and incentives and ensuring a regular flow of customer feedback.

8

KEY ACCOUNT PLANNING

8.1 Overview

In this chapter we look at arguably the most critical process in effective relationship management – the key account plan.

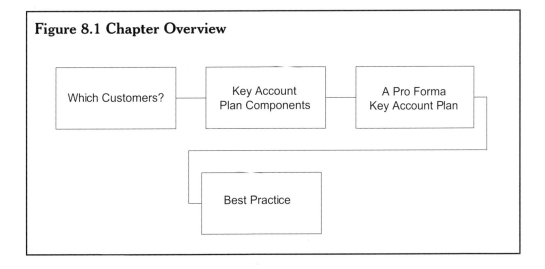

Figure 8.1 Chapter Overview

8.2 Which Customers?

Within the sales function of industrial markets, customer portfolio analysis and key account planning are significant tools for the strategic management of relationships. Embedding the practice of key account management in the organization gives it an opportunity to develop a distinctive competence leading to increased customer satisfaction and profits. Key account customers are those which are important now and those that may be important in the future.

Applying Pareto's law, plans will be considered for the 20% of customers who generate 80% of the business (and/or constitute 80% of the risk). From a practical point of view, it is best to be realistic – planning a small number of accounts properly rather than skating over them all.

Look, for example, at the concentration of customers in the derivatives market. The figures below are the proportion of total customer derivatives business generated by the 20% most active users worldwide and in three major regions:

Table 8.1 Derivatives Usage

Region	Total Derivatives Volume %
United States	92
United Kingdom	82
Continental Europe	90
Global	89

Source: Financial Services without borders, How to Succeed in Professional Financial Services, Greenwich Associates, John Wiley & Sons, 2001.

Here also is an illustrative portfolio that comprises 35 customers with an overall income of £2 million. Rather unhelpfully the 80/20 rule is not clear cut – how would you prioritize these accounts and how might your view change if you were a product manager, for example. Who would be clear candidates for a key account plan and why?

Customer portfolio number	Deposits	Lending	Fees	MT	Asset finance	Int NII	Int fees	Tresaury	Total	%
1	1	12		1	2	2		120	138	
2	6	12	3			50	30	9	110	
3		98	2		2				102	
4	1	75	3	4					83	
5	72	4						3	79	
6			10		60				70	
7		5	9				20	35	69	
8	24	30	1			12	2		69	
9	2	56	2						60	
10	30	24	1						55	
Sub-Total	136	316	31	5	64	64	52	167	835	42

Customer portfolio number	Deposits	Lending	Fees	MT	Asset finance	Int NII	Int fees	Tresaury	Total	%
11			1						1	
13								25	25	
14		40					12		52	
16							20		20	
17		38							38	
18		20							20	
20		25			15	10			50	
21	24								24	
24			2						2	
25	12								12	
28	25		1	15		12			53	
29	14								14	
32		27							27	
35		36			12				48	
Sub-Total	**211**	**502**	**35**	**20**	**91**	**86**	**84**	**192**	**1221**	**61**
Balance	**249**	**248**	**15**	**30**	**49**	**34**	**96**	**58**	**779**	**39**
Total	**460**	**750**	**50**	**50**	**140**	**120**	**180**	**250**	**2000**	**100**

Notes
Figures in '000
Int NII = International Net Interest Income

8.3 Key Account Plan Components

Let us look at the component of a key account plan, recognizing the differences from other plan formats you may be familiar with. Notice the focus particularly on understanding the people dynamics of the customer and the likely influence they can have on your desired business outcomes.

1. Basic Account Information

- Static information: self-evident.

- Other bank relationships – product specialists etc – they should be involved in this account review.

- Current income streams to the bank.

Figure 8.2: The Components of a Key Account Plan

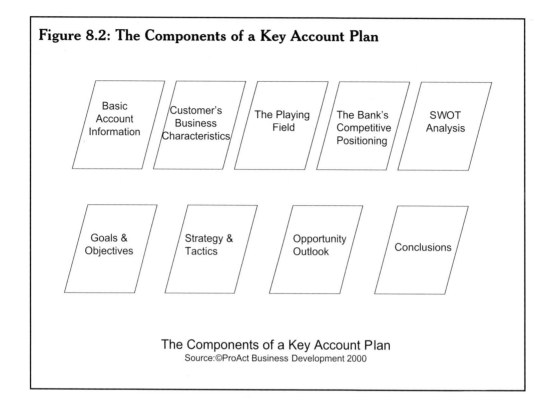

The Components of a Key Account Plan
Source:©ProAct Business Development 2000

- Business description: a thumbnail sketch only.

- Revenues, profits, assets, employees: key statistical data.

- Key performance ratios: an understanding of these should help to surface key challenges and opportunities for the business

- Relationship overview: summary description of the account and the bank's relationship setting the context.

2. Business Characteristics

- Company mission statement: what does this say about the company's purpose and values?

- Company measures of success: how do market share, profitability, sales volumes etc define this?

- Key drivers of performance: trends or issues that are uppermost in the minds of the company's senior management.

- Basis of segmentation: how are the segments defined and what are the value propositions for each segment?

● Customer proposition: what is it that makes their customers want to buy from them?

● The competitive landscape: who are their top competitor's, what do they typically look like and what makes them different?

3. Understanding the People

● Key people analysis: an analysis of the key people by social style, career indicator and levels of accessibility. What are their personal and business drivers?

4. The Bank's Competitive Positioning

● How do we match up against existing bank suppliers, what do they have that we have not got? Are we vulnerable or are their opportunities to expand our share of wallet? What is the competition doing now and what do we expect them to be doing?

5. SWOT

● This is the summation of the previous inputs and is designed to provide the foundation on which your business strategy for this customer is developed.

● The challenge is to be able to summarize this and the other data you have collected in the form of an 'elevator' speech. If you are in a lift with your banking director or indeed the customer, what is it you would tell them succinctly to demonstrate your understanding of the business?

6. Goals and Objectives

● Goal statement: What do we believe we can achieve for the forthcoming year on this account or are there longer-range objectives – three-year facility renewals for example?

● Specific objectives: Defined using the SMART terminology.

7. Strategy and Tactics

● Strategy: An overall statement of intent supported by a series of individual strategies as necessary consistent with the overall strategy. The strengths and vulnerabilities of the declared strategy should be articulated also.

● Tactics: Itemized activities with timing and resourcing that are consistent with the strategy.

8. Opportunity Outlook

● A *pro forma* income projection showing the potential timing and extent of the earnings as an input into your overall portfolio performance.

9. Plan Conclusions

- A summary of the assumptions, risks (with potential responses), the critical success factors and any additional relevant comments.

Source: 'ProAct Business Development Ltd 2001.

This plan should be the combined output of the relationship manager and the product managers. With the product manager on hand, the relationship manager will be able to integrate the product strategies into his own account plan. Product specialists will develop their own product plans covering the areas identified in the table below.

Table 8.2 Components of a Product Plan

Components of a Product Plan

- A thorough analysis of your bank's current product execution, development capacity, and capabilities compared with that of each of your direct competitors.

- A plan for allocating specialist resources, based on the account plans, across the conflicting demands of business development, product development and execution support.

- Accountability for specific events – with dates – to measure product specialist performance against the product plan.

- A review and profitability plan that is tied in with the account plans.

- A sign-off by team leaders and senior management.

- A strategy for introducing the appropriate product specialists to their customer counterparts and getting it right on their product-specific strategy, including how it fits into the overall relationship strategy.

- An analysis of each competitor's strengths and weaknesses, along with tactics for taking advantage of any vulnerabilities as well as defending against their strengths.

Source: *Financial Services without borders, How to Succeed in Professional Financial Services*, Greenwich Associates, John Wiley & Sons, 2001.

A specimen Key Plan Format is shown in Appendix A.

8.4 Competitor Analysis

This is an important area that is often not documented as well as it might be – much of the knowledge may well be in the relationship managers' heads although product managers tend to be more disciplined because they have to. How would you score on the following competitor analysis checklist?

Table 8.3 Competitor Analysis Checklist

Activity	Strongly agree					Strongly disagree
We know the strengths and weaknesses of our main competitors	1 2 3 4 5 6 7
Our bank routinely monitors the activities of our main competitors	1 2 3 4 5 6 7
We subscribe to trade and industry publications in order to find weaknesses that we can take advantage of	1 2 3 4 5 6 7
Our firm devotes a lot of effort to figuring out the strategy of our competition	1 2 3 4 5 6 7
We know the pricing policies of our competitors very well	1 2 3 4 5 6 7
We know which major segments our competitors are trying to serve	1 2 3 4 5 6 7
We know who our major competitors are by market segment and product	1 2 3 4 5 6 7
We are able to weather economic cycles better than our competitors	1 2 3 4 5 6 7
In banking there is really not that much difference among the top few banks in technology development and the functional quality of products	1 2 3 4 5 6 7
We are geared up to respond quickly to our competitors' actions	1 2 3 4 5 6 7
We tend to be a trend-setter in the industry	1 2 3 4 5 6 7
We have a person or group responsible for monitoring the actions of our competitors	1 2 3 4 5 6 7
It costs us less to provide our service than it does our largest competitor	1 2 3 4 5 6 7
We make better use of our technology than our competitors	1 2 3 4 5 6 7

We have a well thought out international strategy	1	2	3	4	5	6	7
We find ourselves frequently adjusting the nature of the product and service support we provide to respond to our competitors	1	2	3	4	5	6	7
Because of the competition we have little control over the prices we charge	1	2	3	4	5	6	7
We provide a substantially different product than most of our competitors	1	2	3	4	5	6	7
We react quickly to competitive moves	1	2	3	4	5	6	7
We are probably more profitable than our largest competitor	1	2	3	4	5	6	7
We monitor the competition so they do not catch us by surprise	1	2	3	4	5	6	7
It is impossible to predict who the dominant bank will be in five years	1	2	3	4	5	6	7
Start-up costs are high in corporate banking	1	2	3	4	5	6	7
Our analysis of the competition is more formal than informal	1	2	3	4	5	6	7
In corporate banking we have to worry about indirect competition as much as direct competition	1	2	3	4	5	6	7
Our top managers frequently meet to discuss the strategies of our competitors	1	2	3	4	5	6	7
We have a frequently communicated and share understanding of the major competitive threats	1	2	3	4	5	6	7
I believe that if you focus on satisfying the needs of customers then you do not have to worry about the competition	1	2	3	4	5	6	7
Understanding our competitors is an integral part of our bank's planning	1	2	3	4	5	6	7

Source: 'The CIM Handbook of Selling and Sales Strategy', Jobber D. (Ed), Butterworth Heineman, 1997.

Some of these questions deal with the process of competitive analysis, some with the potential sources of competitive differentiation. Review them again so you know which questions fall into which camp.

8.5 Best Practice

● A written account plan should:

   – Be 20% past, 80% future.

   – Be an agenda for discussion.

   – Demonstrate alignment of ideas and thinking.

   – Be a live and dynamic document.

● Consider discussing the account plans with the customer:

   – It generates more effective plans.

   – Gains commitment to the plan from the customer.

   – Is a good example of partnership behaviour.

   – Demonstrates professionalism to the customer.

● Need to periodically review plan – should be a live document and not consigned to the bottom drawer:

   – What did we do well?

   – What major changes have their been?

   – Are declared business objectives still valid?

   – What are the three next key actions?

9

BUILDING REFERRAL NETWORKS AND COLD CALLING

9.1 Overview

Although the focus of relationship management is primarily retention, good-quality acquisition also has an important part to play. In this chapter we look at the components of this acquisition process.

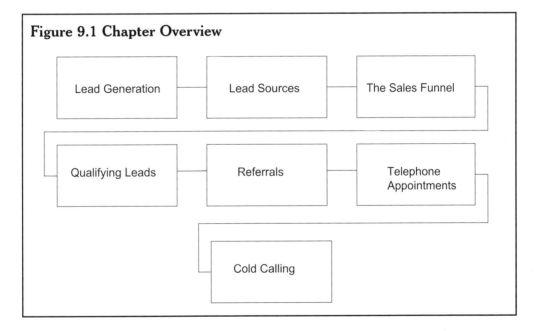

Figure 9.1 Chapter Overview

Lead Generation — Lead Sources — The Sales Funnel

Qualifying Leads — Referrals — Telephone Appointments

Cold Calling

9.2 Lead Generation

Building referral networks and cold calling are an integral part of the lead generation process that in turn is an essential part of the sales process. While the focus of a relationship management strategy is on retention, there is still a need to give a balanced amount of time to new business development.

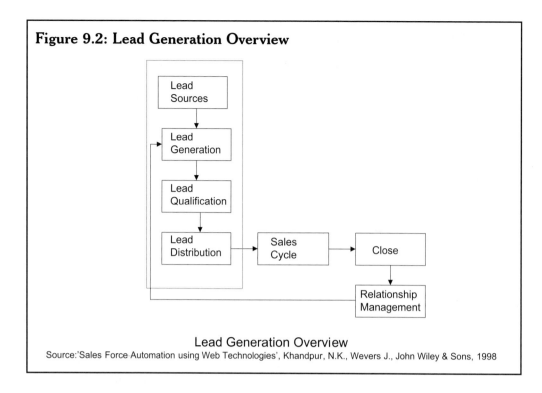

Figure 9.2: Lead Generation Overview

Lead Generation Overview

Source:'Sales Force Automation using Web Technologies', Khandpur, N.K., Wevers J., John Wiley & Sons, 1998

Research by NFO Financial Services (Middle Market Corporate Banking, The 1998 Survey) suggests that over 60% of your customers will have received an approach from another bank in the last twelve months. You need to be out there proactively looking for good quality prospects also.

Some banks have specialist business development teams that work alongside the relationship managers, identifying and qualifying prospects before they are handed over to the relationship manager. They will work hard in the local business communities building relationships with intermediaries and other potential introducers of business. This activity may sit alongside the business development activity that the relationship managers themselves carry out. Often the distinction is made between hunters and farmers – hunters getting the business and farmers developing and growing the on-going relationship. There is an obvious risk if your relationship managers are farmers and your competitor's relationship managers are hunters.

9.3 Lead Sources

A frequent challenge is that of coordinating central marketing activity with local relationship management and sales activity. Usually there is some form of 'traffic management' system in place to avoid oversolicitation of customers. Equally there is a need to ensure that sufficient resources are available at ground level if a central marketing campaign is scheduled.

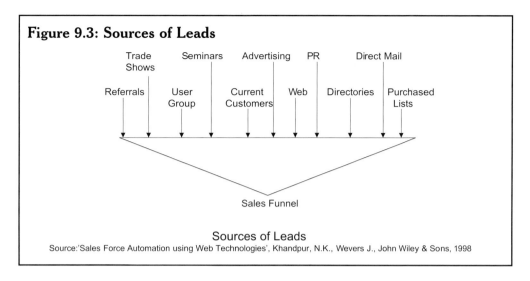

Figure 9.3: Sources of Leads

Sources of Leads

Source:'Sales Force Automation using Web Technologies', Khandpur, N.K., Wevers J., John Wiley & Sons, 1998

Leads are the raw material for this sales process but this needs to be managed in an effective and efficient way. The sources will vary in their levels of usefulness – accurate tracking can help to determine the level of cost effectiveness of the various sources.

Some banks have invested in prospect systems that include a wide range of published and unpublished sources and produce lists for business development teams. If your bank has such a system review the business rules that drive the prospect selection – understand what are the sources used and the filters that are applied to refine the outputs. Local networks and referrals that result from the local profile that the bank has built supplement these.

A typical process then might be as follows:

Table 9.1 Filtering Leads

- Work with readily available lists of companies provided by service organizations such as Dun & Bradstreet, Fame, and Experian to generate a list of potential prospects based on location, size and industry.

- Delete based on industry. Eliminate those industries that do not fit your bank's loan portfolio and business strategy.

- Delete based on location, depending on the scope of your delivery capability.

- Delete based on risk. Eliminate companies that are a poor credit risk.

- Delete based on profiling. Review your current customers to determine the amount of business generated by each one. From this create a profile of the most desirable customers and use this profile to identify and target prospects most likely to generate similar revenue.

- Delete based on revenue potential – use a 'hurdle rate' as a filter.

Source: *Financial Services without borders, How to Succeed in Professional Financial Services*, Greenwich Associates, John Wiley & Sons, 2001.

9.4 The Sales Funnel

The sales funnel recognizes that prospects will be at various stages of development – it is suitably vague about the timeframe also. From your own experience you should have a feel for this together with the various conversion ratios as prospects move through the funnel. In corporate banking these timeframes may run over years, for example, the length of a money transmission contract. In some cases they may be exceptionally short, for example, an approach from a company that has had facilities declined by their existing bank. Miller Heineman have a concept of understanding who 'the best few prospects' are – those where closure is imminent. (Source: 'The New Strategic Selling', Heiman S., and Sanchez D., with Tuleja T., Kogan Page)

Monitoring the timeline is a critical activity. For customers well-established with their banks this can take time. Review these figures from Greenwich Associates and see how they fit in with your own experience – in fact do you have any figures? Talk to your colleagues as well.

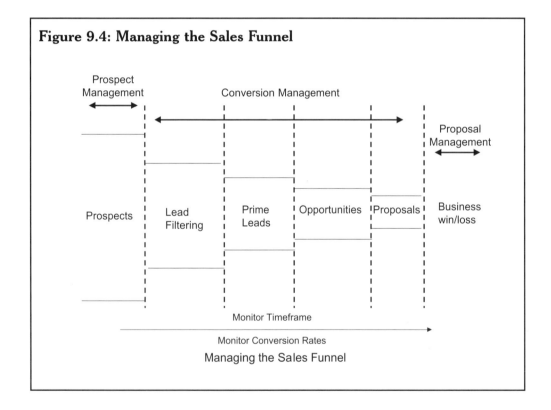

Figure 9.4: Managing the Sales Funnel

Table 9.2 Sales Funnel Time Lines

6 months	18 months	24 months	3 Years
2-3 meetings to:	4-6 additional meetings to:	3-4 additional meetings to:	Close
Verify company's current bank(s)	Meet company owner	Introduce bank senior management	
Verify strength of company's current bank(s)	See financial statements	Employ product specialists	
Verify sales size and net worth (D&B is not always accurate)	Qualify product needs	Introduce to satisfied bank clients	
Verify decision-making and strength of influencers	Determine other soliciting banks		
Terminate or continue	Terminate or continue	Terminate or continue	

Source: *Financial Services without borders, How to Succeed in Professional Financial Services,* Greenwich Associates, John Wiley & Sons, 2001.

9.5 Qualifying Leads

Not all leads are created equal so usually there is often some form of rating system in place to categorize their potential and focus effort. Again this may be a relatively sophisticated system reflecting a number of criteria or just based on the recruiting manager's intuition and using a simple traffic light system of red, amber and green.

The higher the volume of leads the greater the likelihood that this needs to be systemized because it forms an integral part of the sales management process. As with all data, it has to add value greater than the cost of collection, but a comprehensive process would cover many of the following areas:

Table 9.3 Weighting Leads

Prospect Analysis	A weighting	B		A x B
		Possible Lowest Score (Can be minus figure)	Possible Highest Score = 10	
Level of contacts with prospect to date	2	Not yet close to decision maker	More than two levels	
Are we talking to the decision maker?	4	No or decision made by parent company	Sole access	
Accessibility	4	Very difficult	Any time, one of the family	
Basis of decision factors	4	Unknown or favour competition	Established and agreed	
Price	1	Ours above all competition	Better than all	
Timing of proposal	3	Ours still pending	We proposed last	
Prospect's opinion	2	No idea	Outstanding	
Prospect Status/Experience	4	Uses us but unhappy	Our client and happy	
Our experience of the industry	2	None	Bread and butter	
Development required	2	Completely new	None and in constant use	
Attitude to us	2	Biased against	Fully confident	

Note that the factors down the page have different weightings – these are used as a common system but determined in advance by your bank as are the various stages as you go across the table laterally. The outcome is a probability rating ranging from say 25% to 90% depending on the total score.

You also find that some of these factors surface again when we look at the key account management process later.

9.6 Referrals

It is generally recognized that the most cost-effective way of building your client base is through referrals – 'word of mouth' marketing. In consumer marketing this is often called 'member get member'. The benefits include lower acquisition costs and the probability you will be recruiting customers who have the same characteristics as your existing customers and are therefore likely to be more satisfied with your bank.

It is human nature as part of the search process for, say, a new supplier or bank to ask family, friends and respected business colleagues. This is likely to be more persuasive than what the company says about itself. Prospects want to know what people like them think about what you have on offer. This process can be industrialized so that referrals become a predictable part of the new business flow. The term 'viral marketing' has been coined to encompass this activity.

Table 9.4 Low v High Referral Levels

Low level of referrals	High level of referrals
Emphasis on transactional/short-term sales	Emphasis on long-term value of client
Inwardly-focused company	Client-focused company
Closed-book mentality	Commercial transparency with clients
Inconsistent and/or incongruent corporate values and behaviours	Staff and clients feel alignment with corporate values and behaviours
Selling function monopolized by business development and sales staff	Selling – as in meeting customers' needs – is part of the relationship management programme
Ad-hoc referrals	Planned referral generation
Weak or non-existent relationship management process	Relationship management a core corporate strategy

Source: Derived from 'So, you understand referrals, do you?' Sheppard R., Marketing Business March 2002.

Managing the process requires a number of activities. The opening assumption is that your bank is sufficiently credible to be referred. Ask customers what you have to do to make them want to recommend you to others. Make this an explicit statement when you recruit new customers – your expectation is that in due course they will want to refer you to others. Build on success stories – the customer is more likely to be responsive if you have recently delivered exceptional performance. Always acknowledge the referral by saying thank you.

9.7 Telephone Appointments

Making an appointment is very much like a sale. The prospect has been 'sold' the idea that it is worth spending time with you. Think in terms of building interest, qualifying the prospect, overcoming objections and getting the appointment.

Making an appointment is an essential skill for any relationship manager. There are a number of steps to follow:

● Open strongly in vocabulary and tone, be logical, be brief, be to the point.

● Introduce yourself, your bank and check that the person you are talking with is responsible for dealing with the company's banking arrangements – 'I understand you're the person responsible for...'.

● State the reason for your call. Script an elevator speech – what you would say to an influential person riding up several floors in a lift. Be succinct and suggest some benefits that might accrue to the company based on your understanding of their business.

● If time allows do some preliminary probing; position the distinctive features and benefits that your bank has to offer.

● Ask for the appointment – use a closing technique such as 'which day would suit you best, Wednesday or Thursday?'

● Overcome any objections – if there are more than three it is probably worth letting go.

● Ask for the appointment again.

Smile while you dial and when you talk – it lifts the voice. Some people find standing up increases their confidence and the resonance and tone of their voice as well. It always helps when dealing with switchboard operators if you know the name of your prospect – you will have researched this. When speaking to a secretary, remember and use her name (record it in your diary for future reference) – sympathize with the secretary if she sounds harassed. If your prospect is tied up in meetings ask the secretary for a good time to call and/or make a telephone appointment. If the secretary is unhelpful think about ringing early morning, early evening or at lunchtime. Ask questions of any people you deal with – 'I want to introduce by bank to Mr....., is he the right person to talk to?'

9.8 Cold Calling

Technically, cold calling is making contact with prospects without prior warning. It can relate to both telephone calls and personal visits. For the purposes of this discussion we shall extend the definition to include the first call you make to a potential customer also. The extent to which it is used in financial services is clearly contingent on your need to develop leads beyond the mechanisms already available to you. Is it the right way to start a relationship? Possibly not but if, say, a new business park has opened it may well be worth the effort.

Usually there is some form of qualification before the call takes place – even if it is just by observation such as driving around the business park – otherwise it would be extremely wasteful in terms of time.

Some general considerations for spontaneous cold calling:

- Try to get the name of the person you want to speak to – a pre-call to find out the name of a director, say, is a good start.

- If telephoning, getting past a gatekeeper – the switchboard or secretary – is often a problem. Make sure you are well rehearsed and consider telephoning early in the morning or late in the evening.

- If you get a straight no, take it on the chin and move on to the next call – it's not personal.

- Have some knowledge of the company you are calling – its core business, reputation and if possible credit rating.

- If calling in person, leave a business card and promotional material.

If, however, you have the time to be able to plan your approaches in a more considered way, then the following process would help immeasurably.

Table 9.5 Cold Calling Steps

- Send a letter of introduction enumerating the benefits of using your bank and the reasons that justify a visit. Suggest a specific time for a meeting.

- Once you have succeeded in setting up an initial meeting, confirm it, in writing, with an explicit focus on what you and your bank can do to help this particular company.

- Make sure that the solicitation visit is a substantive one that makes good use of the prospect's valuable time. Do not linger. A well-focused first meeting is the best way to get that second meeting.

- Create a short, written plan for the first visit, including appropriate information you hope to glean from the company, and the value and information you will in turn leave them.

- Know in advance what will make the meeting worthwhile for the prospect to ensure that you will be welcome back.

- Determine what knowledge you have that could be helpful to the company. Can you provide insight on interest-rate movements, or offer an observation on their particular industry? If you have reports or other research material to offer, do not hand them over at the meeting. Instead, tell the prospect what is in the report, then a day or so later mail the report along with a brief personal note. This type of 'bridge-calling' turns one sales call into two, and is a highly effective way of ensuring that the calls build on each other toward a relationship from the first transaction.

- Early in the meeting, either introduce one well-chosen good idea or offer the prospect the opportunity to select a topic from an array of three or four choices. Concentrate entirely on that most promising idea, and make the most of it! Establish expectations for the time frame of the reply as well as the format of that reply (such as a phone call, letter or personal visit). Then, meet or beat the expected commitment – so you will be seen to be even better. This can be a tangible and credible means of demonstrating your interest and commitment.

- Trumpet what your bank does best. Many bankers hesitate to laud their operations because they think their bank is not perfect. But no bank is. If you want your sales call to be remembered, walk in the door espousing your bank's key, real virtues and continue from there.

- Always remember: The purpose of the first sales call is to assure a good second call with a specific purpose that is important and useful to your prospect.

Source: *Financial Services without borders, How to Succeed in Professional Financial Services*, Greenwich Associates, John Wiley & Sons, 2001.

10

INDUSTRY AND CUSTOMER PROFILING

10.1 Overview

Your customers expect you to understand both their business and the industry in which they operate. Here we look at some analytical tools to facilitate this understanding.

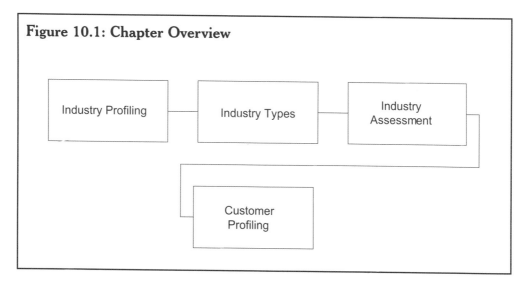

Figure 10.1: Chapter Overview

10.2 Industry profiling

Mainly as a result of the need to manage risk, many banks will have developed sophisticated systems for analysing both customers and the industries in which they operate. Even if you are not an industry specialist per se, customers will expect you to have at least a passing knowledge of the industry in which they operate. Many banks have Intranets that collate this data and the Web means a lot of the information needed will be to hand. Reading the financial press will help to keep your knowledge up-to-date.

An industry is defined from an economic perspective as 'a group of companies producing products or services that are close substitutes for one another'. Broadly industries can be classified as emerging, mature or declining. This classification is obviously dependent on the stage of economic growth of a country and its comparative advantage – compare and contrast, for example, the Third World economies with those of the Asian Pacific 'tiger' economies with more service-oriented economies such as the UK. Here we adopt a Western/UK perspective.

Emerging Industries: The dot.coms have provided a good example of the risks associated with emerging industries. Massive hype obscured the underlying need for a sound business model and an income stream leading to profit. The technology itself was no saviour and in many cases the added value to the customer was not at all clear. In a way that was reminiscent of the South Sea bubble: there was a major re-evaluation of expectations. High start-up costs were barely covered if at all by income streams and even major undertakings such as Amazon and Egg – the Internet bank – found it took several years to reach profitability.

From a banking perspective, the challenge is to sort the wheat from the chaff and find good-quality business.

Mature Industries: Maturity is of course relative. In some respects the mobile telecommunications industry may be described as mature – declining opportunities for new subscribers – but in others it may still be emerging as global networks are consolidated and the continuous march of technology adds more costs and uncertainty. In summary, these industries continue to grow, albeit at a slower pace, have a strong market base and deliver consistent profits – although clearly company performance will vary on a case-by-case basis.

The challenge as a relationship banker is to maintain your own good-quality customers and look for similar quality prospects.

Declining Industries: Typically these will be the so-called 'smokestack' industries associated with the Industrial Revolution such as mining, ship-building, steel and increasingly in the UK many forms of manufacturing. Even in the technology sector companies need to continue to invest in research and development as successive waves of technology render previous versions redundant or less relevant, eg IBM with its mainframe computers, e-mail replacing faxes and so on.

Here the banking focus is on helping the customer to achieve optimal profitability and even re-focus if such business options are available.

10.3 Industry Types

Product Industries

These can be broadly classified as:

1. *Manufacturing*: The processing of raw material into finished products that are then distributed usually though intermediaries – the process is one of adding value to the raw materials. Some production cycles may be short, some such as building aircraft or oil platforms much longer.

Manufacturers can be divided into three groups:

- Processors take raw materials such as oil and refine or modify them. These activities tend to require significant investment in manufacturing and processing equipment relative to the unit cost of the raw material. Processing companies have to operate their equipment at almost full volume and full time to make money.

- Fabricators take processor's output and convert it into something that is usable. Think of the processing of steel from rolled strip to car components.

- Assemblers take a collection of finished parts and turn them into a finished product – cars, houses and domestic white goods, for example.

2. *Wholesaling*: Wholesalers buy from manufacturers and sell to retailers. They act effectively as stocking points for goods and an intermediary part of the distribution channel. Depending on their nature these goods can be slow or fast moving. Finance is usually required to fund the stock prior to payment from the purchaser.

3. *Retailing*: This is where the products are sold direct to the public. Competition will be based on the elements of the marketing mix – which we reviewed earlier, such as location, brand, price and service levels. Again a key issue is likely to be the length of the sales cycle.

Note that these are broad and general classifications only. Typically the trend often now is to try to cut out intermediaries and go direct to the buyer – e-retailing and Dell are classic examples. Other companies may try to own or manage the whole of the process from manufacture to retailing – cars for example.

Service Industries

Britain is now a service economy insofar as more people work in the service sector than in all other sectors of the economy. The government is a major provider of services and there are business and professional services provided by airlines, banks, hotels, management consultants, solicitors, architects, advertising agencies and market research companies. There is also the not-for-profit sector among which are charities, churches and colleges. Some services – which are self-evident – require significant levels of capital investment; others are largely to do with intellectual capital.

10.4 Industry Assessment

The factors affecting the assessment of an industry's strength are brought together in the following assessment tool – it may well mirror some aspects of your bank's credit assessment process. From this a numeric rating could be completed if required.

Table 10.1 Rating Industry Risk

Industry characteristic	Low risk	Moderate risk	Moderately high risk	High risk
Cost structure	Low fixed costs, high variable costs	Balance of fixed and variable costs	Fixed costs moderately higher than variable costs	High fixed costs, low variable costs
Maturity	Mature industry – sales and profits still increasing at reasonable rate	Maturing industry – beyond major growth problems and shakeout of weak competitors	Emerging industry – still growing rapidly; weak competitors just beginning to drop out Or highly mature industry just on the verge of decline	Emerging industry – growing at an explosive rate Or declining industry – sales and profits decreasing
Cyclicality	Not affected by business cycle	Sales rise and fall mildly, reflecting expansion and recession	Sales moderately affected by expansion and recession	Highly cyclical or counter-cyclical
Profitability	Consistently profitable through expansion and recession	Consistent but lower than average profitability during recession	Profitable during expansions; mildly unprofitable during recession	Unprofitable during expansions and recession
Dependence	Highly diversified customer or supplier base	Customers or suppliers limited to several industries, but none represent more than 10% of sales or purchases	Customers or suppliers limited to a few industries; some represent 20% to 30% of sales or purchases	Highly dependent on one or two other industries or customer groups
Vulnerability to substitutes	No substitutes available or likely	Few substitutes available, or high switching costs	Variety of substitutes available, or moderate switching costs	Many substitutes easily accessible, no switching costs
Regulatory environment	Friendly regulatory environment protects or enhances industry health, change in environment highly predictable	Unregulated or slightly regulated, regulatory changes highly unlikely or predictable	Regulations have noticeable adverse impact on revenues or costs; predictable and manageable impact	Regulations have significant and chronic impact on industry health; regulations subject to sudden change
Vulnerability to environmental liability	Industry does not produce or handle a regulated waste material	Industry produces a regulated waste material that is not considered toxic	Industry produces or handles a toxic material	Industry regularly produces or handles toxic material that has potential for severe environmental impact

Source: Omega Performance Corporation 1997©.

You might like to review one or two of the industries you are familiar with in the form of a SWOT analysis.

10.5 Customer Profiling

Product-Market Match

We looked earlier at other bases for segmentation of customers by industry, turnover and product usage and so on together with the components of a marketing audit. A key issue is that of differentiation – recognizing those particular product and/or service features that make your customers want to buy from you. We identified that these are the outputs of distinctive capabilities – including in-depth knowledge of the customers – which successful companies have. The product-market match referred to in the chart from Omega Performance is, therefore, of critical importance and also provides a framework against which to assess competitor offerings.

Table 10.2 Rating Product-Market Risk

Characteristic	Low risk	Moderate risk	Moderately high risk	High risk
Importance	Staple; always in demand; consistent and predictable demand	Deferrable necessity; demand cyclical; purchases can be delayed but not deferred entirely	A luxury; thin market but stable demand	An extravagance; market thin and unstable
Product differentiation	Highly differentiated product; few comparable substitutes; strong patent protection or customer loyalty; excellent reputation for quality	Some differentiation; comparable substitutes limited, perhaps by product complexity; some brand loyalty and good quality reputation	Non-differentiable product with a number of readily available substitutes; good quality reputation	Non-differentiable product with many comparable or better substitutes; no brand loyalty or mediocre product quality
Product capabilities	● What products does the company offer?			
	● Are the products final consumables or intermediate goods?			
	● Who are the company's customers? Who are the ultimate consumers of the product? Who influences their purchasing decisions?			

- What value or benefits do the company's products offer the market? What needs do they satisfy? What motivates customers to buy this product?

• Will there continue to be customers for this company's products?	Market size (annual industry sales) and growth. Vulnerability to style changes Risk of technical obsolescence Dependence on business cycles in other industries
• What are the comparative advantages of this company's products over those offered by competitors?	Low prices Better terms of sales Customer service High quality Band image or unique features and benefits Availability Technological leadership

- Are the company's distinct advantages the ones you would expect, based on its goals and competitive strategy?

- What must the company do to maintain or increase the comparative advantages of its product line?

- Does management expect to introduce new products or change existing product configurations in the next trading period? What would be the effects on product-market match?

- In an ideal situation, what would a company like this one do to minimize the risk of a product-market mismatch? How does this company compare?

Source: Omega Performance Corporation 1997©.

Production Analysis

Although we identified earlier the predominance of service industries over manufacturing industries in the UK, manufacturing remains an important contributor to many of the world economies. It is appropriate, therefore, to understand the basis on which this activity can be reviewed. Many of these factors can be applied to capital-intensive service industries or to those services where bringing trained personnel on stream can take time – for example, the time taken to train nurses and doctors for the National Health Service.

Table 10.3 Rating Production Capabilities

Characteristic	Low risk	Moderate risk	Moderately high risk	High risk
Consistency	Trouble-free operations; down-time not disrupting production schedules or costs	Occasional significant downtime or production problems; low to moderate impact on schedules and costs	Fairly frequent unplanned disruptions in production; moderate to significant impact on costs and deliveries	Constant unplanned production disruptions; heavy impact on costs; major cause of cost variations
Vulnerability to technology	An industry leader using most current technology; not likely to be caught off-guard by changes in technology	Keeps up-to-date with technology changes; slow to adopt new technologies, but not vulnerable to rapid introduction of new technology that would prove harmful	Slow to adopt changes; vulnerable to shifts in technology; would not prove fatal immediately	Technology shifts rapidly; company highly vulnerable; major shifts could prove fatal quickly
Labour relationships	Long history of harmonious relationships	Occasional strikes or work stoppages of brief duration; good working relationship between union and management	Occasional strikes of significant duration; some unplanned or unexpected work stoppages	History of acrimonious labour relations; strikes tend to be long and bitter
Process Issues	● What is the nature of the company's production process?	Basis on which the company decides to produce a product – confirmed orders – long-term contracts – past trends and expected orders Time and place of production of goods and length of production process Method of controlling inventory investment Necessary investment in fixed assets Extent to which the process relies on highly sophisticated technology or highly sensitive and delicate machinery Critical success variables for efficient production and minimum cost		

● Has the company developed any significant cost advantages over the competition?	Amount of effort management devotes to cost reduction, and degree of continuing investment in more efficient equipment to reduce production costs
● Are there any events or conditions that could stop or constrain production, or substantially increase production costs?	Type of events and whether they have occurred before Amount of advance warning Amount of damage (actual damage, lost business or increased cost) that would result Likelihood of these events Steps management can take to reduce the likelihood of such events or potential damage if they occur
● Does management plan any additions or reconfigurations of production capacity during the current business cycle?	Relationship to current capacity Implications for the company's costs and profitability Implications for cashflow

In an ideal situation, what would a company like this one do to minimize production risk. How does this company compare with its competitors?

Source: Omega Performance Corporation 1997©.

Management Factors

Here we look at some of the management factors that are of particular importance. Remember while these will be important where lending decisions are being taken, they also apply to credit accounts as you consider the overall attractiveness of the customer, potential changes in the buying centre, the potential to add value in terms of 'business acumen' to the customer (remember the consultancy role) and the potential opportunities for business development. (You might also apply this to an assessment of your team's strengths.)

Table 10.4 Rating Management Capabilities

Industry characteristic	Low risk	Moderate risk	Moderately high risk	High risk
Experience	Extensive industry experience	Has experienced several industry cycles	Limited experience in the industry with minimal exposure to normal industry problems	Limited experience in the industry without exposure to normal industry problems
Depth	Unusually high management depth with succession in all functional areas provided for internally	Adequate management depth with each critical function covered by at least one qualified successor	Insufficient management depth with some outside recruiting necessary to fill vacancies in secondary positions	Insufficient management depth with vacancies in key spots causing serious exposure
Breadth	Experienced managers in place in all major functional areas	One key functional manager somewhat less experienced than desirable, but learning quickly	One key function without experienced manager; other managers covering	More than one key function without experienced managers; difficulties for other managers to cover
Integrity	Established broad reputation for unwavering integrity in positive as well as adverse circumstances	Good reputation for integrity in local business community	Managers known to bank; no reason to question management integrity, but reputation is not widely known	Managers recently acquainted with bank; no reason to question management integrity, but reputation is not widely known
Board of Directors	Active board composed of nationally recognized business leaders serves as a strong check on management	Some outside directors of moderately important stature exercise average control over management	Outside directors, if any, are not an effective control on management	Inside board that does not discharge normal responsibilities
Track record of meeting goals	Long track record of meeting forecasts and goals	Track record of meeting forecasts and goals about half the time	Inconsistent record of meeting forecasts and goals	Rarely able to meet forecasts and goals; some years are better and some are worse

Source: Omega Performance Corporation 1997©.

10.6 Understanding and Evaluating Customer Business Plans

Categorizing Plans

It is probably worth trying to position the various plans and *pro formas* that we surface in the book because although in many cases much of the content may be similar, they are different documents doing different things for different customers. In broad terms, then, they can be summarized as follows:

Table 10.5 Types of Plans

Type	*Customer Type*	*Focus*
Business Plan	All	Overview of all aspects of the company's activity to varying levels of detail
Marketing Plan	Majority but not for, say, some manufacturers	Although needs underlying economic rationale, focuses on how the company defines its customers, its competitiveness and why and what customers will buy
Credit Assessment	Only those where risk exposure	Much of the data talks to the commercial viability of the business but the focus is on understanding the level and nature of the risk to the bank for lending purposes
Key Account Plan	Top accounts only in portfolio	Focus on developing and planning strategy for deepening relationship and business development with key people in key accounts only

The Need for Business Plans

Dealing with business plans then, business planning is a vital activity for any successful company although, and this is probably a function of the size of the company, it can be overtaken by day-to-day demands. An effective plan forms a diagnostic tool, a benchmark for past and future performance and demonstrates to external suppliers such as banks that a structured and thoughtful approach is being taken to the business.

While 90% of companies complete budgets and forecasts (Source McDonald M., Rogers B., Key Account Planning Butterworth Heinemann 1998) fully scoped business plans are less prevalent. A survey by Share Livewire ('Clear, Concise Plan will prove its worth' Rogers M., Business Magazine, March 2001) found that those businesses that regularly undertook business planning had an average profit margin of 54%. For those that did not the average was only 35%.

Business planning does not offer solutions to business problems. Rather, business planning is a concrete methodology or framework to structure concepts and information about the business. A well-written business plan will give a clear overview. A number of adjectives describe the business planning process – the best are: logical, rational and regimented. A business plan organizes, directs, coordinates, controls and facilitates. Business planning is a systematic method for reducing risk and enhancing success for any type of business operation. The complexity of a business plan will vary with the type of business. And the size of the business plan will reflect the complexity of the business and/or proposition.

While a business plan is everything above, it is also a prediction of the future based on current abstractions, assumptions and estimates. This is unavoidable. In fact, if we could see into the future, there would be no need for business plans. When a business plan is implemented the plan comes in contact with reality. This can be a nasty shock for many business executives, causing a good deal of doubt about their business plan. However, reality is the feedback necessary to reinforce or adjust the business plan to achieve project completion, growth and success. If the plan is not working, then change is inevitable. The plan itself will show the impact different changes will have on other areas of the company. A business plan is never cast in stone. It is simply a management tool to reduce risk and ensure as much success as possible.

Core Components

Business Information

- Name of company
- Location
- Purpose of business
- Legal form of organization

- Business owners

Description of Business

- Detail description of business
- Research about the industry
- Strategy
  - Appealing factors of the business
  - Factors that will determine the success of business

People

- Managerial skills
- Organizational chart
- Job descriptions
- Resumes

Market Analysis

- Market research
- Environment & industry analysis
- Competition
- Strategic focus & peer positioning
- Target market definition
  - Consumer/business markets
- Marketing mix strategy
  - Differentiation
  - Price taker/price maker
  - Routes to market
  - Promotional spend
- Suppliers/partners
- Use of technology
  - Advantages/disadvantages

Financial

- Profit & loss statements
    - Revenue from core activities
    - Economies of scale
- Cash flow forecasts
- Budgets
- Balance sheets
    - Gearing/leverage/capital intensity
    - Working capital needs
    - Capital expenditure
    - Accounting policies including depreciation
- Breakeven forecasts
- Key ratios
    - Efficiency/liquidity/gearing etc

Gap Analysis

Typically this is a question of working through the components of the plan and undertaking a gap analysis. Use what, why, how, where, when and who to probe for gaps. One questioning technique guaranteed to get to the root of anything is the 'Six Whys?' although this can make it feel like a relentless cross-examination! You could try to construct a value chain or use the Mckinsey 7S model as part of this diagnostic process and to stimulate additional insights.

If we use, for example, the 7S model, the following sorts of questions might emerge:

Table 10.6 Applying the 7S Model to Business Plan Analysis

Shared Values	● Is there a published mission statement and set of values?
	● As you talk to people from the company are you conscious of these values?
	● Is the importance of the values embedded at a senior level or is it just lip service?
	● Where do customers and staff fit in these values?
Structure	● Has the structure changed recently – if so why?
	● Is the structure appropriate to the nature of the business and the markets served?
	● Is it responsive to change?
	● How is decision making carried out?
	● Is there evidence of in-fighting between different functions?
	● How decentralized is responsibility and authority?
Strategy	● Is the strategy expressed in a coherent and succinct way?
	● Is the company a leader, a fast follower or one of the pack?
	● Is it viable and sustainable?
	● Is the company product or market led?
	● What contingency plans are there in place?
	● Is there a realistic assessment of the competition?
	● How is the voice of the customer fed back into the organization?
	● Is it acted on?
	● What do customer satisfaction surveys say?
Systems	● Are internal control systems robust?
	● Are the financial metrics sound?
	● How reliant is the company on technology and what are the contingency plans?
	● Are processes aligned to deliver customer satisfaction?
	● Are key performance indicators identified?
	● How often is this data reported?
	● To what extent is it shared?
	● Is there a single view of the customer?
Skills	● What are the core capabilities of the company?
	● Where are the skills bottlenecks?
	● How vulnerable is the business to key skills shortages?
	● Are new skills bought in or developed in house?

Style

- Is communication between management and staff two-way?
- How are change and difficult situations such as redundancies handled?
- Do senior management spontaneously tell you a story about a good customer or staff interaction?
- Are supplier relationships partnerships or adversarial?
- How are mistakes treated?
- Is it a fun place to work?

Staff

- Do staff behave as though they own the business?
- Are staff encouraged to sort out customer issues at the first point of contact?
- Is there a policy of promoting from within to encourage staff loyalty?
- Are staff encouraged to take responsibility for their own development?
- What do staff satisfaction and exit surveys say?
- Is recognition and reward appropriately balanced?
- Do people queue up to work for this company?

The benefits of using such a model is that the natural inclination to go straight to the figures, if not avoided, is somewhat more muted. This allows us to see the business in the round irrespective of whether we are dealing with a lending proposition or not.

11

ORGANIZATIONAL BUYER BEHAVIOUR AND THE DECISION-MAKING UNIT

11.1 Overview

In this chapter we start to develop your behavioural analytical capabilities – using observation and judgement in the context of how companies buy – to better understand how you can better meet the customers needs. Bear in mind also that these tools can be used to map the politics of your own organizations.

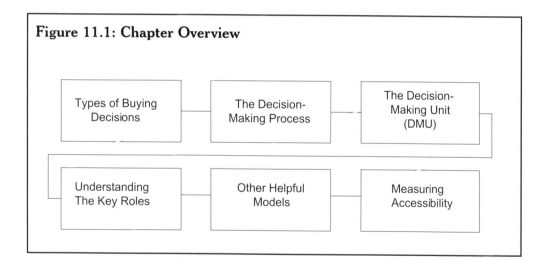

Figure 11.1: Chapter Overview

11.2 Types of buying decisions

The following diagram classifies buying decisions along a number of dimensions that apply to personal and corporate buyers:

New task – the recognition of a purchasing problem that has not been encountered previously. The perceptions of risk and uncertainty will be higher so the search for information will be more extensive.

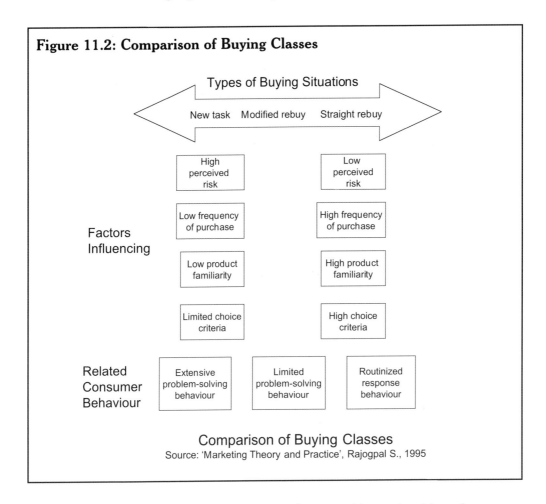

Figure 11.2: Comparison of Buying Classes

Comparison of Buying Classes
Source: 'Marketing Theory and Practice', Rajogpal S., 1995

Modified rebuy – the buyer has previous experience but may wish to review this, such as a more competitive offering, changes in specifications or a sense that performance is not optimal.

Straight rebuy – an accelerated buying process because the benefits of the chosen solution are self-evident.

11.3 The Decision-Making Process

As the diagram shows, organizational decision-making is a stepped process from problem recognition through to the post-purchase evaluation of product and supplier performance. It is influenced by a range of other factors such as the needs of the organization and the individual. These interact in a fluid and dynamic way to produce the buying decision. The individuals involved within an organization may vary from task to task.

This is the cumulative effect is of a series of pressures on the individual or individuals responsible for the buying decision. The risks may be technical, social or even psychological.

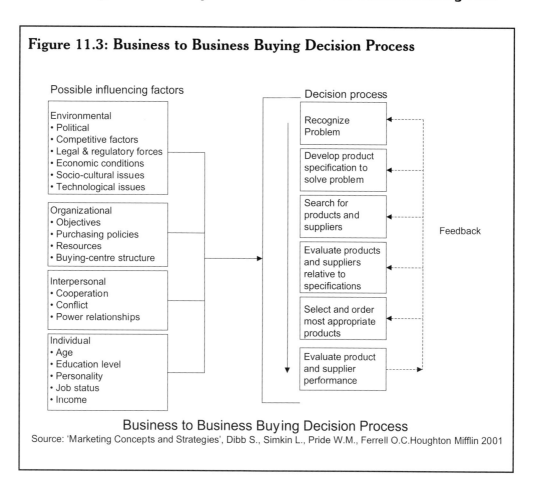

Figure 11.3: Business to Business Buying Decision Process

Possible influencing factors

Decision process

Environmental
• Political
• Competitive factors
• Legal & regulatory forces
• Economic conditions
• Socio-cultural issues
• Technological issues

Organizational
• Objectives
• Purchasing policies
• Resources
• Buying-centre structure

Interpersonal
• Cooperation
• Conflict
• Power relationships

Individual
• Age
• Education level
• Personality
• Job status
• Income

Recognize Problem

Develop product specification to solve problem

Search for products and suppliers

Evaluate products and suppliers relative to specifications

Select and order most appropriate products

Evaluate product and supplier performance

Feedback

Business to Business Buying Decision Process
Source: 'Marketing Concepts and Strategies', Dibb S., Simkin L., Pride W.M., Ferrell O.C.Houghton Mifflin 2001

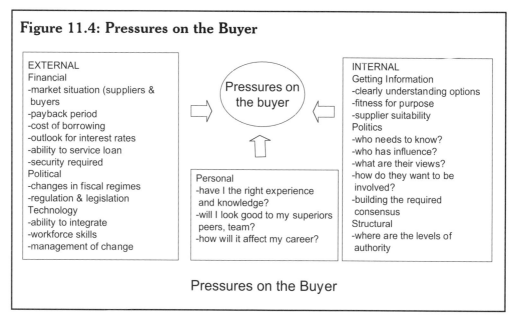

Figure 11.4: Pressures on the Buyer

EXTERNAL
Financial
-market situation (suppliers & buyers
-payback period
-cost of borrowing
-outlook for interest rates
-ability to service loan
-security required
Political
-changes in fiscal regimes
-regulation & legislation
Technology
-ability to integrate
-workforce skills
-management of change

Pressures on the buyer

Personal
-have I the right experience and knowledge?
-will I look good to my superiors peers, team?
-how will it affect my career?

INTERNAL
Getting Information
-clearly understanding options
-fitness for purpose
-supplier suitability
Politics
-who needs to know?
-who has influence?
-what are their views?
-how do they want to be involved?
-building the required consensus
Structural
-where are the levels of authority

Pressures on the Buyer

11.4 The Decision-Making Unit (DMU)

Part of the account-planning process should be to understand how individual corporate customers make buying decisions. In any corporate decision-making process there will be a number of roles being played. The people carrying out the roles may be obvious but more often than not they are not transparent and research will be necessary to identify all those who may have an influence on the buying decision. The people involved and their roles may vary depending on the nature of the buying decision. It may be formal and self-evident or so informal as to be unidentifiable. Clearly the bigger the company the more problematic and the more complex this can be.

How decisions are made will also be a function of the size and culture of the company as Peter Cheverton identifies (*Key Account Management, the route to profitable Key Supplier Status*, Cheverton, P. Kogan Page, 2000):

Authoritarian: key individual (probably boss of small business) – solution may be imposed but risk of alienating others.

Consensus: some form of democracy – majority vote. Harder work having to influence majority. May not know why decision taken whether good or bad.

Consultative: where appointed decision maker will make decision based on views of key influencers in the DMU.

The advantage of understanding the possible roles that members of a buying group may undertake is that it will help to identify them within an organization and plan strategies for overcoming possible resistance while reinforcing those who are in favour. Starting with the organizational chart makes sense – this will help you to identify the influence centres as a prelude to understanding the roles of the key people within them. The buying team will probably vary depending on the product being purchased. In the case of debt instruments, for example, it will probably be the treasury function. For equity instruments or advice-related services it would probably include the finance director, the chief executive/chairman and the board of directors.

Interestingly, research suggests that salespeople rarely reach all the component members of the DMU. This clearly can undermine the strength of the relationship and leave you more vulnerable to defection. The quality of the main contact and the extent of the 'infiltration' into the company are key.

Figure 11.5: Influences Centres for a Large Corporate

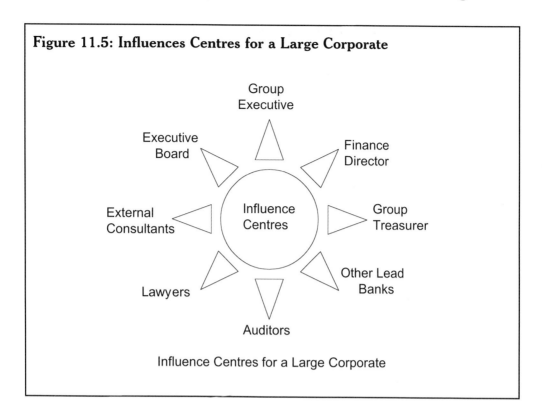

Influence Centres for a Large Corporate

Figure 11.6: Influence Centres for a Mid sized Corporate

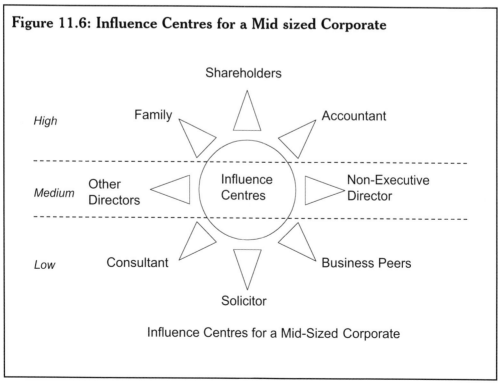

Influence Centres for a Mid-Sized Corporate

Table 11.1 Typical number of DMU members reached

Number of employees	Average number of buying influences (DMU)	Average number of contacts made by salesperson
0-200	3.42	1.72
201-400	4.85	1.75
401-1000	5.81	1.90
1000+	6.50	1.65

Source: McDonald M., Rogers B., Key Account Management Butterworth Heinemann 1998.

11.5 Understanding The Key Roles

There are a number of models for categorizing buyer roles and the one that is both popular and robust comes from Miller Heiman, shown below where four roles are identified. – note, however, that a person may have one or more of these roles.

Economic Buyer: this is the person who gives final approval to buy your product or service. They may be in position to say 'no' when everyone else says 'yes', or 'yes' when everyone else says 'no'. They may be able to release funds from other budgets. An individual, a project team or the board of the company, can play this role. It is essential to find out who

Figure 11.7: Purchasing Roles

Economic Buyer	User Buyer
Controls budget	Will use or supervise
Approaches from cost benefit	on a day-to-day basis
point of view	Want comfort it will do the
Will give final approval to buy	job it is supposed to do

Technical Buyer	Coach(es)
Will be interested in technical	Leads you to other buyer
specifications at early stage	types within organization
Professional gatekeepers	Wants to help you make sale
Quality/functionality key	Probably impacts on their
	own performance measures

Purchasing Roles

Source: 'The New Strategic Selling', Heiman S., and Sanchez D., with Tuleja T., Kogan Page

at the end of the day fulfils this role. For the smaller corporate and commercial customers this is likely to be the owner/manager, in larger corporates it maybe the Finance Director, the Managing Director or, indeed, the Chairman.

User Buyer: these are the people who will actually use (or manage the use of) your banking product or service – it may be the people who will administer the cash management system on a daily basis. These are the people who will also be having the day-to-day contact with your bank. They will be concerned about both the functionality of the product but also how it will affect them personally – on a subjective basis – is it good for me and my job? It is important not to underestimate the influence these people may have – they will certainly be providing feedback to their superiors on how the system is or is not working and their support is required. Inevitably new systems and procedures take a while to bed down and you may need to stay close to the users in the early stages of implementation.

Technical Buyer: this is a rigorous role to have to undertake, and one that from a sales perspective may need a good deal of time and attention. Their role is to apply constructive criticism objectively to whatever is being assessed – they are in a way safeguarding the integrity of the organization. In a relationship banking context this might, for example, include legal people such as solicitors and other professionals such as accountants. They will assess your products or services on its measurable and quantifiable benefits, typically against an explicit or implicit specification.

Coach(es): a coach is your insider in the organization – someone who will act as an extension to your own sales activity. Their motives may be multiple ranging from the commercial good of the organization to their own personal advancement or well-being. They need to be credible within the organization because they are the bridgeheads for your sales activity. Over time you may build up a network of coaches – particularly if they move from one organization to another.

11.6 Other Helpful Models

Identifying the Key Player

We have already identified the extent of emotional and personal influences on the way corporate buyers behave. There are, inevitably, many models for analysing personal behaviour and the purpose here is not to present a definitive model but to encourage you to think both analytically about your behaviours and your customer's as a means to developing and sustaining a better quality mutual relationship.

In practice there should not be more than one playmaker. Matrix management may make this difficult to unravel but at the end of the day usually only one person has budgetary responsibility.

If we start to map these roles (see Figure 11.9), the following picture might emerge:

Figure 11.8: Key Player Analysis

Playmaker	Agent

• Primary decision maker
• Highly influential
• Very personal agenda
• Could be a consultant
  hiding behind a sponsor
	• Supportive for personal
	  or company reasons
	• Conduit into company
	• Personal credibility may
	  be at risk

Neutral	**Enemy**

• By definition neither for
  or against you
	• May be agent for an
	  alternative supplier
	• Antipathetic towards
	  you or your bank

Key Player Analysis
Source: ProAct Business Development, 2000

Levels of Responsiveness

It is all very well having identified the DMU roles of individuals within the organization but what you need to be doing – whether there is a sale in mind or some other development of the relationship – is to influence people to be favourably disposed towards you and your bank. The challenge is to move those people who matter into the 'supporters' camp. The role of the constructive critic is a particularly valuable one.

Figure 11.9: Illustrative Buyer Roles

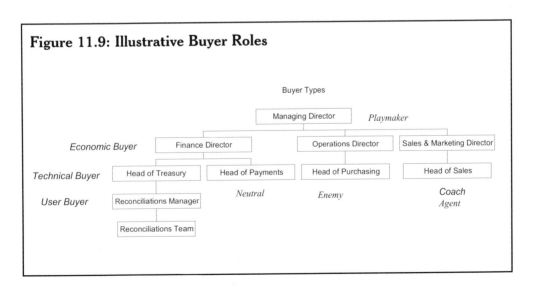

Career Indicator

The relevance of this tool is factoring the potential influence the person you are dealing with has within the customer's company. You may feel by now that this is overanalysing what, for the most part, is a very straightforward and uncomplicated supplier/customer relationship. Clearly the size of the client company is important – but if you are dealing with a company that mirrors the bank in size and structure then these issues are relevant.

Bear in mind that external suppliers to your bank – when you are in a relevant position – may be looking at you in exactly this way. Watch how they attempt to qualify you along some of the dimensions we have been looking at! You may see some similarities here with the Boston Matrix (see Figure 11.1).

The Adoption Curve

This identifies people's responsiveness to innovation – some people like new and different things, others will be more risk averse and prefer a conventional approach as shown in Figure 11.2.

11.7 Measuring Accessibility

We shall look more closely later at the issues of personal behaviour both on the part of the customer and the relationship manager. It is always useful from time to time to step back and review the status of your relationships with the key people in the decision-making unit.

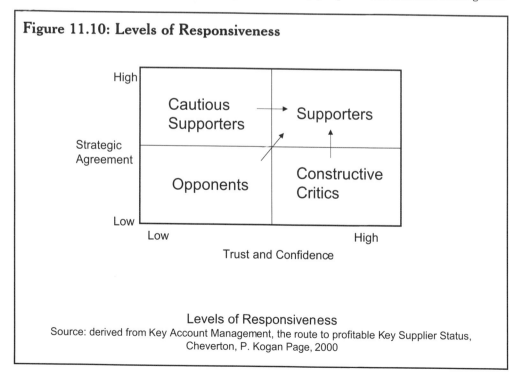

Figure 11.10: Levels of Responsiveness

Levels of Responsiveness

Source: derived from Key Account Management, the route to profitable Key Supplier Status, Cheverton, P. Kogan Page, 2000

Figure 11.11: Career Indicator Characteristics

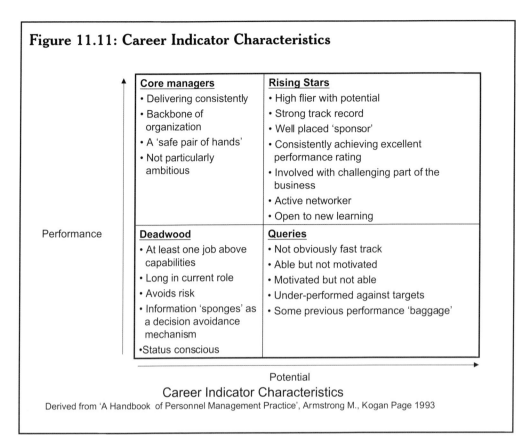

Career Indicator Characteristics

Derived from 'A Handbook of Personnel Management Practice', Armstrong M., Kogan Page 1993

Figure 11.12: The Adoption Curve

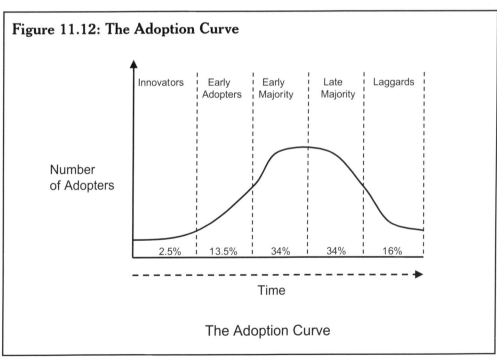

The Adoption Curve

A simple analysis might be along the following lines:

0.   Never had access

1.   Met but no substantive conversation or relationship

2.   Relationship formed, could arrange meeting if sufficiently persuasive

3.   Strong on-going relationship, access straightforward

The following table, however, facilitates a more in-depth analysis.

Table 11.2 Analysing the depth of your relationship

Gives me accurate, verifiable information regarding internal politics and power plays	Yes	No
Gives me accurate, verifiable information regarding relevant and significant company plans such as mergers and acquisitions	Yes	No
Discusses future potential projects with me	Yes	No
Gives me actionable information about competitor activity	Yes	No
Openly refers me to others in the company who are valuable for this or other projects	Yes	No
Understands and can state succinctly our added value	Yes	No
Available to see me without procrastination	Yes	No
Initiates contact with me to discuss the decision-making process	Yes	No
Has stated to me that past actions on my part have helped personally	Yes	No
Has openly advocated our case in decision-making process	Yes	No
Has reviewed account plan and offered suggested improvements	Yes	No
Is candid with me about the personal implications of the business proposal	Yes	No

Derived from Key Player Analysis – Relationship Guide Source: *Proact* Business Development Ltd www.proactbd.com

12

RELATIONSHIP BUILDING ACTIVITY AND COMMUNICATIONS STRATEGY

12.1 Overview

The focus of this chapter is on communications in a number of different guises. Regular, sustained and relevant conversations with the customers using a range of communication techniques is fundamental to an effective relationship in your business (and personal) life.

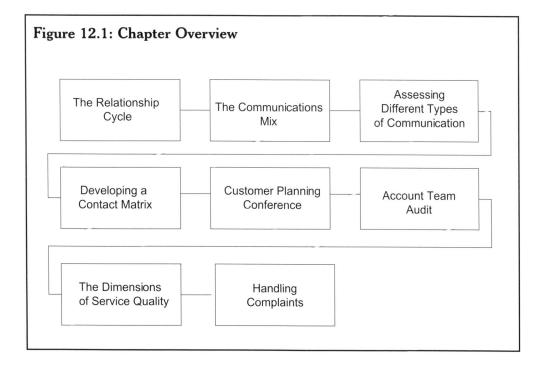

Figure 12.1: Chapter Overview

12.2 The Relationship Cycle

It is customary to think of relationships either in the form of a straight-line continuum or a circular and reinforcing lifecycle. Certainly it can be said that over time the bank and the client become more important to each other. Indeed the information bank will have gained about a customer's business over this time will potentially be a source of competitive advantage. The multiple links of products, services and personal relationships will form the basis of a mutual interdependence and may indeed reduce price sensitivity. This can take time and requires patience on the part of the bank; it may be fruitful only after a long period of consistent effort.

There are numerous causes for the breakdown of relationships which need to guarded against such as:

- changes in key personnel if there is a single point of contact on either side rather than multiple contacts and networking

- deterioration in the relationship caused by such issues as being off sick without adequate cover, failure to deliver, a clash of personalities, or an organizational change like a purchasing function getting involved

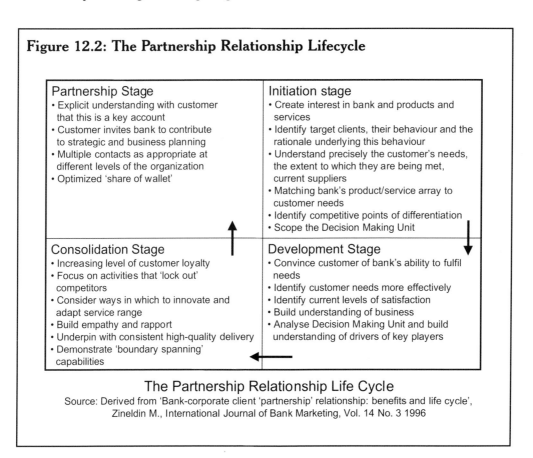

Figure 12.2: The Partnership Relationship Lifecycle

Partnership Stage
- Explicit understanding with customer that this is a key account
- Customer invites bank to contribute to strategic and business planning
- Multiple contacts as appropriate at different levels of the organization
- Optimized 'share of wallet'

Initiation stage
- Create interest in bank and products and services
- Identify target clients, their behaviour and the rationale underlying this behaviour
- Understand precisely the customer's needs, the extent to which they are being met, current suppliers
- Matching bank's product/service array to customer needs
- Identify competitive points of differentiation
- Scope the Decision Making Unit

Consolidation Stage
- Increasing level of customer loyalty
- Focus on activities that 'lock out' competitors
- Consider ways in which to innovate and adapt service range
- Build empathy and rapport
- Underpin with consistent high-quality delivery
- Demonstrate 'boundary spanning' capabilities

Development Stage
- Convince customer of bank's ability to fulfil needs
- Identify customer needs more effectively
- Identify current levels of satisfaction
- Build understanding of business
- Analyse Decision Making Unit and build understanding of drivers of key players

The Partnership Relationship Life Cycle

Source: Derived from 'Bank-corporate client 'partnership' relationship: benefits and life cycle', Zineldin M., International Journal of Bank Marketing, Vol. 14 No. 3 1996

- a breach of trust, inconsistent performance, a single major event, a lack of communication, too many surprises of the wrong sort

- a lack of persistence

    - cultural mismatch, price v value, bureaucracy v entrepreneurial

    - quality problems

    - financial problems.

Achieving a matching perspective

There is a need to understand what customers want at the various stages of the relationship cycle but also to recognize that the needs of the customer, bank and relationship manager may not be completely aligned.

Table 12.1 Differing Views

Buying company view	Supplier company strategic view	Key account manager's view
Integrity	Knowledge of business environment	Selling/negotiating
Understanding our business	Communications	Communications
Product knowledge – technical	Strategic thinking	Understanding customer's business
Product knowledge – applications	Selling/negotiating	Strategic thinking
Communications	Product knowledge – technical	Technical/financial/ markets/credibility

Source McDonald M., Rogers B., *Key Account Planning* Butterworth Heinemann 1998.

Locking Out Competitors

The main purpose of a relationship strategy is to prefer your bank against the competitors – to lock them out. This can be achieved by developing the relationship along the lines shown in Figure 12.3.

Figure 12.3: Deepening the Relationship

Customer's view of Bank	Technology	Accessibility	People	Communications Mix
Strategic partner	Anticipates my needs	Open access to relationship manager	Empathetic – shares my business goals	Mostly face-to-face and very relevant
Consultative approach	Recognizes my needs	Proactive	Looking for solutions	Relevant with some personal overlay
An excellent service provider	7/24 Global availability	Reactive and responsive	Problems quickly resolved	Targeted and timely
A better bank	97% European availability	Noticeably convenient	Noticeably efficient	Targeted and informative
A utility bank	95% national availability	Adequate	Reliable and rules-based	Untargeted, impersonal

Deepening the Relationship

It can also be supplemented in the following ways:

Figure 12.4: Locking Out Competitors

- Use your knowledge of the customer to develop specific services that match needs that competitors do not know about
- Continuously improve product/service quality
- Build and nurture peer-to-peer working relationships
- Be easy to do business with
- Treat the customer as a partner
- Provide fast-track complaint resolution
- Anticipate special requirements
- Integrate common data & information exchange
- Plan/promote jointly
- Structure & renew contracts

Locking Out Competitors

12.3 The Communications Mix

Communications, or promotion as it is called, is one of the elements of the marketing mix that we identified in an earlier part of the book as one of the seven 'Ps'. From a relationship management perspective the challenge is to balance cost and frequency with the actual and potential value of the customer. Often, too, there is a challenge to ensure that the central marketing function does not mindlessly mail the customer – this is part of the relationship manager's gatekeeper and traffic management role.

Because people in banks spend most of their time dealing with people – as opposed, say, to a manufacturing environment – this places a premium upon communications skills. Bear in mind the concept of internal customers as well – those colleagues, groups, departments, branches and business units that depend on the output of other colleagues, groups, departments, branches and business units to meet the customer's needs.

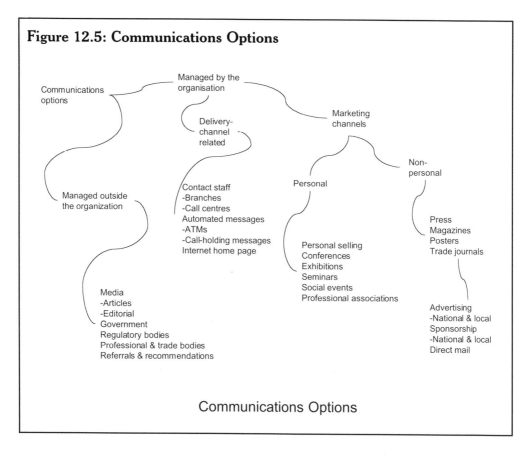

Figure 12.5: Communications Options

12.4 Assessing Different Types of Communications

Research demonstrates that customers make a trade off between the nature of the contact and the perceived value or utility to them:

Table 12.2 The Customer's Perceptions of the Value of Different Communications Methods

Contact Types	Methods use by main bank in past year %	Find most helpful in job %
Telephone calls from relationship team	53	29
Individual letters from main contact giving details of services relevant to your company	48	20
Booklets/brochures about specialist services that can be taken from bank/branches/offices	43	9
Direct mail from bank's head office announcing new services or facilities	40	6
Social events	32	7
Meetings to introduce new services or people relevant to your company's needs	30	22
Meetings to introduce senior bank management to strengthen the relationship	24	14
Meetings to propose ideas and solutions for your company's financial needs	17	17
Use of personal computer to demonstrate products	11	3
Internet Web site	1	1
E-mail	1	1
None of these	5	11
Not sure	Less than 0.5%	2

Source: *Middle Market Corporate Banking The 1998 Survey* NFO Financial Services.

In the light of these figures you might like to consider:

- How does this compare with your own contact strategy?

- What are the actual frequencies by type of contact and what are the implications of this?

- What is the balance between local and central activity?

- How is your relationship activity linked with central marketing activity?

12.5 Developing a Contact Matrix

Again as part of the account planning process there is a need – particularly where specialist product suppliers may be involved – to clearly allocate contact roles and responsibilities. People in the team need to understand their roles and effort needs to be coordinated – generally the more points of contact within organization and account team the better and the whole of account team needs to be involved in working the relationship.

Personal visits are clearly the most effective means of interaction but they are also the most expensive. They also become more important as the customer becomes increasingly closer to a purchase decision. Face-to-face visits may be justified if:

- Personal service is considered essential.

- An important new contact is being made.

- A difficult and sensitive problem needs to be solved.

- A complicated presentation needs to be made.

- In-depth diagnostic work needs to be carried out.

- The customer asks for a sales visit.

- On-site research is required.

Table 12.3 Contact Planner

Number of contacts		J	F	M	A	M	J	J	A	S	O	N	D
Existing customers													
Introducers													
Target customers													
Total													
Customer	Income last year	Target income											
1			F2F	T		FR		T		F2F			T	S
2					T	T	FR		S			F2F	
3 etc.			F2F	T	T		T		F2F		T	T	

Key: F2F = Face to Face; T = Telephone; FR = Facilities Review; S = Social

We have already identified the economics of keeping existing customers and an important part of this is checking with the customer that service levels and any recent sales meet their satisfaction. A frequent phenomenon is that of 'post-purchase dissonance' where the customer is looking for confirmation that they have made the right decision. A timely call can embed a feeling of well-being in the customer and reaffirm that their needs have been met.

12.6 Customer Planning Conference

The level of formality that this takes will depend very much on the nature of the customer. It is called a 'planning conference' because it is more than just a review which on its own tends to be too 'rear view mirror'. Here you aim to get an understanding of where the customer is going in a business sense and understand what opportunities there may be for you to improve your share of wallet. This annual review may from part of more regular reviews that occur during the year.

The key to a good interaction is to prepare thoroughly and be sure to follow up effectively. Make sure you have the key people from the customer's side at the meeting. In summary the agenda – based on a key account plan if you have one – might cover:

- Supplier overview of industry sector

- Customer overview of markets

- Individual business objectives and strategies

- Cross proposals and responses

- Agreed set of plans.

As a guide, 75% of the time should be spent looking forward. This is not a time for monologs and dense slides but is designed to stimulate an open conversation. This forms part of the process of building trust and moving to a partnership relationship.

Make sure the location is mutually convenient and the room is sufficiently comfortable for the meeting. Where you have corporate stationery – pens, pads, signs – use them to 'brand' the meeting.

12.7 Account Team Audit

In the same way that there are structured meetings with customers there should be periodic meetings internally in which performance against the key account plans is assessed. Where appropriate, a product specialist should be included also to ensure that knowledge is pooled, channels of communication are open and the customer's needs are understood and being met as optimally as possible. This would be the time to evaluate in an objective way if systems and processes were hampering 'joined-up' servicing of the customer.

The account team represents a core and significant investment and these kind of performance audits or health checks are valuable. The opportunity could be taken for a full day's review, viewing the event as a major account presentation simulation with some of the risk removed. This is a good opportunity to test management and presentational skills in a non-threatening and supportive environment.

12.8 The Dimensions of Service Quality

It is impossible to overstate the importance of an open and regular dialogue with the customer. Quite frankly in a corporate banking environment this should be face-to-face with the relationship manager. Many banks, however, shy away from this on the basis that responses can be skewed because the customer may feel uncomfortable about being open with the relationship manager. This is an indictment of the nature of the relationship rather than the mechanic for the data collection. Relationship managers should not shy away from the direct 'how is for you' question.

Almost without exception, banks run their own internally managed customer satisfaction surveys, usually carried out by telephone or post and usually using an external agency to undertake and analyse the research. While in theory the surveys should be random, some banks may carry out a prescreening exercise ahead of the survey in case there are exceptional features that will make the survey inappropriate – for example, where there are known asset quality difficulties with an account. There may also be an overall objective to survey all customers within, say, a 12- to 18-month period. Typical areas covered in a customer satisfaction survey or in the construction of a service quality index are shown below:

Figure 12.6 Service Questionnaire Components

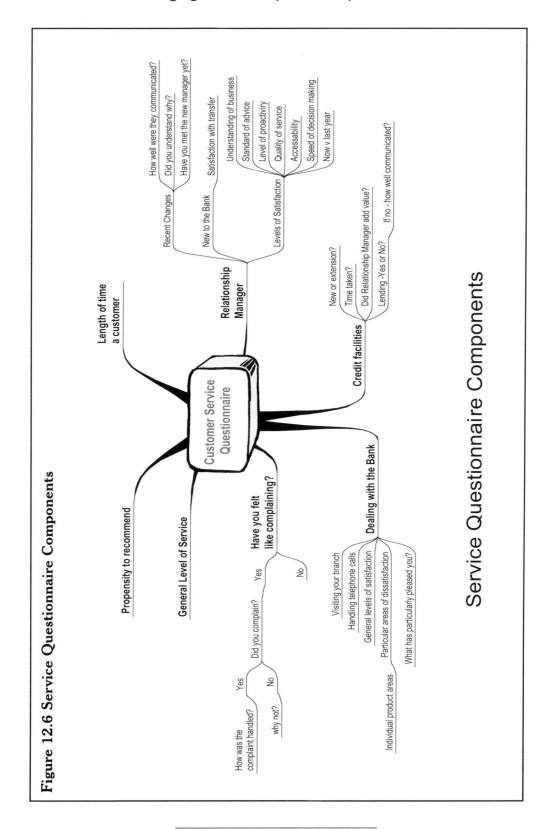

Service Questionnaire Components

As we have already identified, external agencies also carry out surveys. These are randomly selected but in the context of a statistically valid sample and in addition to product usage may delve into the more subjective factors regarding relationship managers. You may wish to compare these outputs with those produced by your own bank – those shown relate to the corporate mid-market.

Table 12.4 Customer Service Priorities

Customer Service Priorities	Most important factors in assessing main bank's performance %	Rating of main bank on each factor* England & Wales %
PEOPLE FACTORS		
Quality of main contact	45	75
Continuity of main contact	45	69
Access to main contact	26	73
Quality of support staff	20	70
EXPERTISE FACTORS		
Understanding your company's needs and requirements	52	64
Overall professional approach	25	69
Proposing financial ideas and solutions for your business	15	49
Specialist expertise in your industry	7	43

Source: *Middle Market Corporate Banking, The 1998 Survey,* NFO Financial Services.
*Performance rating is calculated by assigning a score of the rating given to banks as follows: Excellent 100, Good 67, Not so good 33, Poor 0.

Another set of questions ask about the four or five most important factors when making a final choice between banks:

Table 12.5 Key Factors when choosing a Bank

Factors	England & Wales %
PROFESSIONAL REASONS`	
Understanding the needs and requirements of your type of business	45
Quality of financial and business advice available	18
Proposing financial ideas & solutions for your company	8
Specialist expertise in your industry sector	8
PEOPLE REASONS	
Good personal rapport with the people you are dealing with	40
Quality of people taking part in meetings, briefings, presentations	21
Positive businesslike attitude to clients	17
REPUTATION & RESOURCE REASONS	
Size & standing of bank	21
Range of services offered	19
International capabilities & expertise	15
Recommendation from professional adviser	6
Availability of Internet banking	1

Source: *Middle Market Corporate Banking, The 1998 Survey*, NFO Financial Services.

These tables throw up some interesting questions that you may care to reflect on:

- To what extent are they influenced by their past interactions with their bank and what are the consequences of this?

- How might the responses vary for other segments of the corporate market?

- What gaps are identified compared with what your internal data tells you?

Collecting this data is quite frankly a waste of time if it is not actioned. It is vitally important that it is used not just as a corporate totem pole suggesting that all is well but that it is used as a basis for innovation, modification, problem resolution and recognizing changing customer requirements.

12.9 Handling Complaints

There is now an almost overwhelming consensus that complaints are good for organizations and indeed a shared view that handling complaints well can help to sustain and build customer loyalty. Many organizations are recognizing the need for complaints to be handled at the first point of contact – it is cheaper and impresses the customer, for resolution to be as swift as possible and for the organization not to hide behind rules and regulation.

What determines whether the buyer is satisfied or dissatisfied with a purchase is determined by the relationship between their expectations and the product's perceived performance. This can happen if the product benefits are oversold.

Customers may feel they should have gone elsewhere for whatever reason, so they need to be reassured. This may be a follow-up telephone call to confirm the customer's satisfaction with the purchase as well as thanking them again for the business.

Table 12.6 Diffusing a Complaint

Four methods for defusing a difficult situation	
Smile	Give the customer a warm, sincere hello with a smile
Anticipate	The customer's complaint and head it off with a sincere concerned comment (take the offensive with kindness)
Apologise and assume responsibility	Take the blame for the customer's situation and empathize with them for their problem on behalf of your bank
Action	Solve the problems promptly

Six keys to cooling down an irate customer	
Listen	Carefully and with interest
Empathize	Put yourself in your customer's place. Use positive strokes (see later) that are genuine, specific, timely and sincere
Ask questions	In a mature, non- threatening way, that requires the customer to think about his or her answers
Repeat	Play back to the customer your understanding of the problem
Apologise	Without blaming
Solve the problem	Identify solutions to satisfy the customer's needs or find someone who can

Source: '*Communicating with Customers*', Eunson B., John Wiley & Sons, 1995.

We shall look shortly at assertive behaviour but staff are not paid to take abuse from customers. Some organizations – such as Southwest Airline in the USA – say they put their staff before their customers and indeed this is not just rhetoric. At the end of the day both the customers and staff have rights – although the customer's charter is longer!

Table 12.7 Rights of Provider v Rights of Customer

Rights of the customer	*Rights of the provider*
The customer has the right to:	The provider has the right to:
● Value for money	● Have human dignity respected
● The full and undivided attention of the service provider	● Not to be treated like a commodity or slave
● Open channels of communication for feedback, complaints or compliments	● Not to have intelligence, taste questioned
● To have allowances made for atypical, emotional behaviour caused by stress of actual or potential confrontation	● Be given the opportunity to apologise and explain
● Not to be hassled or stampeded, to be given time to think things over, to cool off	● Be given the time and the opportunity to fix things
● Say no	● Be listened to
● Explanations, apologies	● Not to be blamed for other's mistakes
● Reparation for loss, inconvenience, and then some	● Not to be abused, grovelled to or conned
● Not have intelligence or taste questioned	● Say no
● Not to have time wasted	
● Be listened to	
● Solutions, alternatives, choices, options	
● Expose a problem, and not be treated like a criminal	
● Have promises kept	
● Not to be abused, grovelled to or conned	

Source: 'Communicating with Customers', Eunson B., John Wiley & Sons, 1995.

13

CREATING A PROFESSIONAL IMAGE

13.1 Overview

In this chapter a range of the core attributes and capabilities of a successful relationship manager are introduced. Particular emphasis is given to the way in which relationship managers interact with other people – customers and colleagues alike.

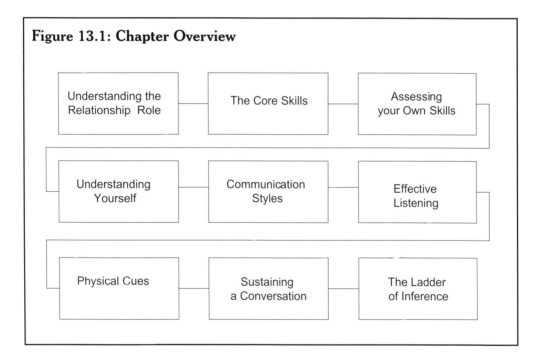

Figure 13.1: Chapter Overview

13.2 Understanding the Relationship Role

The established banks have been financially successful organizations for many generations if not centuries and this has led over time to a high level of confidence in their dealings with customers. It remains a paradox that despite the level of competition in banking, transferring to another bank is still the exception rather than the norm. For corporate customers there may be additional complexity and a fear that – where lending is concerned – the new bank may be less sympathetic if circumstances change and pull the rug from underneath them.

This combination of circumstances can lead to too much power in the hands of the suppliers. Many banks have a growing understanding that the relationship with the customer needs to be on a more balanced footing and indeed this is at the heart of a CRM or customer-centric strategy.

This has profound implications for the relationship manager and the way he or she behaves as they move from a selling approach to a collaborative one.

Table 13.1 Selling and Collaborating Compared

Selling	*Collaborating*
My job is to make customers want what we have	My role is to develop an intimacy of relationship that allows me to fully understand the customer's needs
I work in my own best interests and if that does not suit the customer I will let my company know through periodic sales reports	It is my responsibility to seek an alignment between the company's and the customer's interests
Achieving my sales target is my number one objective	Satisfying the customer in a profitable manner is the number one objective
I will do this with the minimum disruption to my own organization	I will involve and direct the organization as appropriate
I will do this single-handedly (because I have to)	I will achieve this as part of the team
If I encounter internal opposition who am I to argue?	If I encounter internal opposition, I will seek to understand why and seek a way forward, continually trying to balance the company's and the customer's needs
If I encounter customer opposition, I will sell harder	If I encounter customer opposition, I may well be doing the wrong thing
Success will come from my own energy and my ability to present and negotiate	Success will result from my ability to work in collaboration with the customer and to harness the resources of my own organization

Source: *Key Account Management, the route to profitable Key Supplier Status,* Cheverton, P. Kogan Page, 2000.

13.3 The Core Skills

The range of skills that follow are quite awesome in their scope – but do not be put off. Many you will be practising intuitively anyway. Scan them through, then go to the questionnaire in the next section and then come back to them again. Some of them, such as negotiation, we look at in more detail later.

The skills are divided into four main areas

- Personal Qualities

- Thinking Skills

- Technical Skills

- Managerial Skills

Personal Qualities

Integrity: This is needed at an individual and corporate level and in a high-pressure sales environment – which relationship banking is not – can cause conflict and tension. Typically honesty, tact and discretion are the key attributes.

Resilience and persistence: Stress seems to be an inescapable factor of modern-day life. It can be overcome with attention to emotional control and composure, a positive attitude and an innate toughness of character. Clear thinking under stress is a prerequisite for dealing with time-critical customer demands – as is patience at times. You need to be able to handle the inevitable disappointments and setbacks that are part of the relationship manager's baggage.

Likeability: This is an interesting area because it suggests that being good at the role of a relationship manager involves more than just technical skills. It goes beyond having the respect of customers and colleagues to embrace personal chemistry, a sense of humour and the ability to relate with people at all levels. This has an additional dimension – matching the characteristics of the relationship manager with those of buyer; in some cases there may be a period of trialing with the customer before formal appointment.

Capability for self-analysis: it is important that you know your strengths and weaknesses and play to your strengths. One of the most common inducers of stress is trying to be something you are not. Areas for development can be identified in personal development plans but remember it is your responsibility to develop yourself and manage your career.

Sensitivity: This is particularly an understanding of the impact you have on others and their responses to you. It is particularly important, of course, when dealing with people of different countries and cultures. It means showing respect for customers and colleagues whether inside or outside the work environment and being aware of and reacting appropriately to you customer's needs.

Image: Dress, grooming, posture, personality and style all fall under this heading.

Thinking Skills

Consultative mindset: This is an amalgam of many of the skills we talk about in this section but fundamentally it is based on having an enquiring mind, and ability to listen and then frame a problem-solving response in language the customer can understand.

Creativity and flexibility; Many organizations are increasingly recognizing this set of traits as a major source of competitive advantage – but clearly in needs to be framed in the context of the job, say new product development at the specialist level versus reframing a lending proposition. It is not darkroom stuff either – team events are used more often that not. It may be one big idea yes, but it may also be that the dialogue around you triggers a chain of increments.

Strategic thinking and long-term planning: One of the elements of thinking strategically is the ability to take a long-term view – to think in terms of marathons rather than sprints. Another is the ability to see the big picture – the systems-thinking approach that we looked at earlier – rather than become absorbed immediately in the micro detail. These approaches are not mutually exclusive – more a switch of gears as determined by the circumstances and tasks at hand. Understanding the difference between the macro and the micro is also important when planning – effective planning also requires good analytical skills and discipline.

Negotiation skills: we shall look at this area in more detail shortly but it is included here because it has a broader application than just in a customer-facing selling situation. There are very few times in dealing with other people when you are not negotiating in some form or another – indeed if you talk to yourself there is probably no relief at all! This ability to flex responsively to where others are coming from is as important as is the ability to put counterproposals in an open and fair way.

Editing skills: These apply both in verbal and written contexts. The ability to précis and synthesize rather than spell things out in a particularly laborious fashion is not a typically common strength. There is the famous comment of George Bernard Shaw's apologizing when writing a long letter to a friend that he did not have time for a short one – implying that this is in fact would take more time.

Technical Skills

Product knowledge: This includes not just products *per se* but also a thorough understanding of the way your bank does business. It is a balance between knowing the plumbing yourself and knowing a man who can. There is a need to understand how a product works, what it does. Fortunately Internets and Intranets make much of this knowledge readily available. It is probably worth adding that if you are not wholeheartedly committed to your bank's products and services then this will inevitably seep out.

Market/business knowledge: This is an awareness of those external dynamics that we identified in the LePESTCo analysis earlier. At the root of this is understanding your customer's business and the industry it operates in in-depth.

Selling skills: These are characterized as technical skills because they are in essence a series of processes. Even in a relationship management role there are times when you will be technically selling – this is perfectly legitimate. More detail follows in later chapters.

Attention to detail: This is an extremely important but also potentially hugely frustrating area and often one is faced with a value judgement that means that against your better judgement 'something will do'. Well if you are aware of this thinking then it will not do. The bottom line is quite straightforward – if clients and colleagues see and sense that you do not pay attention to the small things then they will doubt your capability to do the more important things well.

Financial: This is the ability to be able to analyse and understand figures and to be able to present a sound financial case.

Legal: This is an understanding to an appropriate level of banking and commercial law, including contracts, employment, competition and consumer protection.

Computer literacy: This includes not just the challenges of mobile working and personal computer skills but also an appreciation and understanding of information systems and technology as it applies to your working and customer environments.

Managerial Skills

Leadership and people management: It is becoming increasingly evident that to be successful organizations need leadership at every level – management is still important but is rarely sufficient in today's fast-paced environment. Most large organizations now operate some form of matrix management which means that although leadership and people management skills are still important they often need to be exercised in a more discrete way in the absence of sole responsibility.

Communication: Remember communication is a two-way activity and that it is very difficult to underestimate just how much communication we all need. Think 'Communicate Communicate Communicate' and this still will not probably overestimate the need, particularly in times of ambiguity, risk and constant or rapid change. The skills set includes verbal fluency, writing and presentation skills as tools for transmitting information, exercising influence and ensuring commonality of purpose.

Administration and organization: In a sense these are the 'hygiene' skills such as reliability, time management, delegation and the more simple planning activities.

13.4 Assessing your own Skills

Spend a few minutes working through this questionnaire and then reviewing the outcome. Indeed you can repeat the questionnaire from time to time to see how your profile is developing.

Table 13.2 Assessing Your Sales Skills

Skill	Rating						
	Low						*High*
1 **Basic Product Knowledge** Understanding basic features and benefits of all products and services well enough to make a competent sales presentation	1	2	3	4	5	6	7
2 **Product Application** Understanding usage of product applications well enough to diagnose and recommend appropriate products	1	2	3	4	5	6	7
3 **Problem Need Identification** Analysing problems and needs of customers who have no pre-defined product requirements; identifying incremental and add-on applications	1	2	3	4	5	6	7
4 **Advanced Product Knowledge** Communicating in-depth product application and technical information with sophisticated experienced users	1	2	3	4	5	6	7
5 **Creative Product Applications** Looking beyond the customer's immediate needs and anticipating or creating new applications	1	2	3	4	5	6	7
6 **Prospecting** Identifying, qualifying and initiating the sales cycle with new and potential customers on a regular basis	1	2	3	4	5	6	7
7 **Territory Planning** Organizing and properly managing sales geography, working territory to minimize travel and sales expenses while maximizing call activity	1	2	3	4	5	6	7
8 **Account Management & Planning** Gathering information and maintaining client-critical information. Understanding the customer's business, including political and power structures	1	2	3	4	5	6	7
9 **Pre-call Planning** Setting specific call objectives. Preparing information and documentation in advance of each call. Mentally preparing for each call. Anticipating objections, barriers, competitive action	1	2	3	4	5	6	7

10 **Opening Skills**
Developing a comfortable level with clients and
encouraging relaxed communication. Using pre-call
planning information effectively to start the customer
talking on matters relevant to the call objective   1 2 3 4 5 6 7

11 **Probing Skills**
Using questioning techniques to uncover customers'
needs, problems, desires attitudes   1 2 3 4 5 6 7

12 **Presentation Skills**
Making an organized presentation based on previous
call information or issues uncovered in probing.
Ability to focus customer on call objectives.
Command of product features and capable of
presenting persuasively.   1 2 3 4 5 6 7

13 **Objection Skills**
Dealing with customer's concerns, fears and
objections, including price. Can get beyond surface
objections and reveal customers' true concerns   1 2 3 4 5 6 7

14 **Buying Signals**
Understanding and looking for customer buying
signals. Responding to buying signals by asking
for the order or seeking a commitment from the
buyer to take some action that will advance the
sales process   1 2 3 4 5 6 7

15 **Closing**
Asking for the order. Understanding the range
of appropriate closing techniques   1 2 3 4 5 6 7

16 **Buyer Psychology**
Altering the presentation style and pace to match the
personality of the buyer. Knowing when to get to bottom-
line issues and when to give time to additional detail 1 2 3 4 5 6 7

17 **Follow-up**
Responding to customer requests promptly and
thoroughly. Following through on promises, returning
phone calls and replying promptly to customer
correspondence.   1 2 3 4 5 6 7

18 **Verbal Communications**
Communicating effectively. Utilizing proper
vocabulary and grammar   1 2 3 4 5 6 7

19 **Listening Skills**
Listening effectively. Giving customers, peers and
superiors proper feedback to ensure understanding.
Avoiding talking over the heads of other people. 1 2 3 4 5 6 7

20 **Written Communications**
Writing letters, reports and proposals effectively. Using
appropriately language and vocabulary. Style concise and
easy to read.   1 2 3 4 5 6 7

21 **Organization**
Coordinating field sales tasks and administrative tasks
in a logical orderly manner, including paperwork, reports,
proposals and itineraries   1 2 3 4 5 6 7

22 **Attitude**
Maintaining a positive professional attitude with
customers, peers and managers   1 2 3 4 5 6 7

23 **Teamwork**
Supporting and making positive contributions during
group interactions and willing and able to support group
goals and objectives   1 2 3 4 5 6 7

24 **Motivation**
Ability to self-start and take initiative in face of adversity
and frequent rejection   1 2 3 4 5 6 7

13.5 Understanding Yourself

Self-Image

One of the areas identified under Personal Qualities was that of self-awareness. Self-image is an important part of this and is shaped by the ideas, attitudes, feelings and other thoughts you have about yourself. These influence the way you relate to others. Once we have formed a mental picture about ourselves it is difficult – but not impossible – to modify our behaviour.

Assertiveness v Aggression

Assertiveness, or self-confidence, is about a high and natural level of openness to a complete range of feelings – positive or negative – where you do not feel inhibited by the potential power, politics and conflict of the people you are interacting with. It means that you can openly express what you mean and allow others to do the same.

It can cover such areas as:

- Giving and receiving compliments.

- Expressing liking and affection.

- Initiating and maintaining conversation.

- Standing up for you legitimate rights.

- Refusing requests.

- Expressing personal opinions, including disagreement.

- Expressing justified annoyance, displeasure and anger.

Self-Assessment Questionnaire

Here is another questionnaire for you to complete. Depending on your perceptions of your level of assertiveness you might ask a close friend, colleague or customer to complete it also to give you a form of 360 degree feedback. Remember for others that perception is reality and what this exercise will do is surface the gaps between what you are doing and what they are seeing.

Table 13.3 Measuring Your Assertiveness

Behaviours	Friends of the same sex	Friends of the opposite sex	Intimate relatives eg spouse, boyfriend, girlfriend	Parents-in-law and other family members	Children	Authority figures eg bosses, professors, waiters	Business contacts eg sales persons	Co-workers colleagues and subordinates	Total score
Give compliments									
Receive compliments									
Make requests, eg ask for favours, help									
Express liking, love, affection									
Initiate and maintain conversation									
Stand up for your legitimate rights									
Refuse requests									
Express personal opinions including disagreements									
Express justified annoyance and displeasure									
Express justified anger									

Scoring
Complete the table using the numerical rating:
Usually 3   Sometimes 2   Rarely 1

After completing total your scores to rate yourself:
180-240 Quite assertive   120-179 Fairly assertive
 60-119 Fairly unassertive`   0-59   Not very assertive

Source: *'Communicating with Customers'*, Eunson B., John Wiley & Sons, 1995.

Saying 'no' is often difficult to do even when people make unreasonable requests. To be able to say 'no' in a firm, polite but effective way is a particular strength. Staying silent is a typical response but this is often interpreted as agreement. Being effective in this area is often linked to feelings of self-confidence or assertiveness.

Being assertive can also be mirrored in a number of other things you do, such as your body language, attentive listening and your general feeling of self-confidence.

13.6 Communication Styles

In addition to developing a good level of self-awareness there is a need also to observe and analyse the way in which your customers' talk and behave as you seek to develop the relationship with them. We identified earlier when we talked about the trait of likeability about mirroring the interests of the customers.

People who have a high rapport with each other often have similar voice tone and tempo, breathing, movement or gestural rhythms and postures. Matching language is another way of raising rapport – matching or synchronizing words. Neurolinguistic Programming (NLP) – which we will not explore in depth here but is well worth further study – divides people into three categories:

- visual – I see what you are saying

- auditory – I hear what you are saying

- kinaesthetic (relating to feeling, taste and smell) my gut feel is that you are right.

As the relationship manager, the onus is on you to adapt your interviewing style so that you are dealing with a customer in a way that reflects his or her preferred style. This means listening closely to the language the customer uses in the rapport-building stages and watching in particular his or her body language. You also will get clues from the layout of the room.

There are many models of varying levels of complexity that can be used to categorize people's behaviour. One that features quite frequently and has the benefit of being intuitive assesses people along the dimensions of responsiveness and assertiveness to produce four behavioural types. Based on these types and their characteristics, different interactive styles can be determined and strategies for dealing with them.

Figure 13.2: Communication Styles

High	**Amiable** •People focused •Good storytellers •Social role important within company •Say what others want to hear • Deliberate about decisions	**Expressive** •Conceptual thinkers •Emotional, extroverted •Spontaneous •Not particularly practical •Don't like being alone •Good persuasive skills •Offices open and creative style
Responsiveness	**Analytic** •Detail & task-oriented •Like organizations, structure & self discipline •Information 'sponge' •Favour best technical solution but not political •Office highly organized	**Driver** •Short of time •Dominant/leader/'my way' •Less mobile, more controlled facial expressions •Factual and independent •Not a good listener •Results/task focused •Offices indicate power & control
Low		

Low   **Assertiveness**   High

Communication Styles

Source: 'Selling by Objectives', Alessandra A., Cathcart J., & Wexler P., Prentice Hall 1988

Driver

● Be clear, specific, brief and to the point.

● Be efficient in the use of time. Stick to business.

● Present the facts logically and plan presentations to be succinct and focused.

● Ask what? questions.

● Provide them with choices and alternatives to help them to make their decisions.

● Provide facts and figures about the probability of success or effectiveness of options.

● Motivate and persuade by referring to objectives and results.

● Negotiate resistance and objections directly because drivers will be very persistent in getting the answers they want.

● If there is a disagreement, focus on the facts not the person.

● Follow up by asking how well the product or service sold is doing in helping the driver to achieve his or her goals.

Expressive

- Introduce yourself in an open and enthusiastic manner.

- Be cheerful, sociable before starting your presentation.

- Use time to be stimulating but leave time also for relating, socializing.

- Talk about people and their goals, opinions they find stimulating.

- Ask for their opinions, ideas regarding people.

- Share your personal feelings.

- Negotiate resistance and objections candidly and confidently.

- Show how your products and services will provide positive support for achieving both the prospect's personal goals and those of the company.

- Do not deal with details, put them in writing, pin them to modes of action. Continue supporting the relationship.

Amiable

- Approach with a warm friendly manner, beginning with a sincere smile and a warm handshake.

- Start briefly with personal commitment. Use time to be agreeable.

- Show sincere interest in them as people, find areas of common involvement, and be candid and open.

- Listen and be responsive. Move casually, informally.

- Patiently draw out personal goals and work with them to help achieve these goals.

- Present your case softly, non-threateningly.

- Ask 'how?' questions to draw their opinions.

- If you disagree look for hurt feelings, personal reasons.

- Negotiate resistance and objections by using testimonials from other people and personal assurances.

- Involve the prospect in the sales presentation as much as possible so that the interaction between you is open, comfortable and relaxed.

- Define clearly (preferably in writing) individual contribution.

- Provide a guarantee that their decision will minimize risks, and assurances that provide them benefits.

Analytical

- Prepare you case in advance. Use time to be accurate.

- Approach them in a straightforward, direct way, stick to business. Support their principles, thoughtful approach,

- Build your credibility by listing pros and cons to suggestions you make. Make an organized contribution to their efforts.

- Present specifics and do what you say you can do.

- Take your time, and be persistent.

- Draw up a scheduled approach to implementing action with a step-by-step timetable.

- Confirm there will be no surprises.

- If you agree follow through. If you disagree make an organized presentation of your position.

- Give them time to verify your actions, be accurate, realistic.

- Provide solid tangible practical evidence.

The import of this analytical tool is that with practice you will become more experienced at recognizing these preferred styles as the customers exhibit them.. The challenge then is to flex your style to meet the needs of the client – for example, if customers talk and move quickly then you should adjust your rate of speech and movement to match theirs.

This model of behaviour we have considered – like all models – serves to illustrate what you could do rather than tell you or prescribe what you must do. You many find in many cases you make these judgements intuitively but this now gives you a framework against which to assess you own and customers' behavioural styles. As with all models you need to exercise judgement – they do oversimplify and generalize but they also have a reasonable level of validity most of the time.

Build rapport through the use of appropriate sociability and interpersonal skills, such as active listening and effective questioning techniques.

13.7 Effective Listening

Researchers at the University of Minnesota concluded that nearly 60% of misunderstandings in the business world can be traced to poor listening and only 1% to written communication. (Source: 'Listening made Easy', Montgomery R.L., Amacom Books, 1981.) After breathing, listening is the most dominant human communications activity.

People talk at a rate of between 130 and 160 words a minute, but can listen at over 800 words a minute. So most people do not listen at all closely – and we are also not likely to retain information that does not match our own views and preconceptions. The effective relationship manager needs to get off his or her agenda and onto the customer's agenda.

Consider how much attention you pay when you are supposedly listening – do the 360 degree feedback approach again:

Table 13.4 Good and bad listening behaviour

The bad listener	The good listener
Daydreams, wanders, 'internally listens while speaker is speaking	Exploits gap between speaking rate and thinking rate by analysing, anticipating and memorising
Doesn't look at the person speaking Is distracted by work, other people, clocks, televisions, noises	Keeps eye contact with speaker Concentrates on speaker
Keeps body oriented away from speaker	Is oriented towards speaker
Gives no feedback (facial responsiveness, friendly grunts)	Gives feedback
Keeps objects (pen, equipment) in hand while speaker is talking	Puts things down, has hands free
Ignores speaker's non-verbal communication	Tunes in to speaker's non-verbal communication
Interrupts	Occasionally reflects and clarifies, but allows other person to complete what he/she has to say
Jumps to conclusions - focuses on symptoms and quick fixes	Is patient. Sees complaints as opportunities for problem solving and learning. Focuses on underlying causes
Is prisoner of gender, power stereotypes (interrupting, quick fixes)	Not a prisoner of gender, power stereotypes
Takes criticisms personally	Doesn't take criticisms personally
Takes all customer's words literally	Doesn't take all customer's words literally

Extract from Eunson B., (1995) *Communicating with Customers*, John Wiley & Sons

Listening needs to be done at a thinking level – paying attention, synthesizing what it is being said, relating it to your own mental framework and guiding the conversation towards a desired outcome.

13.8 Physical Cues

Personal Space

Table 13.5 Personal Space Guidelines

0-18 inches	Intimate – only friends, relatives and close associates are allowed into this space
18 inches to four feet	Casual or personal – observed at most social gatherings, it allows people to talk to each other without feeling threatened
Four feet to twelve feet	Social – occupied by strangers, eg workmen, repairers at home, shop assistants
Over 12 feet	Public – typically used by performers, entertainers and trainers where the audience is seated

Source: Hall, E.T. (1989) *Understanding Cultural Differences*, Intellectual Press.

The Setting

The physical setting or environment has been called the 'servicescape' (Source: 'The Impact of Physical Surroundings on Customers and Employees', Bitner M.J., Journal of Marketing 1992). This comprises the totality of sounds, temperature, lighting, rooms, floor area, buildings, structure, furniture, decorations, equipment and vehicles that both the customer and the relationship manager might encounter. Compare in your own mind, say, the different offices you go into and the overall impression they consciously and unconsciously give you. If your team leader was to do a spot check on your car on the basis that the customer might also see it – what would he or she find?

Body Language

Kinesics describes any movement of the body that communicates something to others, such as shifts in posture, eye, arm, hand and leg movements. Every movement we make crossing arms or legs and shrugging the shoulders is part of body language. Heavy breathing, perspiration and blushing are part of this too. Learning to use non-verbal language is important but it needs to match what you are saying. The customer will quickly pick up any dissonance.

The more confident we feel the more we stand upright. When customers lean towards you they are interested, when they move away this is a negative sign. The same applies if the body going from side to side. Notice how people who share the same opinion in a group tend unconsciously to assume the same body postures.

Voice

A person's voice can be low or soft and deep or high in tone and that conveys differing levels of authority and emotion. Often the more confident you are the faster you will talk – although this may be a sign of nervousness also. Increasing volume and pace can help to emphasize points. Speaking more quietly can also get people to listen more closely.

People generally are very aware of accent – hence the number of Scottish call centres because the Scottish accent researches very positively. Accents are more welcome and accepted now than they might have been historically. You should ensure, however, that obvious colloquialisms are ironed out.

Listen to yourself on tape – clearly you need to be sufficiently articulate and clear in speech to be understood but try out variations in volume, pace and tone. Listen for any mannerisms – a nervous cough, clearing the throat, the ubiquitous 'ums' and 'ahs'. Try some pauses – see how long you can go before you feel the pause is too long and what other people say – it is usually appreciably longer than you think.

Table 13.6 Understanding How You Sound

Voice quality	Potential issues
Volume	Do you speak too loudly or too softly?
Pitch	Is your voice too high or too low?
Clarity	Do you slur your words or do you enunciate clearly?
Resonance	Is the timbre or tone of your voice unpleasant?
Inflection	Do you speak in a monotone, or do you use changes in inflection to emphasize points?
Speed	Do you speak too fast or too slowly?

Source: Revised from Eunsen, B. (1995) *Communicating with Customers*, John Wiley and Sons.

Language

Take care to the use the right words – avoid words with a heavy emotional overload or opinionated and inappropriate words. Clearly obscenities, slang, buzzwords, overly technical and three-letter acronyms, despite their prevalence, should be avoided.

Be sure to say what you mean and avoid 'weasel' words or euphemisms and use numbers where you can to define performance measures but to inform not bamboozle.

Space your ideas – a few at a time and give people the chance to respond. If they go quiet probe the reason why – it may be they cannot hear, do not understand or have lost interest. Be alert to differences in interpretation – people may either exaggerate what they hear or level it down to make it less important than was intended. Make sure you are using a common dialect – that the words you use mean the same thing to the other person and vice versa.

Eye Contact

Eye contact in our culture conveys sincerity and interest, while avoidance suggests shiftiness. Never wear sunglasses when visiting a customer in his or her office – again this could be interpreted as an evasive move.

Remember the teacher's admonition – 'look at me so that I know you are listening to me' – giving this undivided attention is common politeness. It is suggested that many people find it easier to interrupt a speaker when eye contact is established so you can use this to control the conversation.

13.9 Sustaining a Conversation

Have you noticed how children instinctively ask questions – to find things out and learn of course – but that this becomes more controlled and less spontaneous as one gets older? Asking questions allows you to get information, to control the conversation and to steer it in the direction of the objectives that you may have.

Let us look at the different conversational techniques and how you might use them to build rapport – not just with the customer but in any interactive situation.

13.10 Approach

A confident opening is essential and a good tip is to rehearse this in advance. Prospects will respond in many different ways. Some will let you do all the talking; others may be very talkative and deter you from your objectives. The onus is on you to remain focused on your objectives. Remember that you need to be thinking of how to add tangible added value and get the information you need. A good conversation is no more than that if you are not advancing the relationship or the sale.

Probing

A probe is a technique for finding out what a person knows, thinks or feels. It is used to generate and sustain a dialogue and therefore to find out what is on another person's mind. It demonstrates an interest on your part.

Probes are typically open-ended – how, what, when, why – and they invite facts, opinions, and feelings and avoid a simple yes/no answer

- What do you think about...?

- Why do you say that...?

- What are your thoughts on...?

- Tell me about your reaction to...

- What's your opinion on...?

The response you get may be verbal or physical – a gesture, shrug or some other form of body language. If people always volunteered their ideas, wants or feelings there would be no need to probe. There is a need to listen carefully because you cannot intelligently phrase the second probe if you are not listening. Bear in mind that persistent questions may make people uncomfortable.

Getting the Other Person to Keep Talking

Besides asking questions there are a number of other techniques for encouraging people to keep talking and showing that you are listening carefully.

Pauses: a deliberate, purposeful, planned silence of, say, five to ten seconds. Often they create an awkward silence that may provoke the other person to speak – let them fill the gap, not you!

Reflective statements: these play back an awareness and understanding of the emotional content of what is being said without agreeing or disagreeing 'You seem pretty concerned about that'.

Neutral probes: encourage the other person to elaborate – 'Tell me more', 'Help me to understand that'.

Brief assertions: a very short statement, question, sound or gesture to let the other person know you are paying attention and are interested – 'I see' 'mmm' a nod of the head, an appreciative smile.

Making Sure you Understand

The range of techniques here includes:

Closed questions: They are designed to stimulate a one-word answer. Note how they control the options for the answer:

For fact-finding – 'Who should we use for this project?'

Gaining commitment – 'Do you think this idea will work?'

Presenting options – 'Would you prefer Tuesday afternoon or Thursday morning?'.

Leading Questions: This is a query that allows only one reasonable answer. The answer is built into or implied by the question – 'Do you really feel it's a good idea if it doubles our costs?' They help to get agreement by testing assumptions.

Summary statements: This is a brief rephrasing of what the other person has said. They repeat briefly and usually in different words the substance of what has been said – information, ideas and opinions. It may require several sentences but they do not evaluate or express agreement but check understanding and synthesize what the other person is saying. You need to keep your own ideas out at this stage and the focus should be on content not feelings.

- What I understand you to be saying is...

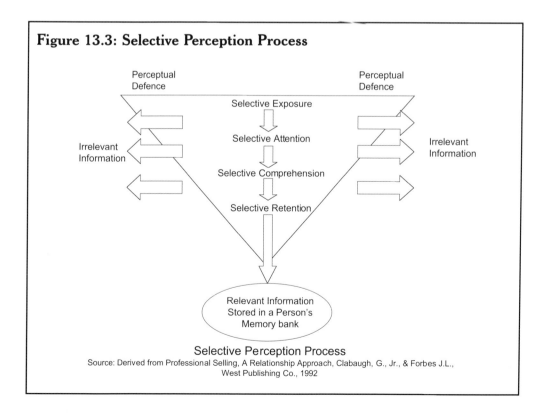

Figure 13.3: Selective Perception Process

Selective Perception Process

Source: Derived from Professional Selling, A Relationship Approach, Clabaugh, G., Jr., & Forbes J.L., West Publishing Co., 1992

- If I've heard you correctly...

- Let me just check and see if I've got this right...

13.11 Beliefs and Assumptions

Much of what we have talked about is about putting yourself in the shoes of your customers – understanding their business and their needs and thinking about them as people. We are all aware of the issues of communication and sensory overload in today's fast-paced world. To handle the potential avalanche that this could create, we all have a set of operating rules – beliefs and assumptions – and a set of perceptual filters that are continually at work to help to handle the information flows.

The challenge is that these assumptions and beliefs built up over the years – and which for most of the time operate at the subconscious level – are incredibly difficult to change. What

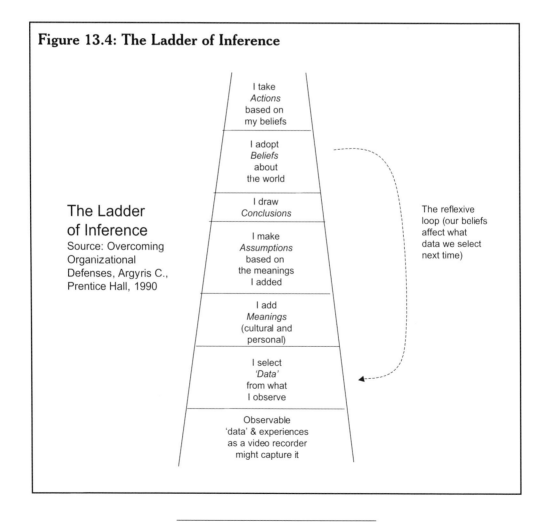

Figure 13.4: The Ladder of Inference

The Ladder
of Inference
Source: Overcoming
Organizational
Defenses, Argyris C.,
Prentice Hall, 1990

I take
Actions
based on
my beliefs

I adopt
Beliefs
about
the world

I draw
Conclusions

I make
Assumptions
based on
the meanings
I added

I add
Meanings
(cultural and
personal)

I select
'Data'
from what
I observe

Observable
'data' & experiences
as a video recorder
might capture it

The reflexive
loop (our beliefs
affect what
data we select
next time)

usually happens is that we filter away information that is at odds with our own beliefs and assumptions. To address this, we need firstly to understand our own perceptual filters. Then we need to develop the capacity to diagnose other people's filters. People will give clues in the way they talk about time – are they focused on the past, the present or the future. Some may prefer to deal in concepts, others the intricate detail. Do they see problems or opportunities? Is the glass half full or half empty?

A powerful concept for encouraging you to become aware of your own thinking and reasoning is the ladder of inference. What it encourages you to do is to make your own thinking and reasoning clearer to others and in turn inquiring into their thinking and reasoning without making assumptions. This has multiple applications – whether you are dealing with customers or colleagues. How many times have you made assumptions about another person's point of view or likely response without really probing to find out where they are coming from? This openness has strong links with assertiveness that we have looked at earlier. This needs to be handled carefully – a fact, no matter how obvious it seems, is not a fact until validated independently.

14

PRESENTATION SKILLS

14.1 Overview

In this chapter we look at a number of different ways a relationship manager may be communicating with the customer from presentations to letter writing.

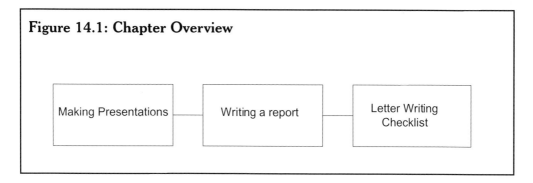

Figure 14.1: Chapter Overview

Making Presentations — Writing a report — Letter Writing Checklist

14.2 Making Presentations

Let's face it, making presentations is not everyone's cup of tea but it is an important part of the relationship manager's communication mix. Presentations may be formal, semi-formal internal or external. Normally there will be some form of visual support depending on the size and nature of the audience.

Pre-briefing

Ensure you know the 'what' of the content and the 'where' of the presentation. To the extent that you need to, do your homework on the audience such as age, sex, roles, and whether they know each other. This will help to ensure the style, structure and content is suited to audience needs.

If you can, and its an audience you are not familiar with, try to speak to some of them ahead of the presentation to get a sense of what their needs might be – this will help to increase your confidence, and minimize the risk of unexpected questions and negative feedback. Additionally it gives you the opportunity to personalize your presentation using a language and style that the group are comfortable with. It is often worth checking on the dress code to so that you are dressed in a way that is appropriate.

If the presentation is part of the sales process you will want to find out what the customer needs and that the audience will include those who have:

- the money or other resource to spend

- the authority to spend it and

- the need to spend it.

Structuring Your Presentation

- Typically and simply your objectives will be to:
  - sell something
  - persuade someone to do something
  - influence a decision.

- Like a good play your presentation will need a beginning, a middle and an end. A common framework is to:
  - start with what you are going to say and outline the content of the session – this conveys the purpose of the presentation
  - say it – here you develop the argument, provide facts, evidence, and examples and communicate the key ideas and facts that the speaker wants remembered
  - conclude by reminding them what you have said by reiterating the main points and emphasizing what you want people to remember to ensure that you leave the audience with a positive and constructive feeling.

- Use humour appropriately but sparingly – but examples, stories and analogies together with vivid statements can help the presentation to become more alive.

- In summary the content needs to be
  - positive and convincing
  - enthusiastic – keep up the tempo
  - flowing
  - logical and emotional – you need to connect emotionally with your audience as well
  - professional – avoid the 'unaccustomed as I am' routine.

- You might want to practise by recording your voice – better still get somebody to video you so you can check speech and body language at the same time.

Delivery Options

There are a number of options with various pros and cons but the important thing is for you to be comfortable with the style you adopt.

Table 14.1 Delivery Support Alternatives

Type	When	Pros	Cons
1. Prepared script	Formal conference. Need to be sure everything is said. Early attempt at public speaking. Where a formal copy needs to be handed out.	Gives you control of the material. Consistency – particularly if doing a number of presentations. Can mark up pieces for particular emphasize. Can practise and predict timing.	Written words are not the same as spoken words. Can come over as stilted and monotone. Need to remember to maintain eye contact with at least some of the audience. One way – difficult to interchange with audience. Tied to a rostrum.
2. Notes – on cards or paper flipcharts	More confident about public speaking. Do not have to be word perfect. Looking to develop dialogue with group.	More spontaneous. Helps to establish two-way dialogue. Can move about more freely.	Need to be able to take speech back to where it was if you digress or the conversation goes in a different direction. Timing needs to be managed by you. May end in a rush.
3. OHPs or acetates	As per 2	As per 2 Can put prompt notes on materials.	As per 2 Need to be careful not to just read from the slides. Do not over elaborate. Need to keep audience sight lines to screen clear. Not seen as particularly professional these days.
4. PowerPoint – note can be used to support 1 & 2 anyway	As per 2	As per 2 & 3 Use of colour, graphics and sound. Can use paper copy of slides if want to have more intimate discussion. Form ready made basis of handouts. Can import material if needed.	As per 2 & 3 Fiddling with technology may distract audience. May need delivery alternative if machine goes down. Risk of distancing the audience – they may focus on the show not the content.

On the Day

Some practical hints:

- Give yourself plenty of time to get there and scout the room and let people know you are there.

- Check that the physical layout of the room is satisfactory – you need to make sure you can be seen and heard by all attending so check the sight lines and sound levels.

- Smile when you walk in to the room – it gives an aura of confidence. Keep smiling – people will smile back. A certain amount of nervous tension is appropriate – it keys you up in a positive way – remember nerves are internal and once you get started they will disappear.

- Check time allocated and that if anybody important has to leave early they get your main message.

Body language

Statistics suggest that body language accounts for 55% of the communications impact, ie what you see or feel, facial expression, clothes, posture, gestures. The voice counts for 40% such as tone of voice, vocal clarity, and verbal expressiveness and the words only 10%.

So given the importance of body language:

Some Don'ts – don't

- grip the rostrum like a long lost friend

- wander away from a microphone or out of the pool of light

- have unnecessary barriers between you and the audience

- fold your arms

- put your hands in your pockets or behind your back

- stand between your audience and the screen.

Do

- keep smiling (again)

- be alert – watch your audience. Bear in mind if audiences go quiet they may be bored and not engaged or they may be thinking and pondering, or English may not be their first language

- scan the room in small groups making systematic sweeps to include all the audience

- see if you can get 1-3 seconds of eye contact per person

- thank people genuinely when they ask a question.

Communicating Effectively

Data suggests that a combination of 'tell and show' works best in terms of audience retention of your message:

Table 14.2 Levels of Communications Recall

Communication method	Recall After 3 hours	After 3 days
Tell	70%	10%
Show	72%	20%
Tell and show	85%	65%

Any slides used should complement and not distract from your speech. Keep them simple and use them to summarize or identify the key points of what you are saying. Use a new slide for each subject and use the six by six rule – no more than six lines of text and six words per line. Make sure you use the same font throughout – avoid scripts because they are difficult to read and use capitals sparingly. Do not use psychedelic colours – a blue background with yellow script and red heading is a good base.

Never read from your visual aids – and do not turn your back on the audience. They will be able to read your slide content quicker than you can say it so your commentary should highlight or expand but not just repeat what is on the slides. If there is detail on the slide give your audience time to read it first before you speak. The risk is that if you give them two forms of communication they will not register either of them.

One of the vexing questions is what to do with handouts – whether to give them out upfront or not – certainly you need to make clear at the beginning if handouts are available so that people do not have to make notes unnecessarily.

The timing of distribution is important. If you do it before it means people know what is coming, they can make notes on slides and can be aware of complex material which you need to be shared then and there. The risk is that they may read on, may not agree with the outcome and may disengage.

Remember that if you use colour slides when you are giving them out as handouts in black and white that dark block colours will come out as black and charts that use colours will not communicate as effectively.

Developing a Dialogue

It is always good to stimulate audience response where possible. If you particularly want a session to be interactive, ask them a question early on. The challenge may be, of course, that they do not respond or alternatively time management becomes an issue. As you gain more experience you will be better able to deal with these outcomes. By all means make it clear at the outset how you will prefer to deal with questions – but remember senior people will expect to be allowed to speak. Do not jump in with your own views – it is best to present your own viewpoint last.

Depending on the size of the room and audience, often when questions are asked everybody does not hear them, so it is well worth repeating them. If a questioner persists to the detriment of others then suggest you continue the conversation at the break.

Closing

End on a high note – people will probably remember best the opening and the closing but more of the closing. Make sure that the audience realizes that this is the end of a session. Conclusions should be explicitly stated and summarized rather than left for the audience to decide. Be clear what the next steps are – if it is appropriate, ask for the order – 75% presentations fail because this does not happen.

Make sure to thank the attendees for their time and attention. When you leave, keep your movements brisk and confident and do not shuffle sheepishly out of the room – finish with another round of eye contact.

Final Thoughts

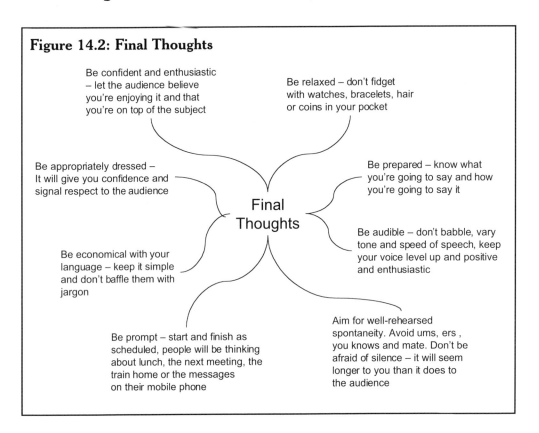

Figure 14.2: Final Thoughts

Be confident and enthusiastic – let the audience believe you're enjoying it and that you're on top of the subject

Be relaxed – don't fidget with watches, bracelets, hair or coins in your pocket

Be appropriately dressed – It will give you confidence and signal respect to the audience

Be prepared – know what you're going to say and how you're going to say it

Final Thoughts

Be audible – don't babble, vary tone and speed of speech, keep your voice level up and positive and enthusiastic

Be economical with your language – keep it simple and don't baffle them with jargon

Be prompt – start and finish as scheduled, people will be thinking about lunch, the next meeting, the train home or the messages on their mobile phone

Aim for well-rehearsed spontaneity. Avoid ums, ers , you knows and mate. Don't be afraid of silence – it will seem longer to you than it does to the audience

Team Presentations

You need to have the respective team roles clearly defined so the session runs smoothly. It is useful to cover off in the introduction who will do what during the presentation if the talking is being shared between you. Introduce the team at the beginning. Clearly it is important not to disagree in front of the client and important to demonstrate your own fluent team working in front of the customer. There should be an opportunity for all of the team to contribute otherwise the client will wonder why the passenger came along. People not talking should watch their body language – they need to at least mimic interest in the speaker and keep 'moving off the ball'.

14.3 Writing a Report

Writing as a Skill

The ability to write well is a major asset and within that the ability to synthesize and edit. Analysing, interpreting and organizing information are also key skills. Spending the right amount of time doing the right amount of research is also a fundamental. You can choose the best or most appropriate information only by gathering and examining all the relevant information. Bear in mind that when it comes to the actual writing you may use only somewhere between a third and a half of the information you have collected – hence the need for the editing skills.

Generally, writing is a learned skill and one in which it is not difficult to be competent. Certainly there are some key rules such as grammar and punctuation. Spelling is less of an issue with word-processing programs but this does not prevent the wrong word being used even though it is spelt correctly – so careful proof-reading is essential.

Some people enjoy writing, some may not but practice is often the key. Writing does require thinking – for example, finding the right words to get what you want to say across in a medium that has more permanence than day-to-day speech. Remember the written word creates a different impact from the spoken word. Rarely when writing do people get it right first time, more usually, particularly for a lengthy document, there are a series of drafts which are revised and edited as many times as its necessary. Like a good case study or conference presentation, it may look seamless at the end but much work will lie beneath the surface.

Bear in mind that content should take precedence over style – does it communicate what it has to as succinctly and effectively as possible?

Organizing and Structuring the Material

1. Working notes

One of the advantages of PCs and word-processing software is that you can just input your material in a stream of consciousness and come back and revise and edit it later. There is no particular need at this stage to think in terms of structure, although if you have to work to a prescribed structure that is fine.

2. Draft a structure

For internal processes such as credit assessment, the shape of the application is usually predefined in a paper or screen format. Report formats can also be driven by software packages that provide a very useful aid to determining the structure. There will be times, however, when a stand alone report may have to be produced and in any event the guidance below also has a broader application.

Drafting a structure may be a two-step process moving from an outline structure to a more detailed one. In any event the structure needs to be logical and help you to present your material in the most persuasive way. There are some helpful rules. Start with what the readers know before taking them into unfamiliar territory. There should be a logical flow rather like a good story that takes the reader incrementally to the conclusion. Group similar material together so that the reader does not have to move from one section to another and back again.

3. Organize your material

Reports should be structured logically from the introduction to the conclusions. An important aspect is continuity of thought and a logical flow from beginning to end. Often it is helpful to have an executive summary at the beginning to communicate succinctly the key points. It is not unusual as you try to establish the flow of information for a certain amount of 'cutting and pasting' to take place as you search for the optimal presentation. It is often recommended that you allow a gap of, say, 24 hours before carrying out the final edit and revision to allow your subconscious to work on it also.

So in this phase, you are dropping your material into the structure you have decided on. This may be an iterative process because you may find the structure does not entirely work or, say, give sufficient prominence to what emerges as the key issues. This will also enable you to stress test the shape and content of the report against its objectives or terms of reference, the extent to which it deals with the critical issues and the clarity and persuasiveness of your thinking.

4. Finalize the content

It is often useful to think about who the recipient might be – even if only doing the 'breakfast table' test – is this something I would want to read in this way first thing in the morning? Is this presented in a way that makes it easy for your credit controller to say yes!

Reports are normally written from an impersonal viewpoint with sparing use of adjectives and adverbs. Short sentences are generally better than long sentences, words with fewer syllables generally better than those with more. As a rule of thumb you should be aiming for sentences with an average length of 15 words. This reduces the 'fog index' – a measure of the difficulty the reader will have in understanding the content.

It is often useful to think about the style and content of the daily national newspapers – would your reader be more familiar with the *Daily Mail* than the *Financial Times*? Pay attention to the formatting and the physical layout – good presentation is important – relevant diagrams and charts often say more than words.

Table 14.3 Calculating the Fog Index

Calculating the Fog-Index

Note: Many word-processing packages will calculate a similar readability index for you

1. Select a sample of 100 words.

2. Count the total number of sentences.

3. Divide the number of sentences into the number of words to give the average number of words per sentence.

4. Count the number of words with three or more syllables, disregarding the last syllable for those ending in *ed* or *es*, compound words such as *marketplace*, and proper names.

5. Add (3) and (4) together and multiply by 0.4

The result is the Fog Index which can be compared with the corresponding reading level:

Less than 10	easy reading
11-12	top 20% of 12 year olds
13	top 20% of 16 year olds
14-16	university student
17	postgraduates

Reports should be logical, well-reasoned documents that present the necessary facts on which to make any necessary decision or form an opinion on a topic. Remember you are conveying certain relevant information to the reader to enable the reader to take a particular course of action. Clearly the starting point is an understanding of the objectives, the reader, and the outcome required. An important element is how the information, arguments and views are presented effectively and without undue bias. Bias can arise from a number of factors: the personality, opinions, values and skills of the writer, the relationship with the reader and limitations of time or scope in the data collection. Bias may also creep in because of the preferred outcome of the writer irrespective of the content and evidence.

5. Report production

Proof-reading is a particularly challenging phase and it is worth getting a colleague to read through the report for you – after a while you see only what you expect to see. Often a report may not print as it appears on the screen – so run off a draft as a precaution. Colours too on the page may come out differently.

Do not under estimate the amount of time that will be required to finalize and physically produce the report. Just the need to print a number of copies can take a seemingly inordinate amount of time, particularly if the deadline is looming – this is typically when printers run out of paper or breakdown!

When discussing the finished output with the recipient it is often difficult to remain objective about the content. 'Pride of authorship' is difficult to overcome but you must learn to separate facts from personalities, recognize that some people will want to see things written in their own style even if you feel it offers no obvious benefit and may also, at the end of the day, simply have a different point of view.

14.4 Writing an Article

From time to time you may be called upon to write an article or contribute to an advertorial, for example, for your local press. In all cases your first port of call should be your own internal corporate communications or press office. He or she in turn may ask you to help in the preparation of a draft article to personalize it to your locality. What should you consider?

14.5 Letter Writing Checklist

And finally, just an aide-memoire on letter writing, memos or indeed e-mails to round out this section. Take particular care with e-mails because spelling mistakes and poor grammar seem to slip in more easily and for some it is more difficult to pick these up off the screen as opposed to on paper in front of you.

Figure 14.3: Writing an Article

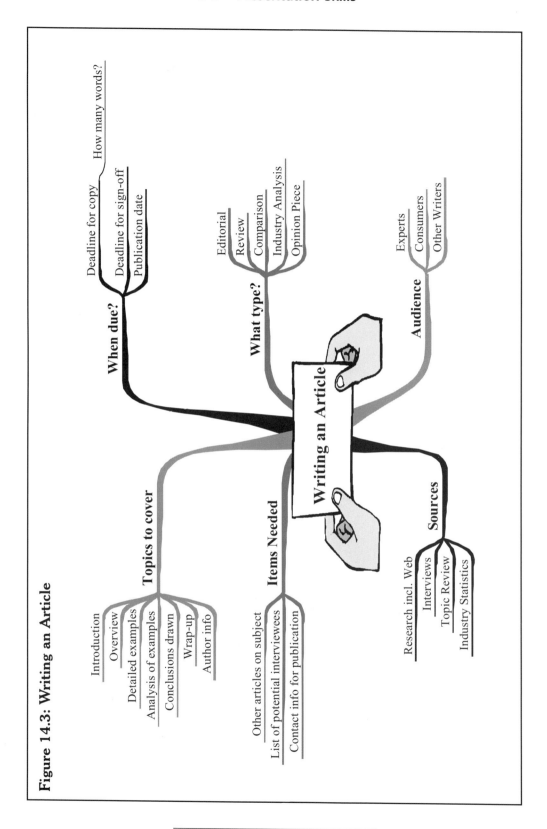

Table 14.4 Letter Writing Checklist

You must know	Before you begin make sure that you:
Your subject	1. Clearly understand the subject.
Your reason for writing	2. Know why you are writing. What does your correspondent want to know and why does he or she want to know?
Your reader	3. Adapt your style and the content of the letter to suit your correspondent's needs and his or her present knowledge of the subject.

You must be:	When writing you should:
Clear	1. Make your meaning clear; arrange the subject in logical order; be grammatically correct; exclude irrelevant material.
Simple and brief	2. Use the most simple direct language; avoid obscure words and phrases, unnecessary words, long sentences; avoid technical or legal terms and abbreviations unless you are sure they will be understood by the reader or are demanded by the needs of the letter; be as brief as possible; avoid 'padding'.
Accurate and complete	3. Be as accurate and complete as possible, otherwise further correspondence could result, resulting in extra work and the loss of time.
Polite	4. In your letters be sympathetic if your correspondent is troubled, be particularly polite if he or she is rude, be lucid if stubborn, be appreciative if he or she is helpful and never be patronising.
Prompt	5. Answer promptly, sending acknowledgements or interim replies if necessary – delays harm the reputation of the bank and are discourteous.

Source: *'Skills', International Journal of Bank Marketing*, Volume 8 Issue 6, 1990.

15

PRESENTING CUSTOMER-FOCUSED SOLUTIONS

15.1 Overview

In this chapter we look at how a relationship manager builds and sustains a trust based relationship with customers and colleagues alike by using a range of appropriate behavioural skills and relationship management processes. Throughout an important distinction is made between relationship management and transactional sales behaviour.

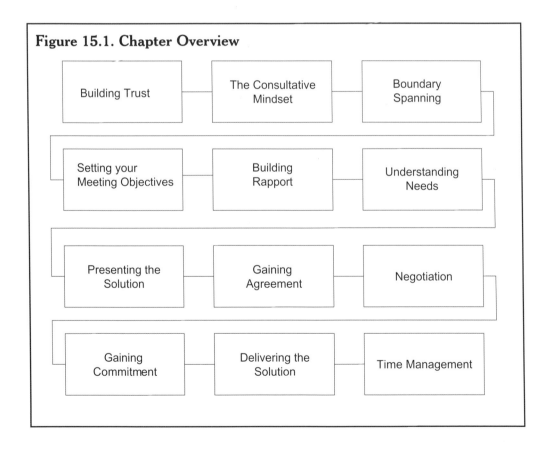

Figure 15.1. Chapter Overview

| Building Trust | The Consultative Mindset | Boundary Spanning |

| Setting your Meeting Objectives | Building Rapport | Understanding Needs |

| Presenting the Solution | Gaining Agreement | Negotiation |

| Gaining Commitment | Delivering the Solution | Time Management |

15.2 Building Trust

Presenting successful solutions relies on a shared bedrock of trust which in the case of relationship banking will hopefully have been built up over time. In a first meeting, clients will be assessing your confidence, capability and professionalism. Trust can be evidenced to some extent by the level of disclosure that we identified earlier and the general way and extent to which information sharing – particularly on an unsolicited basis – takes place. This calls for a high degree of empathy, sympathetic listening and the ability to take an honest look at yourself through your customer's eyes. As we all know from life's experiences trust is extremely fragile, is slow to build and easier to break than create.

The trust-building elements and the benefits of building this trust are shown below.

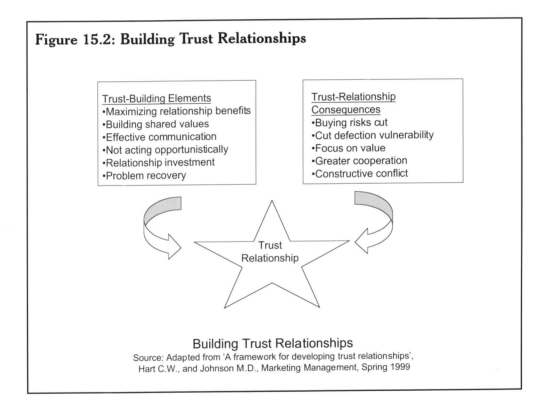

Figure 15.2: Building Trust Relationships

Trust-Building Elements
•Maximizing relationship benefits
•Building shared values
•Effective communication
•Not acting opportunistically
•Relationship investment
•Problem recovery

Trust-Relationship Consequences
•Buying risks cut
•Cut defection vulnerability
•Focus on value
•Greater cooperation
•Constructive conflict

Trust Relationship

Building Trust Relationships
Source: Adapted from 'A framework for developing trust relationships', Hart C.W., and Johnson M.D., Marketing Management, Spring 1999

15.3 The Consultative Mindset

Here we introduce another frame of reference or simply a way of doing things that is consistent with a relationship management strategy.

This is what is termed a 'a consultative mindset' – this is about understanding the customer's mindset, trading environment, concerns and implicit and explicit needs. In short, it is putting yourselves in the shoes of the customer – almost like role-playing. The rhetoric of being customer-focused is simple and straightforward; the reality is something quite different. The biggest challenge you face is thinking that you might be doing the right things now. Some yes, but all, probably not.

Let's look at some of the components of a consultative model as defined by Mick Cope as the 'Seven Cs' (Source: 'Seven Cs of Consulting', Cope M., Prentice Hall 1999). These questions also have a change management dimension that you might like to consider but have been contextualised here to a relationship-banking environment. These questions are relevant either:

- as you look at your client's business in a trading and operational sense or

- in terms of the benefits of the product or service that is being discussed

- as you consider changes within your bank.

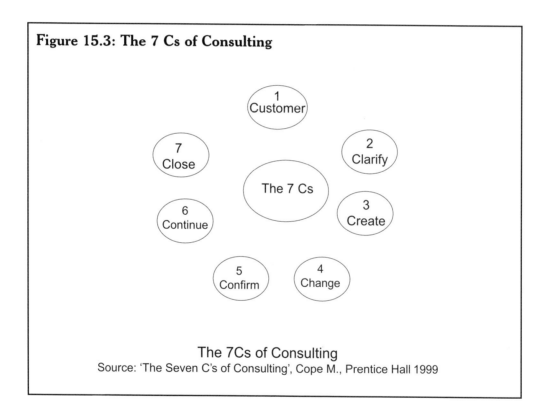

Figure 15.3: The 7 Cs of Consulting

The 7Cs of Consulting
Source: 'The Seven C's of Consulting', Cope M., Prentice Hall 1999

1 Customer – Getting it Right from the Start

Often customers are groping with a problem that they have not yet clearly defined in their own minds. There is a need to consider:

- Are you able to view the problem as the customer sees it?

- Have you tested the clarity of the desired outcome in terms of what the customer wants?

- Have you removed the clutter from the problem by focusing on where and what might be needed?

- Can the issue be successfully resolved and is the timing right?

- Do you have a clear picture of the decision-makers who can influence the initial stages of the buying process?

- Do you have a clear contract that sets out a framework for action and measurement? This is vital as an independent consultant it might mean you do not get paid. As a relationship manager it may mean you undertake a good deal of work for little or no benefit.

2 – Clarify – Understand the Real Issues

The real risk is that you go into 'one size fits all' product mode before you have a clear understanding of the customer's needs or indeed how the product may need to be modified to get an optimum fit.

- Have you gathered information that will determine the real source of the needs, and not just the symptoms? This is where the probing and active listening skills etc come to the fore.

- Is there a clear appreciation of the background and any unspoken issues affecting the situation?

- Do you understand the structural make-up of the company's system? Remember our earlier look at systems and process thinking.

- Is there a clear map that indicates who can influence the outcome of the project – the buying centre?

- Have you determined the extent to which known and unknown factors will have an impact? This might range, for example, from environmental and competitive factors to succession planning within a family owned company.

- Have you clarified how the customer and his or her company want to be kept in the information loop as the project and solutions develop?

3 – Create – Developing a Deliverable Solution

One of the core roles of the relationship manager is engineering the fit between customer needs and corporate capabilities – this may not be a particularly comfortable role as you carry out, for example, 'shuttle diplomacy' between your customer and the credit function.

- Have you ensured that the bank can actually deliver any creative solutions that you come up with?

- Have you understood any potential creative blockages for the customer? This is particularly relevant if the customer has a more traditional outlook and is likely to be resistant to innovation.

- Can solutions be found in the work that others have done such as relationship manager colleagues and product/market specialists?

- Have you a clear process for deciding on the final solution? How are decisions made within the company? Who is going to have the most powerful voice?

- Have you considered the resource required for the potential solutions to ensure the option is viable – including the potential involvement of market/product specialists?

- Are there clear owners for the solution both internally and at the customer level and do they have the capability and desire to own them?

- Have you considered possible threats to adoption of you solution? You may have to use your influencing skills to reposition some of the perceived negative aspects into worthy ones.

4 – Change – Working to Make Things Happen

This section in essence relates to the difference between 'thinking' and 'doing'. It also highlights the 'boundary spanning' and coordinating role the relationship manger will have between the customer and the internal functions of the bank.

- Is there a clear understanding of how the desired outcome will be managed?

- Is there a clear appreciation of where the energy for action will come from and how it will be shared across the different parties?

- Do you know how people can be encouraged to be involved in the effective and continuing implementation?

- How will systems and processes both externally with the customer and internally with the bank cope with the proposed activity?

- Is the planned outcome flexible enough to operate in a dynamic and uncertain environment?

5 – Confirm – Measuring the Effectiveness of Implementation

Ahead of measuring the benefits of implementation is defining what these might be. A key part of the role of the relationship manager is setting these expectations.

- Who will own and manage the measurement process?

- Have you decided at which point or points the measurement will take place?

- Is the relationship between qualitative (attitudes- and opinions-based) and quantitative (numbers-based) measures clear to you?

- Do you know if your performance has been up to the standard expected by the customer? Will you be able to call down any customer satisfaction survey reports?

- Have you clear views of the costs of sale and any on-going support costs?

6 – Continue – Making Sure the Full Benefits are Realized

Do not take your foot off the pedal too soon. Often after completion of a piece of business there is a positive halo effect but there is a risk that subsequently customers become disappointed for some reason or another. There is a need to continue to manage both the perceptions and the reality of the solution you have delivered.

- Do you have a plan to ensure slippage does not occur once the project has been closed, ie that the expected benefits will be delivered?

- To the extent that you can, have you ensured the customer will derive the full benefits from the product/solution? The risk is that if this is not the case it may rebound against you.

- Have you consolidated or developed your relationship with this customer?

- Will the knowledge created as part of the project be captured both by the customer but particularly within and across the relationship management teams and the other parts of the bank that may have been involved?

- Are you better able to categorize the customer's responsiveness to creativity and innovation?

7 – Close – Signing off with Style

Memories fade. Usually formal correspondence between the customer and the bank will relate to technical and procedural issues rather than capturing the real benefits at the time. Make sure there is a letter on the file which reflects the open and acknowledged success between you, your customer and the internal support areas. Better still write up the event as a success story that can then be featured in your internal communications – Intranet or whatever.

- Have you encouraged the customer to reflect on his or her view before presenting your own view of the outcomes?

- Have you formed a view on the success of this piece of business?

- Have you helped the customer/bank to consider what has been learned over and above the planned outcomes?

- Is there a clear indication of any tangible improvements to the operational or commercial viability of the customer and your bank?

- Have you identified what opportunities exist for further work?

- Have you consolidated the overall capabilities of the bank to deliver focused solutions to this customer?

You can see within this activity a number of potential roles for the relationship manager in consultant mode:

- Facilitator: Having the skills to help the customer to explore the problem and solve it himself or herself. It may be that you do not have a product that meets the customer's needs and therefore have to gateway them to another provider.

- Problem-solver: Using investigative skills to disaggregate the problem and provide a solution. For example, providing alternatives such as invoice discounting to a customer with cash flow difficulties.

- Advisor: Based on your experience from the range of customers you have dealt with, these are some of the things that your customer might consider.

- Resource: Usually this is to do with being part of the customer's problem-solving team. For a consultant this would be an explicit role for direct reward, for a relationship banker it would be part of the relationship development role, although due regard would have to be given to the proprieties of the situation.

We shall look at some of the practical skills you will need to be fluent in to manage the required outcomes shortly. Inevitably the consultancy model overlaps with elements of the model interaction process that we shall look at now. You might want subsequently to consider where these overlaps occur so that in your own mind you have a seamless and integrated view of the process.

15.4 Boundary Spanning

It is appropriate at this stage to acknowledge the ambiguity and ambivalence that a relationship manager has to deal with, often on a day-to-day basis, in acting as the 'boundary spanner' or pivotal point between the customers and the bank. We have already identified the need of the effective relationship manager to become a trusted advisor and to be recognized as providing solutions that are in the best interests of the customer.

This occurs at an organizational and operational level:

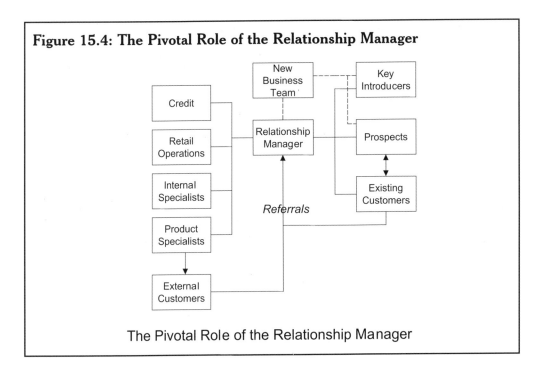

Figure 15.4: The Pivotal Role of the Relationship Manager

The Pivotal Role of the Relationship Manager

And, if not more challengingly, it occurs at an emotional level:

> So, relationship managers have to draw on emotional strengths – 'having continually to smile, show empathy, listen and solve problems'.

Source: 'Communicating with Customers', Eunson B., John Wiley & Sons, 1995.

This concept of total customer commitment surfaces a number of risks. One is the risk of 'going native' – identifying more with the customer than the bank. It may result in the relationship manager making commitments outside of, say, his or her lending authority. Another is that a sense of frustration may occur – which is shared with the customer in a way that is not positive – about the manner in which the bank goes about its business.

If that is not enough, the relationship manager may be categorized internally as a troublemaker – the grit in the oyster, not a team player – as he or she seeks to align the organization internally to the external expectations of the customer. And we shall not even mention pricing!

This puts a premium on the relationship manager's ability to role play – to put himself or herself in the shoes of the internal customers – credit, compliance and so on – as well as the external customers. Breaking out of the monoculture of the bank can offer a wide and powerful spectrum of understanding. Challenging the conventional wisdom of the dominant group – or 'Cowdung' as it has been called (Source: 'Tools for Thought', Waddington C.H., Jonathon Cape, 1977) – is a major strength-sapping activity.

Let us look now at the client-interaction process.

15.5 Setting Your Meeting Objectives

We shall start before the actual meeting when you will have worked on what your objectives for the meeting are. Let us get this straight – setting objectives for an interview is critical. It gives a framework against which to assess the success of the interview and will also help to give the meeting a structure and purpose.

This is an important part of the client-interaction process. Throughout this process you will see that different weightings are given to the different stages for relationship managers as opposed to transactional sellers.

Figure 15-5 – Outcomes of Sales Calls

For a first call the objectives may be establishing your credentials, developing an understanding of the customer's potential needs and earning the right to keep the dialogue going. The customer may have invited you in with something specific in mind such as a factory extension, increased working capital or the introduction of a product specialist. Alternatively this may be a high-value customer where you are sustaining the dialogue to maintain the relationship.

Note in this case the distinction between an advance and a continuation, as shown above.

In any event, as part of the pre-research, you must do your homework before the call so that you do not ask unnecessary questions. Make sure you look at the customer's website if there is one. Make sure you are up-to-date on any servicing difficulties there may have been. Check to see that the mandate you have is current.

Think through the call and imagine what a positive outcome will look like and feel like. It can help before the call if you also plan your questions – what potential problems might the customer have? How would your products help to address these problems? Think about questions that may guide the conversation in the direction you need to go to achieve your objectives.

15.6 Building Rapport

Creating a good initial impression is always important – after that, although you will be continuing a dialogue with an existing customer, do not let complacency or overfamiliarity creep in – treat everyone as a 'first date' in that respect. Keep your opening topical and relevant and do not spend too much time on the pleasantries. 'Appropriate sociability' is the key – after all time is valuable for both parties.

The handshake is usually the first and only physical contact during a customer call. As you will know from your own experience, it can communicate warmth and strength or indifference and weakness. Be firm, maintain eye contact, make sure your hands are dry – recall the body language points from the section on presentation skills: they are equally relevant here.

Make sure for a first meeting and confirm at subsequent meetings that the customer has your contact details by giving out or offering another business card. Get a card from the customer if he or she has one – this will give you the customer's name spelt correctly and the title and position in the company.

Some cultures such as the Japanese and Chinese make a point of taking time to carefully read the card then and not just slipping it in the pocket or tucking it into a folder automatically. This makes sense anyway – it adds to the customer's perceptions of how you value them and the time they are giving to the meeting. It goes without saying that any collaterals and sales support material you use in the meeting should be both up-to-date, company approved and in pristine condition.

Look for any clues in the office environment that will help you to understand the customer's behavioural style; note the tone and pace of his voice. If he (or she) looks as though he has just rushed in from another meeting or a crisis on the shop floor then give him time to settle back down. Aim to create an environment and feeling of ease and start to mirror the customer's body language, pace and tone of voice.

Often at that this stage it will be useful to reprise the purpose of the meeting so that you are both on the same wavelength and confirm how much time you have. Take the customer's cue on how much time is available and plan the meeting mentally to cover your objectives. If at the end of the day the customer seems happy to continue talking and it is relevant then fine. Other customers – such as busy corporate officers – will want the meeting to run to time and if you do this it may make getting back to see them easier.

This is the stage at which the empathy starts to surface. Persuasion skills are much less to do with the rational and much more about personal feelings and emotion. Being liked and trusted is as important as being a subject matter expert. Get a handle on the customer's perceptions – these are what will count at the end of the day. Start to understand the personal motivations as well as the business motivations. Good personal chemistry is important – common interests, common circumstances and common acquaintances; never underestimate the value of the people networks.

15.7 Understanding Needs

It is worth making a distinction at this stage between those situations when:

- you are an 'order taker', ie the customer knows what product he or she thinks she wants and the options available are fairly prescribed anyway. Here the sales task is relatively straightforward and there is no need to be overcomplicated apart from making sure the customer fully understands what he or she is getting.

- there are a richer variety of options and indeed you move into a more sophisticated problem-solving mode.

We develop here how you would handle the second set of requirements. Here, through the use of a series of structured questions that you have predefined, you develop your understanding of what the customer's needs might be. This is the first stage of the SPIN(r) technique (Spin Selling, Rackham N., McGraw-Hill, 1985) – the situational questions. You may be familiar with other or indeed trained in other solution-focused selling programmes, but bear in mind they must be grounded in relational not transactional techniques – so make sure you understand the principles.

The challenge is to be patient, not to rush in with a preformed solution before the 'discovery' process has been adequately completed. Indeed, if you ask the right questions the customer will end up persuading himself. There is a need to thoroughly uncover the customer's situation in the sense of unmet needs and develop it until it reaches a critical mass. Problem questions – the second stage of the SPIN(r) technique – ask about specific difficulties or problems as perceived by the customer.

Take, for example, electronic banking. This offers many benefits to the customer who may be resistant to the technology or to the impact on systems and people within the business. A deeper understanding of these areas of resistance will result in a better and more persuasive positioning of the service benefits in due course.

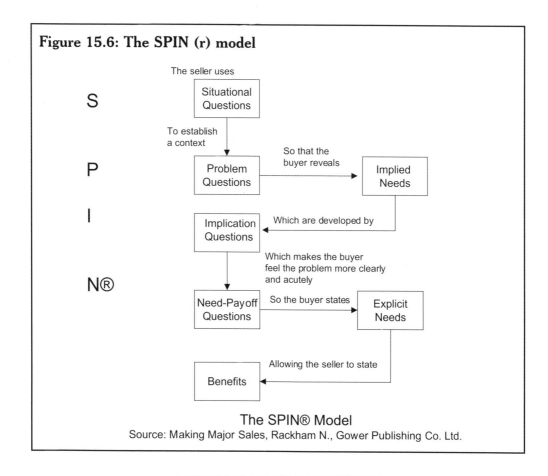

Figure 15.6: The SPIN (r) model

The SPIN® Model
Source: Making Major Sales, Rackham N., Gower Publishing Co. Ltd.

At this stage the message is to hold back on product specifics and presentations. Be creative in defining the problem. Search for those most affected and understand the nature of the impact. Get an in-depth understanding of the implied needs. These are the 'implication' questions – understanding how the problem affects the effective running of the business.

It also helps at this stage if you can get some sense of what criteria the customer will be using to assess the fit of what you will be proposing. This gives you the opportunity to tailor the features and benefits to their particular needs at the next stage and if possible play to your strengths. Use open questions such as 'Why is that important?' 'How would that help?' and 'Would it be useful if?' If you can convince your customer of a key criterion in an area where your products are strong then you will have a competitive advantage. You may also avoid the fundamental impasse where the customer, despite the persuasiveness of your presentation, just says no. You need to avoid this if at all possible by fully understanding the customer's needs and positioning the benefits accordingly.

This leads in to the last stage of the SPIN(r) approach – the Need-payoff questions, which ask the customer if the relationship manager has correctly identified the customer's explicit needs. These questions begin with a benefit statement and show the pay-off in terms of addressing a key need. If the need has not been correctly identified then the SPIN(r) process is repeated.

15.8 Presenting the Solution

In many ways all you may have done up to now is to have helped the customer come to an understanding that he or she has a problem. At this point, the customer may not be able to go further because this may have the effect of triggering a set of internal processes that come into play given the magnitude and potential severity of the issue. No matter, this is a significant advancement along the relationship development continuum.

The Value Equation

If you are dealing with the decision-maker then anyone making a decision to purchase – whether it is a product or a service – must balance two opposing factors. One is the seriousness of the problem that the purchase would solve. The other is the cost of the solution – in summary the value equation. Remember we identified the sorts of pressures that a decision-maker would be under when we examined the decision-making unit earlier.

Features and Benefits

At this stage you might start to talk about features and benefits of your potential solutions. Note the language which is not just semantics – we are talking about solutions not products. Features are dry – facts, data, information about a product which may appeal to

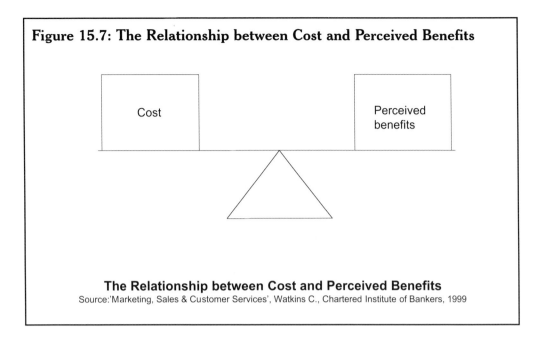

Figure 15.7: The Relationship between Cost and Perceived Benefits

The Relationship between Cost and Perceived Benefits
Source:'Marketing, Sales & Customer Services', Watkins C., Chartered Institute of Bankers, 1999

the functional buyers but are unlikely to be compelling for others. This might be described as product-centred sales behaviour.

Benefits show how features can help a customer; they are more powerful and can be framed in a way that meets and explicit need of the customer. To transform a feature into a benefit use the phrase 'which means that':

Table 15.1 Features & Benefits

Feature		Benefit
Cash Management Services		
Out-of-hours access to banking information	which means that	Company has flexibility to manage books outside banking hours
On-line access to accounts		Accelerates decision-making process, re disbursement of cash

An important aspect of features and benefits are those that apply to your bank – it may be such things as size, global reach, liquidity, credit appetite, speed of decision-making and so on – these, of course, are couched as features not benefits so apply the 'which means that' metric. These benefit statements can be scripted as a joint exercise among product and relationship managers. Well-designed and focused benefit statements can be a valuable tool to help customers to understand and appreciate the bank's capabilities.

Bespoking the Product

At one level this bespoking relates to the way in which you position the benefits of your solution against the needs of the customer. But probably a more important aspect is the extent to which the solutions specialist or relationship manager can in fact construct the offering in a way that relates to the individual needs of particular corporate customers. For example, the potential range of options, such as the availability of:

- various lending vehicles such as overdrafts, fixed- and variable-rate loans, invoice discounting and other forms of asset finance.

- money-market solutions offering short-term investment opportunities in sterling, euro and US dollars through the money markets, structured deposits, money-market funds, commercial paper and other securities.

- structured investment products reflecting the amount, timing and duration of the investment, the investment objectives, the risk tolerance, cash flow needs and whether the company wants to be an active or passive investor.

The challenge for the relationship manager is to pick the bundle that best fits the needs of the customer against the needs of the bank in terms of yield and risk management.

15.9 Gaining Agreement

In some cases this may be a 'slam dunk' – the American basketball term for a sure-fire score. In most cases there will a process of negotiation to get the best fit for the customer and you. This process will be helped immeasurably if you have been able to foresee and cover off before this phase potential objections that the customer may have. Remember this is not about confrontation – the desired outcome is a 'win-win' situation.

Many sales courses teach that objections are disguised buying signals insofar as they indicate buyer interest and all you have to do is bat them away using your superior selling skills and all is well. In this area of major sales and relationship banking, however, – as in a number of others – the number of objections *per se* is not an indicator of success. If you have successfully prevented objections there should be fewer at this stage.

When dealing with objections, the first step is to listen carefully and acknowledge the objection by restating it back to the customer. Then move on to clarifying the objection using your questioning techniques to get to the bottom of it. For example – if the charge is that your price is too high:

- What aspects of the price are they referring to – interest rates, fees, activity-based rates, and so on?

- Is it too high in relation to the competition?

- What do they consider to be a fair price?

- Is the customer aware of the total value received?

- Is this a cover for other objections that have not been voiced or a being shielded – the need to refer to others for example?

Be honest in responding to the customer's objections. Bear in mind, however, that attempts to talk customers out of criteria they regard as crucial usually fail and do not lead to lasting relationships of mutual trust. Admitting to the validity of an objection can boost the customer's self-esteem and shows respect for his or her opinion.

It is appropriate, however, to look at techniques for overcoming objections and gaining agreement:

1. Using additional knowledge to counteract the customer's point of view – perhaps additional product benefits or service-related enhancements.

2. Agreeing to the validity of the objection then translating it into a reason for selling the product.

3. The 'yes but' approach – indirectly denying statements and restating the objection in a positive manner.

This process may lead to completion of the sale – it may serve simple to clarify the areas of disagreement at which point it is appropriate to move on to a more structured negotiation approach.

15.10 Negotiation

Everyone negotiates – probably more often than they are aware of. Negotiation is more than just a formal bargaining process – it is any conversation with a purpose. In every negotiation the potential for agreement sits side by side with the potential for conflict. Negotiation is not about thinking on our feet or forcing our opponent into corners. It is about reaching a mutually beneficial agreement that opens up further opportunities.

Skilled negotiators need planning skills, the ability to think clearly under pressure, good verbal reasoning and a high tolerance for ambiguity and uncertainty. They should be assertive not aggressive and be able to test their own assumptions and the customer's intentions (see Ladder of Inference) in an open and non-threatening way.

In many situations there is a danger of negotiating too soon – this should be saved until late into the engagement process. The risk is that the earlier you give concessions the less impact they will have. It has to be recognized that there maybe showstoppers – the customer may need a different product or radically different approach.

Some do's and don'ts:

- Sort out issues of conflict as quickly as possible – don't procrastinate.

- Be sure you have the necessary authority – and make sure the person you are dealing with has the requisite authority also.

- Don't bluff your way through if the customer has more expertise than you – get a more senior person or a specialist.

- Collaborate don't confront – mutual gain should underline every movement of the negotiation.

- Understand 'what your best alternative to a negotiated agreement is' (BATNA). What is the best outcome if you don't negotiate? If there are more options and they are better than what you can agree from this particular negotiation then the higher your negotiating power.

- Understand also the customer's BATNA – are there competitive offers that he or she might turn to – do we know who these are from and where we might be vulnerable?

Table 15.2 Competitive v Collaborative Behaviour

Competitive behaviour	*Collaborative behaviour*
● Behaviour is purposeful to pursue own goals and targets	● Behaviour is purposeful to achieve common goals
● Secrecy is of supreme importance	● Open and frank
● Do not let them know what you really want lest they know what you are willing to lose	● Undisguised representation of needs
	● Predictable but flexible
● Be unpredictable, mix strategies, surprise with off-balance manoeuvres	● Not threatening
● Use threats and bluffs	● Behaviour focused on achieving solutions to mutual problems
● Suggest apparent commitment to a position	● Ideas considered on own merit – hostility and friction not introduced
● Stereotype the other person as the 'bad guy'	● Whatever is good for others is good for self

Source: *Derived from 'Successful Negotiation Skills', International Journal of Bank Marketing*, Volume 10 Number 1, 1992.

In practice skilled negotiators focus on:

1. Areas of Maximum Leverage

One error is to assume that the negotiation centres only on price. What are the broader decision criteria – how important will a concession on price be to the customer? It pays to think in terms of ranges rather than fixed points. There is a need to be realistic based on you are competitive positioning and where the customer might be coming from. Too high and they may walk out, too low and you may unnecessarily be giving away margin. Another error may be to too narrowly define the range of solutions that are available – is there another solution to the problem outside of the direct competitor's, eg outsourcing an activity rather than continuing with in-house investment.

If you are competing with another bank there is a need to consider how vulnerable you may be and, as the model above illustrates, bear in mind that negative statements about your competitors will generally damage your credibility more than the competition. Where you need to, make concessions in small increments and be slower in conceding as you get nearer to your limit.

Always be aware too of your BATNA. Think in terms of the best outcome you could

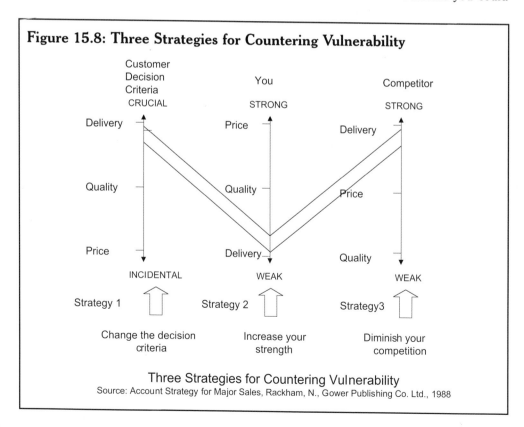

Figure 15.8: Three Strategies for Countering Vulnerability

Three Strategies for Countering Vulnerability
Source: Account Strategy for Major Sales, Rackham, N., Gower Publishing Co. Ltd., 1988

achieve if you did not negotiate. What other options would be available to you and are they more attractive compared with what you can agree at this negotiation? This might occur, for example, where there is a cap on exposures within a particular industry segment. What is negotiable and what is not negotiable? What are the range of variables and their weightings for the respective parties?

2. Planning and Using Questions

Planning is essential ahead of the meeting – what happens before is as important as what happens during the meeting. What will be the strategies of the respective parties? Will the meeting be confrontational or collaborative?

Remember again your questioning techniques – skilled negotiators ask lots of questions – over twice as many as those who are less experienced.

3. Separating Understanding from Agreement

Skilled negotiators confirm they understand what the other side is saying but do so without suggesting acceptance or agreement.

4. Rigorously Testing for Misunderstandings

You need to achieve an agreement that works. Take care – failure to establish a common understanding of a key point during negotiations can lead to expensive trouble afterwards.

5. Reaching an Outcome

Psychologically, the more time you invest in a negotiation, the more important a successful conclusion is to you. Similarly by causing your customer to invest more time, energy or resources, you increase his or her need to conclude rather than abandon the deal.

Pressure generally has a negative impact on the customer as the size and importance of the transaction grows – overly aggressive closing techniques may make this worse. A wrong decision for the officer of a large corporate might be career damaging – concerns like this often remain below the surface with other psychological issues in the customer's mind.

It is better to get the issues out on the table than let them stay hidden and unresolved. Telling someone not to worry does not resolve fears. Unresolved concerns can damage your chances of success. You will probably only get away with forcing the customer once – this approach is not conducive to a continuing good relationship.

It may well be that the differences are irreconcilable – that's life.

15.11 Gaining Commitment

Typically in most sales training courses this is referred to as 'Closing'. There is some debate, however, over the part closing techniques have to play when dealing with corporate customers in a relationship-banking context.

Characteristically there are two approaches to getting business. The first is sales-oriented, which trains sales people in high-pressure selling techniques and is based on aggression and supersmooth presentation. The range of closing techniques is worked through until the customer succumbs. Professional and sophisticated people are less likely to buy if they detect an artificial closing technique.

The second approach is customer-oriented and focuses on customer problem solving, having uncovered customers' needs and having found appropriate solutions. Indeed, the bigger the decisions the more negatively people react to pressure.

At the end of the day, however, for most products and services you must ask for the business and you must obtain some form of commitment. This is best done by your proposing the commitment in an appropriate way.

Relevant approaches might be:

Direct Appeal: This is a simple request for the business that avoids any ambiguity.

Summarization: A summary statement that draws together the major benefits of the transaction to the customer. This is especially useful if there have been several meetings because it draws the main points together.

Buying Decision Review: This reviews the buying decision areas of need, price and time. Each decision area can be reviewed and the customer's understanding and commitment confirmed.

Balance Sheet: An interactive balance sheet approach summarising the pros and cons of the transaction, dealing with the elements on an item-by-item basis. This particularly appeals to rational and logical buyers who think in scientific way.

Emotional Close: This appeals to the customer's desires for pride, prestige or freedom from fear. It is a way of demonstrating empathy and recognizes that people do make decisions based on emotional as well as rational factors.

Test your own perceptions about closing techniques now:

Table 15.3 Perceptions about Closing Techniques

Question	Strongly disagree	Disagree	Uncertain	Agree	Strongly agree
Closing is the most valuable of all techniques for increasing sales	1	2	3	4	5
Trying to close a sale too often will reduce your chances of success	1	2	3	4	5
Unless you know a lot about closing techniques you will be unable to sell effectively	1	2	3	4	5
Even at the start of a sale it never hurts to use a trial close	1	2	3	4	5
Weak closing is the most common cause of lost sales	1	2	3	4	5
Customers are less likely to buy if they recognize that you are using closing techniques	1	2	3	4	5
You cannot close too often when selling	1	2	3	4	5
Closing techniques do not work with professional buyers	1	2	3	4	5
The ABC of selling is Always Be Closing	1	2	3	4	5
It is your other behaviour earlier in the sale, not your closing technique, that determines whether a customer will buy	1	2	3	4	5
You should try to close every time you see a buying signal	1	2	3	4	5
From the moment you enter the customer's office, you should act as though the sale has already been made	1	2	3	4	5
If the customer resists your trial close, then it is a sign you should have closed more forcefully	1	2	3	4	5

No matter how good your other skills, unless you have good closing techniques you will never succeed	1	2	3	4	5
Using closing techniques early in the sale is a sure way to antagonize customers	1	2	3	4	5

Source: *'Making Major Sales'*, Rackham N., Gower Publishing Co. Ltd., 1987.

Add your scores up by taking the number, 1-5, for each item. If you score over 50 you have a favourable attitude towards closing. But studies have shown that in major sales-sales people with the best results scored less than 50.

15.12 Delivering the Solution

Saying Yes

Normal courtesy demands that you thank the customer for the business. There is an opportunity now to set the customer's expectations over the timing and nature of the next phases. Typically paperwork and processes are set in train and the customer needs to be aware of this to the extent they affect him or her.

Make sure this is clearly understood before you take leave of the customer and that there are no ambiguities – these can come back to haunt you later. Do not overpromise – if anything be conservative about timescales – if it happens quicker this will increase satisfaction levels.

Make sure you monitor the progress both internally and with the customer to ensure expectations are being met.

Saying No

There are inevitably going to be times when you have to say 'no' to customers – maybe you cannot match the pricing, maybe you cannot bespoke the product in exactly the way the customer wants it, maybe the credit risk is unacceptable. This is quite legitimate because the needs of all the stakeholders – customers, staff and shareholders – need to be balanced. This message maybe unwelcome and perhaps unexpected – although you may have had the opportunity to manage expectations upstream of the final decision.

Here your assertiveness skills come to the fore – a 'no' has to be delivered in a professional and convincing way. Empathizing with the customer is important – understanding the impact of a refusal from their perspective. Pure logic may not overcome emotion and you need to be aware of this. Language is important – using positive words rather than negative words. If, at the end of the day the customer decides to transfer the business, then exit in good grace and be sure to make sure the door is left open should any subsequent opportunities arise.

Table 15.4 Saying 'No'

Five proven ways to say 'no' in an acceptable way

1. Say 'yes it can be done' then give the real cost:, ie extra margins, fees, paperwork, timescales etc to give the customer the opportunity to say 'no thanks'.

2. If there are several elements – lead on those you can do before saying 'no' to those you cannot do. Lead on the yeses to create a fund of goodwill to absorb the 'no'.

3. Offer alternatives: soften the blow by offering positive alternatives where possible.

4. If an unusual request, at least consider it – say you'll discuss it with the team and advise. Often customers will accept the 'no' if they think their request has been fairly considered.

5. Do not undermine your position – by saying things like 'It's Head Office, its company policy, 'I'll ask my boss' or 'if it was up to me'.

Source: 'Customer Care means saying 'No' sometimes', Cooke, P. Customer Management Jan/Feb 2001.

Summarizing the Sales Process

In summary we have looked at a client interaction process that follows a typical sales interaction but it has several important differences in terms of how the time is used and spent. This reflects the essential nature of a relationship approach.

15.13 Time Management

Across the relationship cycle, effective management of time is a key priority. As a relationship manager you must learn to manage your own time effectively. With experience you will develop the skill of categorizing outstanding activities in a way that should manage away most of the fire-fighting typical of so many roles. Effective managers control their use of time proactively rather than be at the beck and call of others.

One of the key criteria is likely to be time spent in front of customers. Keep a running diary or time log of how you spend your time and in particular how it relates to your key customers and prospects. From time to time it may help to analyse in more detail how your time is spent. Compare a day working in the office with a day working from home – what lessons can you learn about how to spend your time more effectively?

Figure 15.9: Effort Blocks of the Selling Process

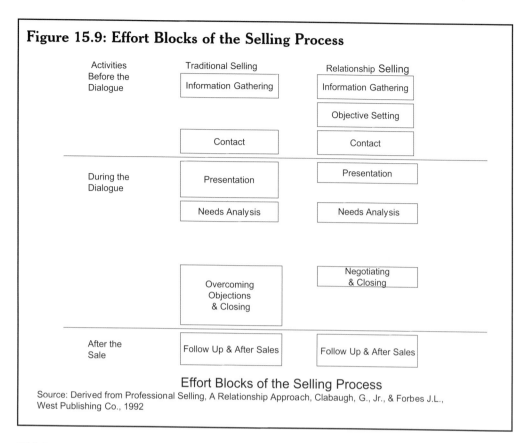

Effort Blocks of the Selling Process

Source: Derived from Professional Selling, A Relationship Approach, Clabaugh, G., Jr., & Forbes J.L., West Publishing Co., 1992

Table 15.5 Analysing Your Time

Analysing how you spend your time

- Make a note of everything you do in a day, recording activities that take, say, more than ten minutes.

- Accurately and rigorously make a note of all the things you do that take up your time unnecessarily (ie time stealers).

- Make sure that when you are recording these details you continue to do so in a way that incorporates any peaks and troughs in your work activities. This may mean that a day may be insufficient – you may need to record a week or a month.

- Begin to categorize the amount of time you spend doing your priority activities – how much is planned and how much is unplanned?

Source: *'Personal Development and Team Management'*, James D., Financial World Publishing, 2002.

Your effectiveness can be improved in principle by:

- Focusing on those activities that really matter.

- Making sure you play to your strengths.

- Increasing delegation where the support is available – part of your coaching role.

Understanding how you work best as a person – are you a morning person, do you need the stimulation of others or peace and quiet, do you prefer to see a task through from beginning to end in one go?

Table 15.6 Time Management Checklist

Time Management Checklist

- Are you giving adequate attention to current activities, to reviewing the past and to planning the future?

- Are you dividing your time correctly between different aspects of you job? Is there, perhaps, one part of your job on which you spend too little or too much of your time?

- Have you allowed for the effect of changes that may have taken place in the content of your job, on your objectives and on the organization of your work?

- Are you certain that you are not doing any work that you ought to have delegated?

- Who are the people that you ought to be seeing? Are you spending too much or too little of your time with them? Are you avoiding certain people?

- Do you organize your working week, as far as possible, according to priorities, or do you tend to deal with each problem as it turns up without stopping to think whether there is something more important that you should be working on?

- Are you able to complete tasks or are you constantly interrupted? Are these interruptions an essential part of your work?

- What have you done recently to further your own development? How long is it since you read a book or an article in your field of work?

Source: *'Managers and their jobs'*, Stewart R., Macmillan 1967 and Pan Books 1970.

Simple techniques for more effective time management include writing 'to do' lists and prioritizing them and setting aside a specific block of time to make telephone calls and dealing with your e-mails – do not become am e-mail junkie! Build some slack into your

---

Figure 15.10: Categorising Activities

	URGENT	NOT URGENT
Important	FIRST PRIORITY •Crises •Pressing problems •Deadline driven projects, meetings, preparations	SECOND PRIORITY •Preparation •Prevention •Planning •Relationship building •Empowerment
Not Important	THIRD PRIORITY •Interruptions •Some telephone calls •Some meetings •Many apparently close pressing matters •Many popular activities	DON'TS •Trivia, busy work •Some telephone calls •Time wasters •'Escape' activities •Irrelevant mail •Excessive e-mail/Internet use

Categorizing Activities
Source: Derived from 'Picking up good habits', Smith M., Financial World December 2001

Figure 15.11: Time Analysis

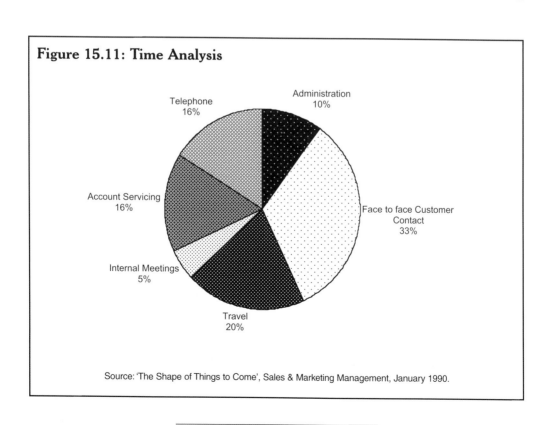

Source: 'The Shape of Things to Come', Sales & Marketing Management, January 1990.

day so that you have a margin for overruns and the unexpected. Many people pride themselves on 'wall-to-wall' meetings in their diaries but it important to be discriminating about the meetings you attend – why do you need to be there, what particular value will you add? We shall look at running effective meetings later.

Do not let other people consistently interrupt you because they themselves are poorly disciplined. Remember to allow some time for the unexpected – a call from a customer, an internal emergency and so on. Try to handle a piece of paper once only and aim for a 'right first time' approach. Delegate where possible – but do not abrogate your responsibilities.

Finally, some figures on how salespeople – as opposed to relationship managers – spend their time – how does this fit with your experience?

16

WORKING IN TEAMS

16.1 Overview

In this chapter we look at the role of the team leader, issues of leadership and motivation and then explore the dynamics of team working and meetings.

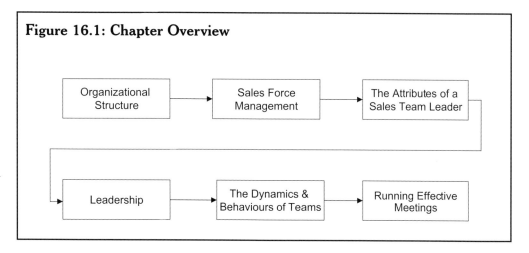

Figure 16.1: Chapter Overview

16.2 Bank Structure

It would probably be quite a challenge – if not an impossibility – to reduce the whole of your corporate banking structure to a single page of this book and for it to remain legible. Typically structures will coalesce around geography, specialist markets (for example the different industries) market segments (a sub-division of the market say by sales turnover bands) and products (derivatives, cash management, electronic banking etc.) depending on the degree of specialism required and the size of the bank.

It might be argued that the development of organizational theory has not kept pace with the development in size, complexity, scope and challenges of running modern organizations such as global banks. Most banks will have some form of cross-functional working in an effort to address these challenges that may include some form of matrix management. Matrix management is where there is a multiple command system – many managers having two bosses.

Functional, product, market and divisional structures overcome this but in a sense there is a reverse matrix with one customer 'being the boss' of different market and product managers, ie a relationship manager and a product manager. It is not unusual in these circumstances for there to be debates about 'who owns the customer' and the issues of traffic management arise – which surfaced in the section on prospecting earlier.

It is clear, then, that delivering a seamless service from multiple sources to a single customer requires shared objectives, the highest standards of communication and effective team working. Before looking at the particular dynamics of teams it makes sense to look at where responsibility for their management falls.

16.3 Sales Force Management

For the purposes of this section we shall regard the terms sales manager and relationship team leader as the same – indeed this may well be the role of a Corporate Director. Additionally sales management may cover the responsibilities of market and product managers also. If the term sales manager is used this does not imply any particular emphasize because, as we know, any sales activity is set in the context of relationship management.

Sales managers are responsible for getting planned business development objectives achieved through the efforts of their people and not for them. They must develop others and not do the job for them. This activity embraces the analysis, planning, implementation and control of the sales force. It also includes setting sales-force objectives, designing sales force strategy and recruiting, selecting, training, supervising and evaluating the firm's salespeople. The challenge in doing this is to build a team that is stable, productive and satisfied.

Three key areas of focus are objectives, strategy and structure.

Salesforce Objectives

Salespeople perform many tasks from finding new customers, communicating information, developing the sales funnel to sales completion and initiating and developing relationships. They also collect market research on customer's needs, potential business opportunities and competitive intelligence These components are very much a moveable feast and, as well as varying across companies, may also vary depending on their stage of development.

The challenge is to find the right 'bundle' of activity relative to the customer's needs, and match it with the capabilities of the organization. Inevitably this will vary over time as sales forces undergo restructuring to improve efficiency and effectiveness. Typically, one of the key measures is time spent in front of customers. In a relationship context, issues of underlying profitability and customer satisfaction levels balance pure sales activity.

Sales Force Strategy

This is really concerned with the way in which the company goes to market and the mix of contact activities that can be used to initiate and sustain the sales process. This will include direct mail, telephone appointment setting, face-to-face meetings, seminars and conferences. Careful measurement will provide data to determine the most cost-effective way of attracting the best quality business by value, profitability and persistency so that the 'cost of sale' can be measured.

In relationship management, the account manager is typically an intermediary between the customer and different parts of the organization. As a result a premium is placed both on influencing skills from an internal perspective and team working.

Sales Force Structure

Sales force structures are predominantly defined by one or more of:

- geography;
- the nature of the customer segmentation;
- customer numbers and density;
- the number of products and their complexity.

These factors all in turn – as we have identified before – influence the 'bundle' of activity undertaken by the salesperson.

Relating this to your own bank you may see global multinational customers serviced from a major global financial centre such as London or New York, key national customers serviced from London and Birmingham and mid-sized corporates serviced from regional centres such as Derby, Sheffield and Newcastle. Product specialists may also be domiciled centrally or regionally, again depending on the complexity and usage of the products. There is a need to strike a balance between cost and the customer's servicing expectations.

Another issue is the way in which the sales process activities from prospecting through established relationship management are resourced.

Many banks have dedicated business development teams whose role is to identify and nurture prospects for eventual migration to a relationship manager. Relationship managers may still have a new business development target of their own but the essence is sub-division of the tasks to match the nature of the marketplace and the capabilities of the individuals. Some key account managers may be more successful in the early stages where selling and negotiating skills are important, other better at developing partnering and synergistic relationships. Often the terms hunters – the business development role – and farmers – the relationship management role – are used but they are not necessarily mutually exclusive.

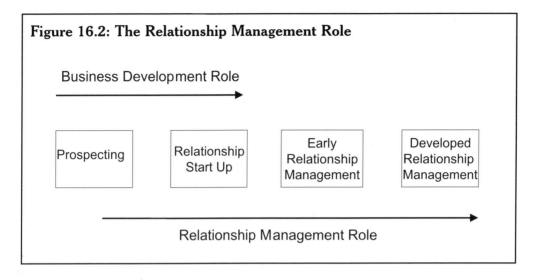

Figure 16.2: The Relationship Management Role

On top of this, depending on the client's needs, product specialists may be drafted as part of the 'virtual' team. Bear in mind that there is scope for a potential mismatch if the customer wants one key relationship manager orchestrating the bank's offerings while the bank wants to offer product specialists. There is no one right answer and different banks may address similar customer groups in different ways.

The more uniform and straightforward the products, the higher the volume, the greater the commoditization – many competitors offering the same thing – then the greater the challenge to take costs out of the business and downsize the sales force. A customer intimacy approach such as relationship management, however, would demand higher levels of one-to-one contact and portfolios would be influenced by the size, importance and complexity of the customer's requirements. Banks may legitimately decide against taking this approach because of the additional costs.

16.4 The Attributes of a Sales Manager

We reviewed the attributes of a successful relationship manager earlier and deal here with the higher-level skills of a team leader. Make no mistake, this is one of the key roles for leveraging performance in the bank – a pivotal job having a major effect on sales effectiveness.

Let us group the skills in three areas:

1.Planning Monitoring and Control

● Strategic business and market planning.

● Project management.

- Set the goals and identify the team's objectives.

- Organize the team around its two critical tasks:

  - creating an in-depth understanding of the customer;

  - managing customer development plans.

- Establish criteria to measure team performance.

- Develop information analysis techniques and reporting procedures.

- Generate options for business-winning action.

2. Resource Management

- Performance management planning and assessment.

- Techniques of motivation.

- Recruitment and selection.

- Leadership.

- Coaching.

- Training.

- Understanding of team dynamics.

- Higher-level interpersonal skills.

- Good communication skills.

- Change management.

3. Conceptual Skills

- Managing innovation and creativity.

- Problem solving.

In summary, a person of thought, a person of action and an ambassador for the bank. We look at some of these areas in a little more detail now.

16.5 Leadership

Increasingly, given the trend towards flatter organizational structures and self-directed workforces, the issue of leadership is receiving more attention. Managers and supervisors are being expected to take on more of a leadership role. Here we shall focus on leadership style rather than just listing the traits and characteristics of leaders (you may wish to consider this as a separate exercise by thinking of three well-known leaders and comparing and contrasting their traits).

Team leaders are responsible for directing his or her team to achieve the desired business goals. In a sales team this will be the role of the sales manager. In a relationship team, sales will be an important part of the role but the portfolio of responsibility is wider and, as we have discussed earlier, sales is only part of a relationship management strategy.

Leadership Styles

Essentially leadership is about getting others to do things through influencing their behaviour. This has a task dimension, such as achieving the set goals, and a people dimension, such as mobilizing the team and its individual members. It will also depend on the environment and the actual leader.

Table 16.1 Managers v Leaders

Manager	*Leader*
Administers	Innovates
Focuses on systems and structures	Focuses on people
Relies on control	Inspires trust
Has a short-term tactical view	Has a long-term strategic perspective
Asks how and when	Asks what and why
Does things right	Does the right things

Source: *'Global Mindsets for Global Managers'*, Rhinesmith S., Training and Development October 1992.

There is no one leadership style appropriate to all situations. Managers must be prepared to adjust their style depending on the circumstances – success comes from building 'appropriate versatility' (Source: 'Style leaders'. Watkin C., Financial World, July 2002) and the use of 'tough empathy' (Source: *The weak shall inherit the earth'*, Jones G., and Goffee R., Financial World, July 2002).

It is possible to act along a continuum from authoritarian to democratic but it is not suggested that one is better than the other. In some circumstances you may have to tell a colleague to do something, in others a more consultative approach may be appropriate. This might reflect, for example, their levels of competence, confidence and motivation. It will certainly mean distinguishing between those who can/can't do as opposed to those who will/won't do.

Styles can be categorized as:

● *Autocratic:* the leader makes decisions without any input from the team; decisions are quick but team members will feel left out.

● *Benevolent autocratic:* the leader creates a more positive environment through the use of rewards and incentives, for example, but the direction is still top down.

● *Consultative:* views are sought from the team but authority remains with the leader and is not shared.

● *Participative:* This is characterised by involving everyone in the decision-making process. It increases the team members' sense of involvement but can be time-consuming as a shared outcome is negotiated.

In all cases good communications, satisfaction in the work and positive attitudes must be present.

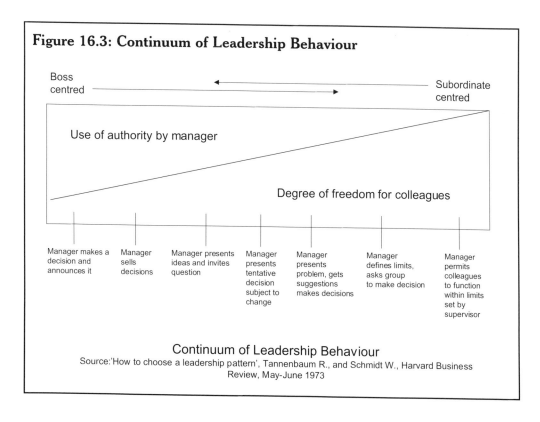

Figure 16.3: Continuum of Leadership Behaviour

Boss centred — Subordinate centred

Use of authority by manager

Degree of freedom for colleagues

| Manager makes a decision and announces it | Manager sells decisions | Manager presents ideas and invites question | Manager presents tentative decision subject to change | Manager presents problem, gets suggestions makes decisions | Manager defines limits, asks group to make decision | Manager permits colleagues to function within limits set by supervisor |

Continuum of Leadership Behaviour
Source:'How to choose a leadership pattern', Tannenbaum R., and Schmidt W., Harvard Business Review, May-June 1973

Contingency Approaches

These take the view that leadership traits and styles need to be adapted to the context of the working environment. The most effective leaders fit their style to the situation, which includes their own preferred style of operating and personal characteristics as well as the nature of the task and the group.

So while the optimal leadership traits and styles can be learned and applied, they may require adaptation to the pressures of the working environment. This can be represented as follows:

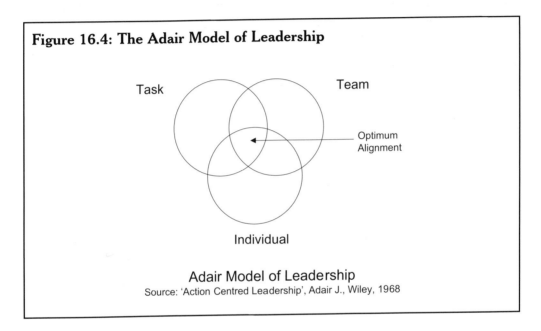

Figure 16.4: The Adair Model of Leadership

Task   Team

Optimum
Alignment

Individual

Adair Model of Leadership
Source: 'Action Centred Leadership', Adair J., Wiley, 1968

Looking at the three components of task, team and individual:

Task needs: to make a profit, provide a service, and deliver a defined outcome.

Team needs: delivering the synergy, efficiency v effectiveness, managing constructive conflict to deliver a superior outcome.

Individual needs: the alignment of personal needs from basic to self-realization and actualization (as per Maslow) with group needs.

What cannot be trained or developed is situational or contextual knowledge that relates to specific companies and environments. Leadership skills, therefore, require modification and adaptation in all situations to achieve a balance if authority and influence as well as direction and purpose are to be truly effective.

Winning the Popularity Stakes

Being a team leader is always challenging, but for a team leader, respect comes before being liked. Respect comes from personal integrity – keeping promises, leading by example, and being scrupulously fair with no favouritism. 'Walking the Talk' is particularly important; any differences between what you say and expect others to do and what you yourself do will soon become transparent.

A participative style is a strength but it does not mean at the end of the day that if a tough decision has to be made it is avoided – with leadership comes responsibility and accountability. For example, the team will expect leaders to deal promptly and appropriately with issues such as poor performance and discipline.

As always communication is of the essence – here we are taking about effective two-way communication. One way of communicating openness is MBWA – 'Management By Walking About' – meeting with the team in a relaxed, informal and sometimes unstructured way. Seeing people and talking to them on a daily basis, however, should not be seen as a substitute for the more formal one-to-one or group meetings that should also take place.

Effective team leaders are also able to review their own performance – consider a SWOT analysis, for example:

Table 16.2 A Personal SWOT Analysis

Strengths	*Weaknesses*
What you can do well which is supported by evidence – high scores in competency ratings, for example.	Developmental areas that you know you have to work on – capture in a personal development plan
Opportunities	*Threats*
Sources of support and development such as training, external qualifications, mentoring, coaching etc.	Lack of time, unsupportive line management, budgets

Source: Derived from *'Managing People in Organizations'*, James D., CIB Publishing, 1999.

Perhaps the greatest challenge to a leader is remaining positive at all times. Think how often the tone of the office or a meeting is set by the way the most senior person walks in – facial expression, body language, demeanour and so on – you will have the same effect as a team leader and your team will take their cues from you. Try the following questionnaire, asking your team to complete it as well, and repeat the exercise periodically:

Table 16.3 Assessing Your Own Team Behaviour

Attribute	Always	Sometimes	Never
Positive			
Enthusiastic			
Decisive			
Appropriate sense of humour			
Confident			
Business-focused			
High levels of energy			

Source: *'Managing People in Organizations'*, James D., CIB Publishing, 1999.

16.6 The Dynamics and Behaviours of Teams

Organizations are made up of groups of people working together. This may follow both the formal structure but is also increasingly likely, as we have discussed, to be cross-functional or virtual as, for example, product specialists are drawn in. Understanding how these groups or teams behave is an important part of the team leader's management skills toolkit.

The structure of the day-to-day relationship team will depend on the number and nature of the relationships and the roles that need to be performed. The role of each member will be defined and there is likely to be a hierarchy of authority. Nonetheless the team needs to be flexible in the way it goes about its business – think of it as a problem-solving unit dealing with the needs of its customers.

The Role of Teams

Teamwork is managed, planned, systematic coordination of effort by a group with a common goal, for the purpose of achieving that goal in an optimally productive way. There may be reporting teams – vertical groups made up of a superior and subordinates or peer teams – people of the same level. Peer teams may be more problematic given the potentially different goals the individual members may have. They may be permanent or temporary, depending on the nature of the task.

Teams differ from groups in that groups are looser collections of individuals without the cohesiveness and interdependence of teams. Teams fulfil a number of important formal and informal functions meeting the needs both of the organization and the individual. Indeed, employees can feel isolated and unhappy if they are not part of a cohesive team. Teams offer then a range of benefits such as:

- Task completion based on the combined effort of a number of individuals working together with multiple viewpoints and specialized knowledge.

- Making work more palatable through cooperation, job rotation and modifying formal working arrangements.

- Meeting social needs for friendship, support, companionship and helping to reduce stress.

- Providing a means of evaluating opinions and attitudes, and confirming one's identity and status. They give the individual a sense of belonging as well as providing guidelines on acceptable behaviour.

There are certain common factors in effective teams:

- Shared experiences: the more effective teams have similarities among their members in terms of background, status, objectives, norms and values. Similarity in levels of skill and ability also lead to greater cohesiveness.

- Size: between five and seven members is considered to be the optimum size. This gives enough individuals for there to be variety and multiple viewpoints.

- Interdependence: where members are supportive of each other teams tend to be more effective. Constructive criticism can be helpful but destructive and excessively critical comments tend to destroy rapport and support among members.

- Group roles: if individuals play different roles within a group then this can make it more effective.

- Communications: formal and informal communications are improved and people are not inhibited from speaking or expressing an opinion.

Team Members

Effective teams need a mix of people with different characteristics, such as those who can get things done and those who are concerned with social workings of the group. In his book 'Management Teams: Why they Succeed or Fail' (Heineman 1981), Dr. Meredith Belbin identified eight key roles:

1. *Chairmen:* control the way in which a team addresses the key tasks, recognizing the capabilities of the team members to make best use of their strengths and weaknesses. Responsible for creating the team environment and ethos.

2. *Shapers:* direct attention to the setting of objectives and priorities and look to impose some shape or pattern on group interactions in pursuit of the tasks in hand.

3. *Company workers:* turn concepts and plans into practical working procedures and carry out agreed plans systematically and efficiently.

4. *Plants:* good for new ideas and strategies because they relate to major issues. Also good gap analysis of present processes.

5. *Resource investigators:* tuned in to relevant events outside the team and maintain contacts that may be helpful as the project develops.

6. *Monitor-evaluators:* analyse problems and evaluate ideas and suggestions so that the team is better placed to make decisions.

7. *Team workers:* support members in their strengths and underpin members in their shortcomings, improve communications between members and foster team spirit.

8. *Completer-finishers:* ensure that the team is protected from mistakes, look after work that needs a higher level of attention and maintains a sense of urgency in the team.

To be an effective team there should be a balance of all of these roles. Some members will adopt a primary role; most will have an alternative back-up role as well.

Team Building

Most teams will already be in existence but it is worth considering the process a new team goes through when starting up. There are a number of fairly distinct stages of development that are captured in the diagram. Bear in mind that there is unlikely to be a smooth transition through the stages – at times you may have to go backwards to go forwards. Remember also that not everybody will be in the same place at the same time.

Improving Teamwork

There are a number of ways in which teamwork can be improved:

- Pick people who will fit the culture and work well with others but who are still capable of taking their own line when necessary.

- Keep on emphasizing that constructive teamwork is a key core value of the bank.

- Assess people's performance not only on the results they achieve but also on the degree to which they uphold the value of teamwork.

- Encourage people to build networks – things get done of the basis of whom you know as well as what you know. It is no good being right if you cannot carry others with you. Informal channels are important here rather than relying on reports, memos and committees.

Figure 16.5: Stages of Group Development

Performing	Forming
• Interpersonal problems resolved	• Bringing together of group of individuals
• Roles flexible	• Members trying to create their own identity
• Focus on completion of objectives	• Some anxiety
• Work-focused use of energy	• Dependence on the leader
	• Need understanding of situation and task
	• Understanding norms of behaviour
Norming	**Storming**
• Group cohesion developed	• Start to present views
• Standards of behaviour established	• Disagreements and arguments may occur
• Open exchange of views	• Conflict
• Mutual cooperation	• Emotional resistance to the demands of the task
• Sense of group identity	• Resistance to control
• Social pressure to isolate nonconformists	• Group may collapse

Stages of Group Development

Source: 'Development sequences in small groups', Tuckman, B. Psychological Bulletin 63, 11965

- Set up multidisciplinary teams with a brief to get on with it.

- Clamp down on unproductive politics.

- Describe and think of the bank as a series of interlocking teams (or systems) united by a common purpose.

- Do not be alarmed is there is disagreement – remember the value of constructive conflict.

- Hold 'away days' and conferences for work teams so they can get together and explore some of the real issues without the pressures of the day-to-day jobs.

- Use training programmes to build relationships (and reinforce values). This can often be a more beneficial result of a course than the increase in skills that was its ostensible purpose.

- Set overlapping objectives for managers and their teams.

Source: 'A Handbook of Personnel Management Practice', Armstrong M., Kogan Page 1993.

How would you assess the performance of your team or a team of which you are a member against the following criteria?

Team Behaviour Audit

Table 16.4 Team Behaviour Audit

1	The atmosphere tends to be informal, comfortable and relaxed	Yes	No
2	There is a lot of discussion in which everybody participates	Yes	No
3	Discussions stay focused on the task of the team	Yes	No
4	The task or objective of the team is well understood and accepted by the members	Yes	No
5	There is an open discussion of the task/objective so that it is framed in such a way that all team members can commit to it	Yes	No
6	Members listen to each other; every idea is given a hearing	Yes	No
7	People do not appear to be afraid of being considered foolish by putting forward a creative thought even if it seems fairly extreme	Yes	No
8	There is disagreement which is not suppressed or overridden by premature group action	Yes	No
9	The reasons for disagreement are carefully examined and the team seeks to resolve them rather than dominate the dissenter	Yes	No
10	Most decisions are reached by a kind of consensus in which it is clear that everybody is in general agreement and willing to go along	Yes	No
11	Formal voting is at a minimum; the team does not accept a simple majority as the proper basis for action	Yes	No
12	Criticism is frequent, frank and relatively comfortable	Yes	No
13	There is little evidence of personal attack either openly or in a hidden fashion	Yes	No
14	People are free in expressing their feelings as well as their ideas, both on the problem and the team's operation	Yes	No
15	When action is taken, clear assignments are made and accepted	Yes	No
16	The team leader does not dominate it	Yes	No
17	The group does not defer unduly to the team leader	Yes	No
18	There is little evidence of a struggle for power as the group operates	Yes	No

Source: 'The Human Side of Enterprise', McGregor G., McGraw-Hill, 1966.

An increasingly popular way of assessing team performance and in particular that of the team leader is 360-degree appraisal. In the case of a team leader, for example, direct reports, peers and his or her superior will be asked to complete a structured questionnaire on the individual concerned. This produces a performance review 'in the round' and can be used as the basis for a performance gap analysis and personal development. This can be enhanced if the team leader also completes a questionnaire, because there is then a means for comparing how one thinks one is performing and behaving against the perceptions of others. There are a number of proprietary models for measuring leadership and team performance as well as culture – see, for example, www.denisonculture.com.

Managing Conflict

Conflict is intrinsic in society, organizations and groups. It can be within a group but also among groups that need to work together. Some conflict can be positive in the sense that it knits teams together and generates greater loyalty among its members. The team tends to become more highly structured and organized as well as more task oriented. While people need to pull together it should not be at the expense of creating a vanilla climate where nothing exciting or challenging happens.

The negative consequences of conflict can, however, sometimes outweigh these gains and the team leader may have to try to find ways of reducing the tension.

16.7 Running Effective Meetings

The Need for Meetings

Meetings are an essential tool for coordinating effort, making sure everyone is on the same wavelength, getting things done, problem solving and developing teamwork. Because they are people intensive they are costly so it is important to ensure that they 'add value' to individual, team and business performance. All of the practices of good meetings are relevant, of course, in a customer as well as a corporate context. Increasingly these calls may be by some means of conference facility – say telephone or video – to save on travel time and costs.

Meetings need to have a clear results-oriented purpose: the right attendees need to be well prepared. It should be properly chaired and have agreed action-based outcomes. A key element is careful preparation leading to a well thought-out and carefully planned agenda. This is effectively the route map for the path the meeting will take.

Figure 16.6: Why Meetings Fail

- The meeting was unnecessary
- The purpose of the meeting was not clear
- The meeting was badly planned and ill-prepared
- The meeting was held in a poor environment
- The meeting was disrupted
- The wrong people were present and the right people were absent
- The chairperson was not adequate
- Nothing was decided

Why Meetings Fail
Source: 'The Perfect Meeting', Sharman D., Century Business, 1993

Critical Success Factors

The ground rules for success are:

- issue the agenda and key papers in advance;

- be punctual in beginning and finishing;

- have clear and shared objectives;

- structure the agenda ;

- avoid lengthy presentations;

- allow sufficient time for questions and make sure everybody contributes;

- nominate a scribe to record actions to be undertaken but generally avoid verbatim minutes or overly detailed notes.

Note: recording the outcome of meetings is clearly a position of power which should not be abused if you wish to continue to hold the trust of others. It is also a good developmental activity for the appointed team member – encouraging them to actively listen, edit from the material available and present a succinct outcome.

Many companies have aide-memoires on the walls of their meeting rooms to remind people of best practice – have a look and see if these are any in your office and what they say.

There is a particular skill in structuring the agenda with the toughest issues in the middle and those where a more open discussion is needed towards the end. If nothing else it will ensure that those who arrive late and those who leave early are there for the key issues.

Figure 16.7: The 6Ps of Meetings

1. Planning
-clear objective
-known purpose
-right people
-venue/facilities/timing

2. Publication
-adequate written notice
-date/time/duration etc.
-objectives/purpose

3. Preparation
(of chairperson)
-necessary information
-fluency with agenda
-timing of items

4. Process (of meeting)
Chairman to:
-remind attendees of objectives
-confirm agenda appropriate
-discuss evidence/interpretation/action
-encourage participation/discussion
-summarize

5. Participation (of members)
-Contribute: prepare, research ahead
 of meeting, constructively join
 discussions
-Concentrate: maintain interest at all times
-Cooperate: realize part of whole even
 if decisions contrary to own views

6. Put on record (by chairperson)
-summarize decisions before meeting ends
-agree action who/what/when
-circulate minutes promptly
-communicate decisions of meeting
 to all relevant people
-signal next meeting

The Six 'Ps' of Meetings
Source: 'Skills', International Journal of Bank Marketing, Volume 9 Number 3,1991

Figure 16.8: Structuring an Agenda

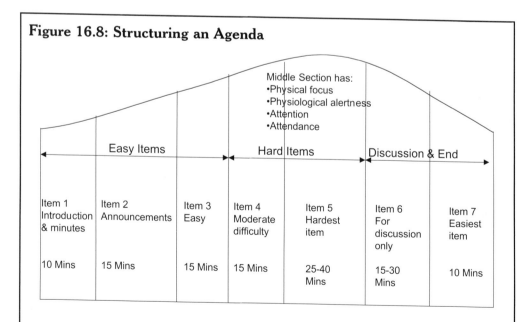

Middle Section has:
•Physical focus
•Physiological alertness
•Attention
•Attendance

Easy Items   Hard Items   Discussion & End

Item 1 Introduction & minutes	Item 2 Announcements	Item 3 Easy	Item 4 Moderate difficulty	Item 5 Hardest item	Item 6 For discussion only	Item 7 Easiest item
10 Mins	15 Mins	15 Mins	15 Mins	25-40 Mins	15-30 Mins	10 Mins

Structuring an Agenda
Source: 'Effective Meetings: improving group decision making', Tropman J.E., Sage Publications, 1980

You should think carefully about the environment for the meeting and if necessary 'stage manage' it. Increasingly in open-plan offices, meeting rooms are at a premium. You may end up having the meeting around a desk, in a coffee bar area or indeed in chairs adjacent to a walkway or corridor.

Where you have a room or a more formal presentation area, you may not go as far as drawing up a seating plan but you should remember that those at the end of the table are usually in positions of control as are those to the left and right of the chairperson in a 'U' shaped setting. Clearly there is a need for you to be seen and heard by all who are present and this is no different from the basic rules of delivering an effective presentation.

On a practical note, it is often quite useful to have a flipchart to capture points as they occur in a discussion. This has a number of benefits – participants can see that their comments have been captured, it is easier to relate action points to what has gone before and it provides a basis for whatever is to be distributed after the meeting. Another useful tool is a PC and screen to use Mind mapping software, which fulfils the same purpose.

The Chairperson

Effective chairing is a skill in its own right. Effective chairpersons avoid getting involved in the content of the meeting but focus on how things are going to be achieved from a process perspective. Non-verbal behaviour (which we have looked at previously) is important as well for setting the right tone for the meeting through an effective introduction. Two elements of control are required:

- procedure: following the agenda, keeping to time

- process: facilitating the discussion, involving the participants.

Chairpersons do not dominate the meeting or force their views through over the views of others – think assertion not aggression. There may be some areas where you are the subject-matter expert and need to be more involved in the discussion. It is quite legitimate to delegate the chair to an alternative for the purpose of the discussion but you must be prepared to accept his or her authority as regards the meeting and your contribution!

A particularly positive activity by the chairman is to summarize the outcome at the end of each agenda item to ensure that what has been agreed is understood by all concerned. This summary can pull together the threads of what may have been a wide-ranging or detailed discussion so that there is a shared understanding. It may be that the chair has lost part of the plot, so corrections can come from the other attendees.

Within a relationship team where the same people are meeting regularly, for example, it can often be a good idea to rotate the chairmanship from time to time. This is a useful development tool and gives team members the opportunity to practise these skills in a user-friendly environment.

Facilitation Skills

Facilitating is a key skill not just for a chairperson but in a wide range of other social interactions also. Essentially it is the ability to help and encourage others (using, for example, open questions) to express their views in an environment that they will not find intimidating or threatening. At times it means subjugating your own views and even being prepared to having them directly challenged. If something contentious is raised, do not feel the need to answer it yourself – throw it open to the group. If the discussion becomes circular then summarize where it is at and 'park it' for the time being. If a discussion becomes particularly negative ask contributors to begin their contribution with positives before carrying on.

Difficult Situations

These will inevitably arise; they may be small in number but on an 80/20 basis potentially expensive in terms of time and nervous energy. Typically these situations might include:

Irrelevant contributions: the contributor needs to be reminded of the objectives of the meeting;

Rambling contributions: the chairperson needs to handle this sensitively but bring the meeting back to the topic in hand;

Continued interruptions from the same person: needs to be reminded that it is only courteous to listen while other people have their say;

There is a meeting within a meeting: there is a need to reinforce the protocol that only one person should be speaking at any one time;

Someone arrives late: you can stop the meeting then and there to summarize what has gone before or wait until the discussion on the current topic has finished;

Someone senior takes over the meeting: this clearly puts a premium on assertiveness and is best resolved by agreeing respective roles ahead of the meeting. If not a tactful reminder of the agenda as it stands may help, or a quiet word at a coffee break.

Non-contributors: these are the people who say nothing when you would expect them to be contributing. They may be 'out of their depth', feel too junior or just have no interest. Forewarn them that you will be asking their views as you go to a particular topic area and then keep them in the loop.

Aggressive people: these have the potential to destabilize the meeting; either there will be a full blown row or people will just switch off. The chair needs to step in quickly and firmly. Disagreement is acceptable provided it is substantiated key fact – outright personal attacks are not.

It is often informative to listen to the radio or watch programmes on television where people are being interviewed or there is audience participation. These maybe confrontational – to make them more newsworthy – which would not be appropriate for the environment in which a relationship manager or his team operates – but the questioning techniques, the facilitation skills and the ability to deal with awkward contributors are frequently dealt with in an apparently effortless way.

Writing up the Outcomes

If you are holding a regular meeting, say of your relationship team, simple agreed action points may be sufficient. Many meetings, however, still require minuted outcomes and this is another area – in addition to report writing, for example, in which your skills of synthesizing and summarizing in a clear way will be used.

A good note of the outcomes or set of minutes will:

- Follow the agenda.

- Use simple and clear language.

- Have numbering and/or headings and sub-headings that take the reader logically through the outcomes.

- Note opposing views in a factual, non-personal way and in a way that is not inflammatory or contentious.

- Stand alone without references to other documents unless they are particularly key.

17

MANAGING AND MOTIVATING TEAMS AND TEAM MEMBERS

17.1 Overview

In this chapter we look at a number of the higher-level people skills that team leaders need to have, such as developing trust, coaching and motivation.

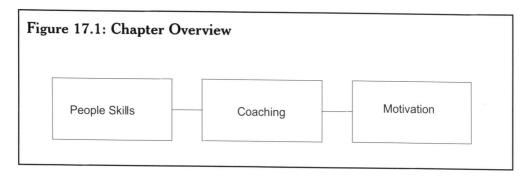

Figure 17.1: Chapter Overview

People Skills — Coaching — Motivation

17.2 People Skills

The Core Skills

We have already identified that developing empathy with customers is a key part of the role of a relationship manager. We have also illustrated a number of ways in which this can be achieved, ranging from better understanding of them as people to structured questioning techniques. It is self-evident that many of the required skills in this external facing environment are also highly relevant internally as you deal with the colleagues in your team or across the other support areas of the bank.

People skills is an umbrella term that covers the ability to understand human behaviour, communicate, motivate and to work with people as individuals.

There are a number of key components:

Observation skills: the ability to observe what people do in the work environment and to understand why they do it.

For example, thinking about some of the needs identified by Maslow's hierarchy it is possible to infer intrinsic needs from the behaviour you see.

Table 17.1 Assessing People's Needs based on Observed Behaviour

Security	Social	Esteem	Self-realization
Lacks self-confidence	Friendly, outgoing	Uses 'I' and 'Me'	Eager to learn
Slow to speak	Optimist	Likes to be the centre of attention	Frank and open
Cautious	Exaggerates		Tells it how it is
Does not take sides	Talkative	Not a good listener	Steady, serious worker
Indecisive	Unstructured thinker	Inflates own reputation	Looks for challenges
Follow the leader	Not objective	Firm views on everything	Willing to take chances
Rarely volunteers	Tries hard to please	Name dropper	
Prefers to work alone	Very loyal	Poor looser	Shares ideas
Works to rule	Disorganized	Ostentatious	Responsive to others
Pessimist	Uses lots of superlatives	Treats slights as serious insults	Debates ideas not people
	Seeks out team projects		

Source: '*Improving Productivity Through People Skills*', Lefton R.R., Buzzotta V.R., Sherberg M., Ballinger Publishing Company 1980.

Communication skills: once you have diagnosed your own and other people's behaviour you must devise a communications strategy for finding out what the other person thinks and getting your own ideas across. This ability to exchange ideas is central to effective problem-solving and decision-making.

Motivation skills: the creation of an environment in which people do what they are capable of doing because there is a compelling reason to do so. Before they pitch themselves into their work people must know what you want them to do, why it is important and what they are going to get out of it

Building Trust: trust is the conviction held by the other person that you genuinely want to help them. It is the confidence that you will make every effort to say and do what is in their best interest. Credibility depends on trustworthiness. Trust builds day by day – it develops and deepens over time.

Some Do's and Don'ts

- Don't score points at the other person's expense – avoid sarcasm, condescension, treat them with respect.

- Create a supportive problem-solving climate – don't manipulate or lay down the law.

- Focus any discussion on facts not personalities.

- Create win-win situations – you may win a shouting match only to find it is not worth the price in terms of the resentment it leaves behind.

- Use first person statements instead of second person when communicating.

  - Not 'You let me down' but 'I'm disappointed'.

  - Not 'You keep on making the same mistake' but 'I'm frustrated, because this has happened several times'.

- Adapt your communication and motivation skills to meet the different needs of different people – recognize that each individual is unique.

These skills need to be continually practised.

A Model Meeting

How many times have you come away from a meeting – probably with a boss – feeling you have been railroaded into an outcome you did not really agree with and not having been able to put your own point of view across? As a team leader you cannot afford to have your people disaffected in that way – there may be a short-term benefit in terms of getting something done but in the longer term it just builds up resentment.

In cases like this a better outcome is likely if there is a perception of equal status between the parties, adequate time is given to airing different points of view, conditions are created that favour openness, and mutual understanding is increased through effective communication.

Let us have a look then at a model process that can help to create this quality of interaction.

1. Setting the Scene

- Check your team members' readiness for the meeting – be appropriately sociable. Let them settle if they have just rushed from a previous engagement. Recognize any sensitivities – a family illness or a pressing deadline. If necessary and possible consider reconvening the meeting if they are particularly agitated.

- Outline the purpose of the meeting, in particular the benefits to the individual and to the bank

  - ask a question to find out how they feel about proceeding and whether they have anything else on their agenda;

  - assess again their state of readiness.

- Make sure they are focused, ready to listen carefully, consider your ideas and take part fully in the discussion. This needs to be a dialogue to which both parties contribute.

2. Understand their Views

- Let the team member put his or her views first. It could be the merits of a particular lending proposal, it could be a performance assessment review or dealing with a complaint. But in all cases let the other person give his or her version first.

- Suspend any sort of judgement at this stage.

3. Present your views

- Tell the team member what you know and think about the subject. Identify those area where you agree and those where you disagree.

- Again, do not be judgemental and do not get personal.

- Do a status check to confirm understanding and get a reaction.

- Finally summarize where you agree and disagree. Expect disagreements.

4 Deal with any resistance

- Help the team member surface any negative emotions to try to reduce tensions. This is rarely done spontaneously in a business interaction.

- Problem-solve any differences – explore the evidence.

- Break things down as much as possible and work through them line by line – do not generalize and discourage your team member from this also.

- Keep going until you see eye-to-eye on as many things as possible – recognize it may not be all of them.

5 Formulate an Action Plan

- Ask the team member to propose the solutions.

- Work out the final resolution selecting the soundest solutions from the alternatives available.

- Emphasize the benefits to the team member and the bank.

- Confirm activities and commitment.

Next time you have a meeting share this framework with a colleague and try to work through it. As always, practise makes perfect.

17.3 Coaching

Coaching is an increasingly popular and effective technique for developing individuals' capabilities on the job. While in principle it is planned, it also has an element of informality not found in more formal classroom situations. Often the trigger is a development need identified by the performance review process.

It can be defined as: 'The use of managerial insight and know-how to elicit self-analysis by the subordinate for the purpose of:

- deepening the subordinate's understanding of how he or she functions on the job and why

- getting his or her commitment to mutually accepted goals for maintaining or improving performance, and

- getting his or her commitment to a plan of action for achieving these goals'.

Source: *'Improving Productivity Through People Skills'*, Lefton R.R., Buzzotta V.R., Sherberg M., Ballinger Publishing Company 1980.

Coaching develops skills, attitudes, talents and dispositions. It can be initiated by the team leader of the team member who says 'I'm having a problem with...'. It applies equally to professional and 'life skills' and requires managerial insight and know-how. There is a need to know enough about the work to offer guidance, enough about human behaviour to guide the employee to an understanding of his or her performance problems and know how to motivate and elicit collaboration. It goes without saying that successful coaching relies on a high level of trust.

The process starts by encouraging self-analysis with a series of probing questions. Self-discovery is powerful because when we work out things for ourself we retain it longer, we understand it better and it is more likely to result in a committed change of behaviour. The role is similar to that of a mentor who guides the subordinate to a point where he or she realizes for himself or herself what is going on and what needs to be done about it.

Unlike mentors, however, coaches do not offer advice on how the individual may overcome problems in his or her job. Instead they provide a framework and a forum by which the individual can come up with the answers for himself or herself. It can particularly add value to reinforce the learning and capture the value after formal training events.

In setting objectives for the people being coached:

- keep them simple.

- revise them frequently – use successive approximations.

- link to actions to advance the relationship – they must be expressed as an action – what do I do on Monday?

- define the problem from the customer's perspective – what is it you are helping the customer to solve?

- put actions into a timeline that relates to the customer's buying process. (A selling strategy that is out of step with how the buyer makes decisions will not work.)

Coaching is hard to implement. Managers are usually reluctant to adopt coaching on a systematic basis, pleading lack of time or alternative priorities. Typical barriers are:

- Short-term competing pressures squeeze out coaching. There is a need to build it into the objectives of team leaders and make it part of the appraisal and reward systems.

- Lack of focus – it is better to realistically to find time to coach one or two people rather than the whole of the team – start on the average performers because they give you greater leverage rather than the poor performers. Start also with somebody who you know is receptive.

- No adequate frame of reference – the coach needs to know what good looks like and be able to articulate it.

- Fear of coaching 'I was reluctant to try it in case I couldn't think of anything useful to say'. If you carry out coaching training, have managers and their direct reporters in the same training session.

- A lack of reward or financial reinforcements – it is often not seen as part of the job and/or not adequately measured – how can management tell if good coaching is being done?

Large sales are different from small ones and, therefore, require a different form of coaching. Experience counts for more in small sales because the longer salespeople do it the better they get because of the number of calls and the immediacy of the feedback, ie sale or no sale. In relationship management and the extended sales cycle the coach needs to be involved at the planning stage, not just accompanying on calls. If the team leader goes on calls then his or her presence must be properly explained so that the customer does not defer to her and/or she takes over the meeting. If there are particular skills or expertise gaps then pre-agree these topic areas and inform the customer at the outset.

Some Do's and Don'ts

- When coaching, don't underestimate the potential for the relationship manager's discomfort – think back to when you took your driving test. Check his or her state of readiness before starting the review.

- Start by acknowledging the pressure and picking out a positive – overcome the tendency to focus on what has not worked.

- Use your questioning techniques as with a customer – How did you feel that went? Why? What did you feel went well? What areas are there for improvement?

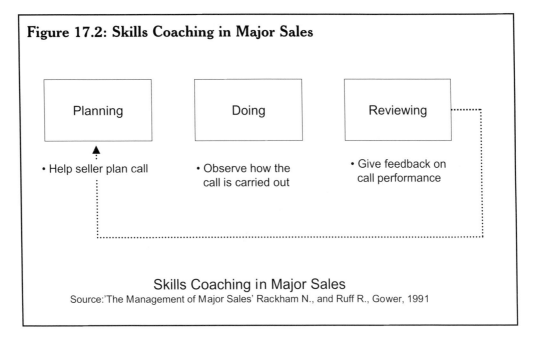

Figure 17.2: Skills Coaching in Major Sales

Planning

Doing

Reviewing

• Help seller plan call

• Observe how the call is carried out

• Give feedback on call performance

Skills Coaching in Major Sales

Source:'The Management of Major Sales' Rackham N., and Ruff R., Gower, 1991

● Don't dump and overwhelm – edit your comments to get the key points on the table and spread the learning points over a number of sessions.

● Make sure you are persistent and systematic in your following up.

17.4 Motivation

The idea underlying motivation is that there is some force within individuals that drives them to achieve a job goal or objective in order to satisfy their needs. These job goals may relate both to what has to be done in business terms – say improved asset quality – and the way in which it is done in behavioural terms – say improved team working. This drive can be stimulated in a number of ways. Motivation theory, however, is a complex area characterized by a many different views, opinions and models. Put simply, however, it is about getting better performance from ourselves and others.

As a relationship team leader it is important that you have a reasonable understanding of some of these models and the tools that can be used to enhance performance. The context in which these tools are used is important – remember we are talking about developing and sustaining customer relationships rather than driving sales volumes *per se*.

Need Theory

One of the best-known models is Maslow's Hierarchy of Needs – we have already looked at this in the context of service quality and in particular the need for empathy. This model, like all models, oversimplifies, but it has both the attraction of being intuitively appealing and the disadvantage of not being supported by empirical evidence. Let us accept it at face value as a useful overview of a number of issues, in particular what the internal drivers of motivation might be, such as self-actualization.

There are overlaps between this approach and a number of other theories you may like to explore such as Frederick Herzberg's 'motivation-hygiene theory' and Douglas McGregor's 'Theory X and Theory Y'. The underlying commonality is that they suggest people will act positively to achieve what they perceive to be desirable goals such as responsibility, recognition and achievement.

Much depends, however, on how people respond individually to a range of internal and external drivers. The mix of internal and external drivers is optimized to attract and retain good-quality staff and to obtain the required standards of performance.

Expectancy Theory

The individual will determine the benefits (or penalties) to him or her of doing (or not doing) what the bank wants. This will be influenced by preferences, but also by expectancy – the belief that a particular act will be followed by a particular outcome – higher performance payments or promotion, for example.

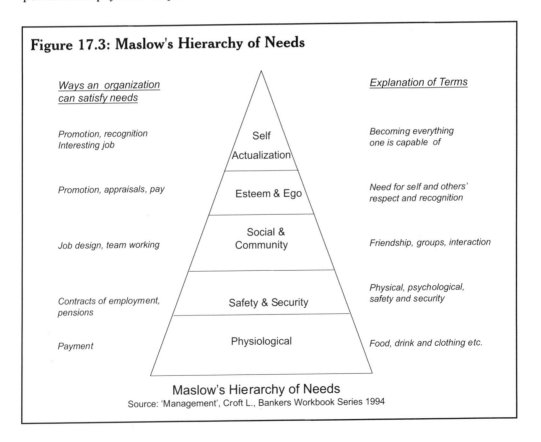

Figure 17.3: Maslow's Hierarchy of Needs

Ways an organization can satisfy needs

Explanation of Terms

Promotion, recognition Interesting job	Self Actualization	Becoming everything one is capable of
Promotion, appraisals, pay	Esteem & Ego	Need for self and others' respect and recognition
Job design, team working	Social & Community	Friendship, groups, interaction
Contracts of employment, pensions	Safety & Security	Physical, psychological, safety and security
Payment	Physiological	Food, drink and clothing etc.

Maslow's Hierarchy of Needs
Source: 'Management', Croft L., Bankers Workbook Series 1994

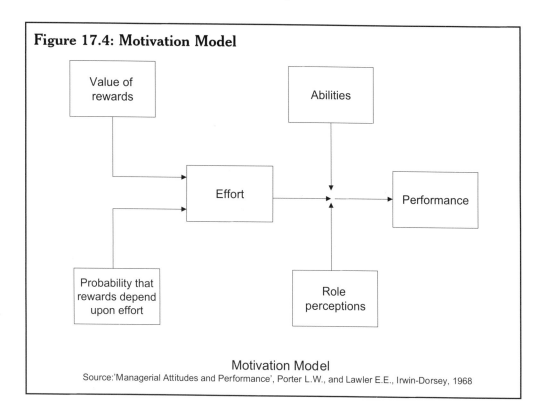

Figure 17.4: Motivation Model

Motivation Model
Source:'Managerial Attitudes and Performance', Porter L.W., and Lawler E.E., Irwin-Dorsey, 1968

However keen people are to do something they will not be able to do it if they do not have the required abilities. This is summarized in the formula

$$\text{Performance} = \text{Ability} \times \text{Motivation}$$

Source: '*Work and Motivation*', Vroom V.H, John Wiley & Sons, 1964.

Targets and Motivation

Some organizations deliberately set highly demanding targets on the basis that if this leaves them with an undershoot then at least what they get is more than what they would have had in the first place. Expectancy theory, however, suggests that targets have to be seen as achievable for them to have the right impact. This is reaffirmed by some work carried out by David McClelland in the late 1950s which suggested that even individuals with a strong need to achieve – who typically would have jobs in a sales environment – were likely in practice to choose only moderately challenging tasks and realistic goals in relation to their abilities and skills.

Another feature of these people with a strong need to achieve was that they continually seek feedback on their performance. This has particular implications for team leaders given the 'major sales' environment of corporate relationship management. Other ways of measuring performance together with high levels of feedback will be necessary to sustain the motivation of these people.

The Role of Money

Money, in the form of pay or some other form of remuneration, is the principle external reward. It is a powerful force because it is linked directly or indirectly to the satisfaction of many needs. It addresses a number of the levels of Maslow's hierarchy from the bottom to the top. In the case of rewards, there has to be a reasonable expectation that they are achievable and fair and equitable or people will just switch off.

At the end of the day, the bank has to make assumptions about what people want when deciding how they should be motivated. This is the challenge of motivation because of the inadequate understanding of the process and the fact that the value of rewards is very much in the eye of the beholder.

In many organizations today there is much debate around the issue of work/life balance, particularly in professional firms and other services such as consultancy where long hours are traditionally worked. In some organizations the balance can be pretty much all work, no life. This has a very definite impact on the level of motivation of staff.

To counter this many organizations are looking more at the benefits of the overall package supplied to meet the needs of employees. The benefits packages are designed to allow the individual to determine what is important to them – ie what their drivers will be.

Two such areas are voluntary benefits, where the individual can opt to use them if appropriate, and flexible benefits that are part of what is traditionally referred to as the 'package'. Voluntary benefits include elements such as preferential rates for products and services, eg discounted insurance (for car/home/pets), holidays at discounted rates, the ability to buy products such as electrical items at significantly lower than the standard retail price. Many employers do not have the purchasing power to negotiate these deals on their own, so go to specialist providers.

Flexible benefits are different because they are an integral part of the package. Such benefits include the ability to 'buy' or 'sell' holidays, flex life and health cover as personal situations change, get a car upgrade/downgrade. These all contribute towards an overall remuneration package that can be flexible enough to meet the diverse and exacting demands of the individuals who work within the organization.

This has a number of inferences for the team leader in terms of combining good selection with good training and coaching and management of the internal and external factors. To deal with team members effectively you must know their needs. They may tell you what salary and benefits they want but they may not tell you what the internal drivers are such as security or recognition, and these need to be uncovered. The team leader will need to go a step further and be more creative in thinking about the whole benefits package. Job enrichment through job redesign to broaden responsibilities might be one response. We shall look at this again when we consider performance management later.

Motivation through Corporate Organization

Research consistently points to the personal value of recognition alongside other reward elements. These may be monetarily based, may have some element of razzmatazz such as sales conventions, may result in awards and certificates which are proudly displayed or may be more low key and personal such as hand-written 'thank you' notes

This has much to do with the culture of the organization – what works in some companies may not work in others so care needs to be exercised when importing schemes because they work elsewhere. There needs to be a culture where symbolic awards are recognized as having an intrinsic value before majoring on non-financial rewards. The challenge is to build a culture in which modest rewards are recognized and valued by your management and relationship managers alike as symbols that are associated with performance excellence.

18

RECRUITMENT, TRAINING AND PERFORMANCE MANAGEMENT

18.1 Overview

In this chapter we continue our look at the people issues associated with managing a team of relationship managers.

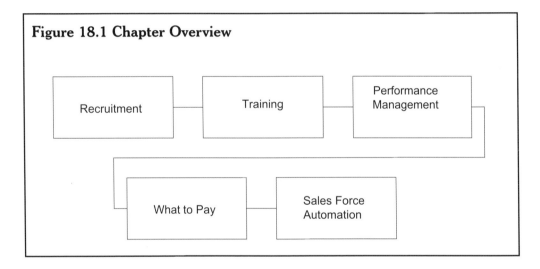

Figure 18.1 Chapter Overview

18.2 Recruitment

Being an Employer of Choice

Many organizations now aspire to be 'employers of choice' but the fact of the matter is that many are unprofessional both in their recruitment and, indeed, induction processes. Evidence of the increase in importance of such issues can be seen in the increased amount of column-inches given to this subject, see for example the *Sunday Times* 'Top 100 firms to work for'.

This is a difficult time for both the recruiter and the applicant. As the team leader this is a perfect time for you to demonstrate all your people skills. Applicants will naturally be nervous – this may be the first time they have interacted with the bank. Whatever the outcome is, it is your responsibility to ensure that their personal dignity remains intact and that their perceptions of the bank are enhanced – remember they can do as much damage as a dissatisfied customer. Get the simple things right – time, place, applicant's name and timely follow up. Think about some of the companies you have applied to – how did you feel about what you went through?

We are assuming that recruitment is carried out under the auspices of the HR function which will keep you sufficiently advised on personnel practices and issues such as contracts of employment, disciplinary and dismissal procedures, discrimination and health and safety at work. You will probably also have a job description and an understanding of the competencies that will constitute successful performance in the role. Remember that recruitment is costly, both in the time it takes to recruit a new member and their subsequent development, but also in terms of the impact a poorly-performing relationship manager can have on the rest of the team.

The early stages of screening may be carried out by an agency or your own HR department. In some cases the recruitment process may start with you but probably be prescribed or guided in a way that delivers consistency. At the end of the day, you may expect to have the final say given that the recruit will be on your team and the personal chemistry allied to technical capabilities will be important. A word of warning – it is estimated that around 70% of application forms and CVs contain an element of deception. (Source Director Magazine April 2002.)

Interviewing

Interviewing practices vary from one-to-one interviews, interviewing panels, selection boards and group selection, often in the form of assessment centres.

Interviews are the most usual method of selection. The purpose of the interview is to predict whether the candidate will be successful in the role he or she is being interviewed for. The interview allows a measure of rapport to be established between interviewer and interviewee – the major shortcoming, however, is that of bias and a lack of personal chemistry in spite of the candidate's ability or vice versa.

Table 18.1 Interview Checklist

Do	Don't
Plan the interview	Start the interview unprepared
Establish an easy and informal relationship	Plunge too quickly into demanding questions
Encourage the candidate to talk	Ask leading questions
Ask open questions to get the candidate to talk	Talk too much yourself
Cover the ground as planned	'Butterfly' around topic areas
Probe where necessary	Jump to conclusions on inadequate evidence
Analyse career and interests to reveal strengths, weaknesses, patterns of behaviour	Pay too much attention to isolated strengths or weaknesses or allow the candidate to gloss over important facts
Maintain control over the direction and time taken by the interview	Be too congenial and have a good but unfocused conversation

Source: Derived from 'A Handbook of Personnel Management Practice', Armstrong M., Kogan Page 1993.

Remember that in any interview the candidate is effectively the customer – shows of corporate strength are unnecessary. If the interview is by panel agree the topic areas that each member will pursue. It is also an exchange of information – the candidate is there also to learn about the company.

One of the challenges is overcoming the 'halo' effect – responding more positively to candidates who in some ways mirror you. This may mean that you are reluctant to ask 'hard' questions. This discriminates against other applicants who, for whatever reason, do not get the same response. To keep your interview process fair and objective you should develop and use a set of structured questions so that the same are asked for each applicant and, perhaps, assign someone as a note-taker to scribe the responses to each question so that a consistent set of notes can be used afterwards for comparison.

Personal and technical capabilities need to be well balanced against the requirements of the role as demonstrated by current high performers. From the job description and the required competencies you should be able to develop a specific set of requirements. In this context some of the retail recruitment maxims of 'hire a smile' and 'hire for attitude' are equally appropriate

Think too in terms of behaviour-based questions. What an applicant has done is a better indicator of future job success than what the applicant believes, feels, thinks, or knows. The following questions are useful in this context:

1. Tell me how you increased teamwork among a previous group with whom you worked.

2. Describe what you liked and disliked about how you were managed in previous positions.

3. Recall a time when you made what you consider a mistake or a bad decision on the job. How did you handle the situation?

4. In your past work life, what kind of co-workers or clients rubbed you the wrong way? How did you respond?

5. Tell me about a time when you set specific work goals for yourself. How did things turn out?

6. Describe a time when you had to criticize or discipline the performance of someone who worked with you or for you. How did you handle the situation? What was the result?

7. Walk me through the major highlights of your career so far and tell me where you want to go next.

8. Tell me about a work emergency or crisis of some kind in which you were involved. What was your role? What did you do?

9. We have all felt stress in our work lives. Tell me about work-related situations that cause stress for you. How do you typically handle such stress?

10. In your most recent position, what did you learn? How did you apply this learning?

11. Tell me about a challenge you faced in a previous work situation. How did you respond?

12. Every manager has to learn to delegate well. Describe a work situation in which you delegated responsibility successfully. Then tell me about a time when your delegation of responsibility did not work out well. How did you handle that situation?

13. What approaches worked best for you in the past in communicating with your boss? With your co-workers? With your subordinates?

14. Tell me about a time when you took charge as a leader in a work situation without being formally assigned to that role by your boss.

15. Tell me about a time when you felt you went beyond the call of duty in helping a client.

Source: *Internet* Arthur H. Bell Professor of Management Communication, McLaren School of Business, University of San Francisco.

Psychometric Tests

Psychometrics tests are a way of providing an objective means of testing individual abilities or characteristics – objective in the sense that the same test is taken by everybody and that over time, given sufficient people have taken the tests, relative abilities can be assessed.

Tests cover:

- intelligence – such as verbal and numerical reasoning;

- aptitude – assessing the ability of the individual to perform a job or specific tasks within a job;

- personality – looking at behaviour, levels of organization and coordination and interaction with the environment.

Given the range of tests on the market it is important to select the right test for the right task. A typical personality test is the Myers-Briggs Type Indicator that can be used for:

Individual development: identifying leadership style, developing managerial potential, time and stress management and executive coaching

Team building and team development: improving communication, enhancing team problem solving, valuing diversity and resolving conflict.

Organizational change: understanding and dealing with responses to rapid change, understanding team and corporate culture.

Education and career counselling: identifying learning styles and motivations, improving teaching and training methods and providing career guidance.

Relationship counselling: improving the quality of relationships and interactions.

It describes an individual's preferences on four dimensions. As the table shows, the person is either:

Table 18.2 Myers Briggs Personality Type Indicators

E Extroverted Prefers to draw energy from the outer world of activity, people and things	or	I Introverted Prefers to draw energy from the inner world of reflections, feelings and ideas
S Sensing Prefers to focus on information gained from the five senses and on practical applications	or	N Intuitive Prefers to focus on patterns, connections and possible meanings
T Thinking Prefers to base decisions on logic and objective analysis of cause and effect	or	F Feeling Prefers to base decisions on a valuing process, considering what is important to people
J Judging Likes a planned organized approach to life and prefers to have things decided	or	P Perceiving Likes a flexible, spontaneous approach and prefers to keep options open

The various combinations of these preferences result in 16 personality 'types', such as ENTS or INTP, each associated with a unique set of behavioural characteristics and values, which provide a useful starting point for individual feedback, self-exploration or group discussion. Many companies from experience are able to determine the characteristics of the people who are most successful and use this as a template for these kinds of tests.

These tests need to be used with care. They need to have been developed by a reputable psychologist, must be specific to the needs of the bank and be interpreted by trained and accredited personnel. If you suspect that a potential employer will use some or all of these tests there are guides available which give you the opportunity to practise in advance!

Assessment Centres

Assessment centres will try to create critical events and activities that will be demanded by the job and will include group exercises, role-plays, in-tray exercises and other forms of practical simulation. They may last from one to a number of days. Assessors typically will be line managers with a ratio of one assessor for each two candidates.

A well-conducted assessment centre can be a better predictor of suitability than interviews by managers carried out in an unskilled way: It has been reported that:

'the probability of selecting an above-average performer by choosing at random is 15%, appraisal data and interviews might raise this to 35%, but if the management information and assessment data are integrated, the probability could be raised to 76%'.

Source: *'A Handbook of Personnel Management Practice;* Armstrong M., Kogan Page 1993.

18.3 Training

Induction

It is surprising how many companies – having suffered the costs and time of the recruitment process then leave new staff to 'jump in at the deep end' with no further guidance beyond Health and Safety manuals and details of the company pension scheme. A well thought-out induction process recognizing the knowledge and anxiety of the new recruit can do much to address the potential stress in the early days.

The induction process then should aim to:

- Put the new member of staff at ease;

- Provide information about working arrangements;

- Indicate the sources of core information such as the company Intranet that form the basis of the induction training;

- Advise the employee as to the nature and extent of any probationary period.

It is often a good move to nominate someone to 'buddy' the new recruit – to show him or her around and make sure he or she settles in as well as possible.

Training

We identified earlier the range of skills that a relationship manager requires and also those for a team leader. Take time to review these and note in particular the nature of the additional skills needed for a team leader or sales manager. Essentially the need for training will be driven by either a corporate desire to improve the skills of a particular population, eg relationship managers, or the needs of an individual as identified by the personal development plan.

Here we shall compare the skills required by a consultative seller with those required by a business partner.

Table 18.3 Consultative Selling & Business Partner Skills

Consultative Seller

- Consultative Selling Skills
- Psychology in Sales Skills
- Key Account Management Skills
- Negotiation Skills
- Advanced Sales Skills
- Fundamental Sales Skills
- Product Knowledge
- Industry Knowledge
- Business Knowledge

Business Partner

As above +
- Strategic Selling Skills

The additional focus on strategic selling for a business partner reflects in particular the longer-term sales cycle associated with major sales.

Training Effectiveness

Lord Leverhulme was quoted as saying that he was aware that 50% of his advertising budget was wasted but he didn't know which 50%. The same could be said of training – except the figures are worse.

There are a number of ways to address this. Firstly, best practice is – having identified the need and the course – to sit down with your team member before they go on the course to establish clearly what the objectives of the training are. Secondly, and probably more importantly, the new skills must be actively coached on return from the training event.

18.4 Performance Management

Management by Objectives

The most common process used for performance planning is management by objectives (MBO). This originated from Peter Drucker's work on the role of management in large corporations, which determined that management has to deal with two dimensions – those of economics and time. Management's role is to organize resources to achieve the required performance – and this is expressed in the form of objectives. These objectives or goals will be many and varied, and part of management's role is to prioritize, ensure the necessary focus and then evaluate the results.

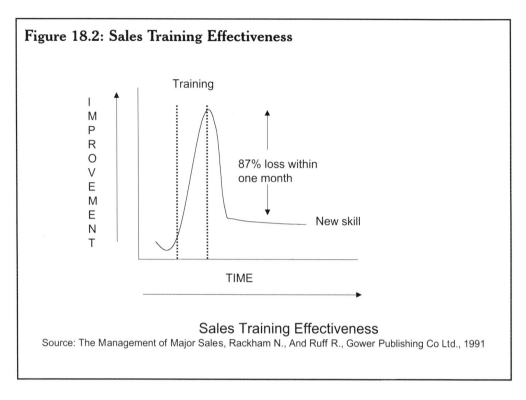

Figure 18.2: Sales Training Effectiveness

Sales Training Effectiveness
Source: The Management of Major Sales, Rackham N., And Ruff R., Gower Publishing Co Ltd., 1991

This objective-setting process has a number of benefits:

● Business activities can be broken down into a series of manageable tasks.

● These tasks can be tested against actual experience.

● This allows performance to be predicted.

● Decisions can be tested real-time.

● A basis is provided for improving performance in the future.

In practice the manager and team member in consultation should determine the performance objectives – the notion of the team member 'owning' the objectives is particularly important. These objectives may relate to work issues and/or areas of personal development and have the benefit of taking the focus off the team members personality and focusing it on what was or was not done.

Another benefit is that, because evaluating past objectives and setting new ones are done at the same time, the manager is able to focus on the future and not just the past. This plays to the manager's role as a coach that we have already identified as a key part of the team leader's role. One of the biggest challenges with MBO is where – say in a team context of product manager and relationship manager – objectives need the support and cooperation of others to be achieved.

Objective Setting

Clearly for MBO to be successful, time and attention needs to be given to identifying the key results areas and the process of goal setting. Here we define an objective as:

'a statement of what an individual is expected to achieve on a continuing and progressive basis over a period of time'.

Table 18.4 Types of Objectives

Types of Objectives
● Targets or budgets that state in quantifiable terms the results to be achieved over a period of time, eg the job holder is expected to generate x income, or process all complaints within 24 hours, or operate within a budget of y;
● Tasks or projects that define a particular task or project which has to be completed by a specific date;
● Performance standards that describe the observable behaviour that indicates that the job has been well done.
Source: '*A Handbook of Personnel Management Practice*', Armstrong M., Kogan Page, 1993.

Note the area covered by the third objective here. Many organizations are giving increasing attention to the way things are done in addition to what is done and this is particularly important both in a customer-facing context and also in terms of the way you interact with your colleagues. Some companies will now dismiss people if they do not practise the values of the company even though they may achieve their quantitative business objectives.

Table 18.5 Illustrative Team Leader Objectives

Performance Target	*Measurement*
Financial To increase income in X Area by X% as agreed with the Regional Director for the year January to December 200X	Target achieved
To design, agree & implement a local business plan, which is communicated to all staff in X Area.	Business plan produced, agreed and implemented. Director to review progress against plan during 1:1s

To design, agree & implement 'target growth' plan. Plan to be in place by end of March 200X	All staff understand local business plan when asked during Director visits
To have a new business acquisition strategy in place with Business Development teams and local Product Partners by end of March 200X for delivery by year end.	Plan in place and communicated to all involved. Progress against plan reviewed by Director during 1:1s

Customers

To instil customer led-culture through

- Improving Customer Experience plan
- Leading by example
- Recognizing appropriate behaviour in team at the time & publicly
- Field visits with all Relationship Managers (at least 2 per quarter – 1 of which must be a prospect)
- Customer meeting Previews/Reviews with all Relationship Managers (at least 2 per quarter – 1 of which must be a prospect)
- Personal discussions with selected customers (minimum 10% of customer base) to review Relationship Manager's service and skills

- Director provides examples of desired behaviours both for self and others
- 360-degree feedback on Director to review leadership
- Customer Service Index
- Contact Reports on personally solicited customer feedback

People

All staff to have Personal Development Plans in place by end of March 200X and reviewed minimum quarterly

Director reviews Staff Opinion Survey

All high-potential staff to be identified by end of April 200X

All action plans to be reviewed monthly with Director

Staff Satisfaction Index to improve by X% and/or achieve minimum level of X%

Staff Opinion Survey (focuses on Management Practices/Communication/ Employee Involvement/Performance Management)

Internal Effectiveness

Credit

- To work with Credit to ensure action plans are in place for all Relationship Manager's credit skills to be at benchmark level
- X% improvement on scores by end H1 through training/coaching

- Reduction seen in numbers of Relationship Manager's rated below benchmark level
- All action plans implemented effectively and reviewed by Regional Director during 1:1s

- To ensure all Relationship Manager's understand risk/reward & Credit responsibilities:
  - Report on time
  - Comply with terms of Sanction
  - Don't exceed authority
  - Professionally monitor customer MI through

- Feedback from Credit to Regional Director

- Output from:
  - previews/reviews; field visits;
  - challenging Relationship Manager's during 1:1s

Operational Excellence
- To ensure all audits completed and areas of operational risk are reported within acceptable tolerances (98%)
- To ensure Know Your Customer is implemented and reported on to 100%
- To ensure all findings are resolved and not reported on subsequently

- Reports/audits/findings

- Feedback from local Key Control Manager

- Spot checks reviewed with Regional Director

What to Measure

It must be possible to measure the outputs from the objective-setting process above to assess the extent to which the objectives have been achieved. This may be expressed as targets, budgets or 'deliverables' as we have identified above. Clearly there should be as little ambiguity as possible and bear in mind even computers do not get it right all of the time!

By their very nature major sales occur infrequently – so measuring sales alone is unlikely to be a dynamic. Earlier at the account planning stage we identified the need to set call objectives that might lead to an advance (where action is agreed that moves the sale forward) or a continuation (where the discussions will continue but no action has been agreed). These offer activity goals as a basis on which to assess performance alongside portfolio profitability.

It follows that measurement should be aimed at developing those constituents of a relationship management culture that we have talked about previously. Many banks are looking at more rounded performance reporting through performance wheels, cockpit dials and the Balanced Scorecard. When you look at the components it may be contrary to think in terms of the 'vital few' but all or a subset of these should constitute the key performance indicators.

Table 18.6 Components of a Balanced Scorecard

Customer Perspective	*Financial Perspective*
Innovative & creative responses to customers' needs	Outperform against target
Customer satisfaction/attitudes	Understand & appropriately price risk
Complaint handling	Portfolio value
Customer retention by segment	Share of wallet
Customer acquisition	Cross-sales ratios
External research rankings, eg Greenwich	Cost of sales
Key customers profiles	Interest margins
Number of referral introductions	Fee income v interest margin income
Strong local profile	Fee income profile
Local market share	Bad debts and provisions
	Sector/country exposure

Internal Business Perspective	*People Perspective*
Compliance with credit rules	Leadership and motivation
Credit application efficiency	Instil a high performance culture
Adherence to key control systems	Demonstrate by example
Use of key relationship management processes	Focus on continuous improvement
Maintain product, industry, and trading area knowledge	Improve performance by use of MIS, observation & coaching
Maintain effective team working with other relationship and operational units	Team working
Maintenance of data quality	Performance improvement plans
Process improvements	
Compliance and regulatory requirements	

If we drill down into one or two of these areas a little more provocatively – how do you think your bank would score on the following criteria?

Sales Effectiveness

In a high-volume sales environment quite often there is close management of what people are doing – activity management such as effective calling programmes, conversion ratios and the value of sales made. This is sales efficiency, getting in front of the right customers, for the right amount of time at a cost that is acceptable to the organization and delivering the required results. Paraphrased this might be described as working harder, not necessarily smarter.

Figure 18.3: Exploring Customer and Staff Focus

Customer Dialogue	Disagree Agree
We are easy to do business with	1 2 3 4 5 6 7
We are fun to do business with	1 2 3 4 5 6 7
We use more than just numbers to understand customer satisfaction	1 2 3 4 5 6 7
We continually educate our customers as to what we will and won't do for them	1 2 3 4 5 6 7
Customers spontaneously tell us how we can improve the way they do business with us	1 2 3 4 5 6 7
Customers feel we know them individually	1 2 3 4 5 6 7
100% of customer complaints are solved at the first point of contact	1 2 3 4 5 6 7
As a customer, speak to any of our staff and you'll immediately know they're on your side	1 2 3 4 5 6 7
We aim to create a WOW customer experience and if it sometimes goes wrong that's an investment we're prepared to make	1 2 3 4 5 6 7
Performance Management	**Disagree Agree**
Staff understand the direct impact they have on the bottom line	1 2 3 4 5 6 7
We measure staff behaviours as part of performance	1 2 3 4 5 6 7
Poor performance is dealt with visibly and immediately	1 2 3 4 5 6 7
We spend as much time analysing good performance as we do poor performance	1 2 3 4 5 6 7
All staff understand completely what good performance looks like	1 2 3 4 5 6 7
Staff have daily performance data	1 2 3 4 5 6 7
Recognition is given more frequently than reward	1 2 3 4 5 6 7
Staff at all levels are trained to apply process analysis tools	1 2 3 4 5 6 7

Exploring Customer and Staff Focus

Figure 18.4: Sales Effectiveness and Account Characteristics

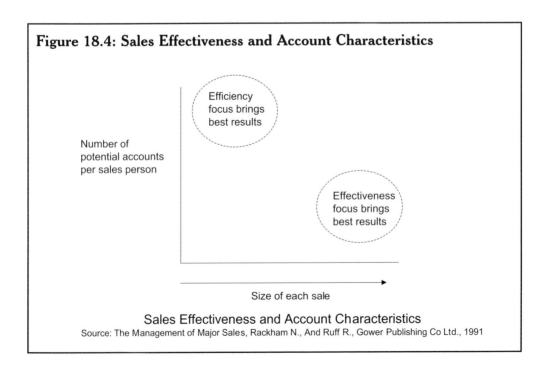

Sales Effectiveness and Account Characteristics
Source: The Management of Major Sales, Rackham N., And Ruff R., Gower Publishing Co Ltd., 1991

Working smarter is about improving sales effectiveness. – which is to do with improving what you do once you get in the door. In major account sales, as we have identified, the dynamic is different – multiple calls with infrequent sales. So what you do when you are with your customers has higher value. This means behaving differently with your customers and here the coaching role of the team leader or sales manager comes into play.

You will have some quantitative data that suggests which relationship managers are doing better than others – new business written, retention levels and overall portfolio income. Asking your top performers how they do it is rarely helpful because experience suggests very few top performers in their field can describe what it is that makes them successful.

So normally you will have to go out with them on calls and work on analysing their behaviour to develop an effectiveness model looking at specific behaviours, having first thought about what these might be:

● Why are they high performing – is it by accident or design?

● What questioning techniques do they use?

● How do they demonstrate their listening skills?

● What level of evident empathy is there between the relationship manager and the customer?

● What best practice is there which should be recycled among the team?

Having collected this data, the next step is to go out with average performers and repeat the process. Then, in comparing the behaviours of the two groups, you seek to establish

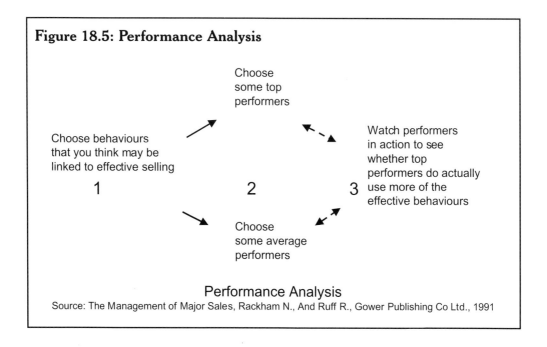

Figure 18.5: Performance Analysis

Choose some top performers

Choose behaviours that you think may be linked to effective selling

1

2

3 Watch performers in action to see whether top performers do actually use more of the effective behaviours

Choose some average performers

Performance Analysis

Source: The Management of Major Sales, Rackham N., And Ruff R., Gower Publishing Co Ltd., 1991

which behaviours differentiate the high performers from the average. Then you have the basis for a coaching programme.

18.5 What to Pay

Many banks have recognized the need to move away from straight salary schemes to more performance-related pay. This has been influenced by the concept of shareholder value, the need to motivate and energize the workforce and retain high performers. This has properly been constrained by the need to balance service with sales, the desire for relationship rather than transactional activity and the need for quality as well as quantity in building assets.

In summary, there are two simple rules at work here:

●   what you pay is what you get;

●   what you measure is what you get.

Both of these rules are extremely powerful influences on behaviour and are generally determined in principle at a corporate level to deliver the desired corporate results.

Reward schemes need to be flexible, transparent, equitable, and easy to administer and fulfil the prime requirement of influencing behaviour. Not all the sales force will necessarily respond in the same way and this needs to be factored into any scheme design. For this reason, incentive schemes should be researched among the participants ahead of implementation to test the potential impact on performance.

Table 18.7 Characteristic of Sales Force Compensation Schemes

Compensation/ Remuneration method	% Use	When especially useful	Advantages	Disadvantages
Straight salary	17.4	Compensating new salespeople; company moves into new sales areas that require developmental work. Salespeople need to perform many non-selling activities.	Gives salesperson maximum amount of security; large amounts of control over sales force; easy to administer; yields more predictable selling expenses	Provides no incentive; necessitates closer supervision of salespeople's activities; during sales decline selling expenses remain at same level
Straight commission	6.5	Highly aggressive selling is required; non-selling tasks are minimized; company cannot closely control sales force activities	Provides maximum amount of incentive; by increasing commission rate, sales managers can encourage salespeople to sell certain items; selling expenses relate directly to sales resources	Salespeople have little financial security; sales manager has minimum control over sales force; may cause salespeople to give inadequate service to smaller accounts; selling costs less predictable
Combination	76.1	Sales territories or portfolios have similar sales potential; company wishes to provide incentive but still control sales-force activities	Provides certain level of financial security; provides some incentive; selling expenses fluctuate with sales revenue	Selling expenses less predictable; may be difficult to administer

Source: *'Marketing Concepts and Strategies'*, Dibb S., Simkin L., Pride W.M., Ferrell O.C., Houghton Mifflin 2001.

The payment mix can be related to the desired areas of performance and a number of hurdles put in place to ensure that business priorities are recognized.

Many companies now think in terms of a 'cafeteria' approach to reward packages that can comprise a number of self-selected elements.

Reward schemes may be individual or group or a combination of both. Group schemes

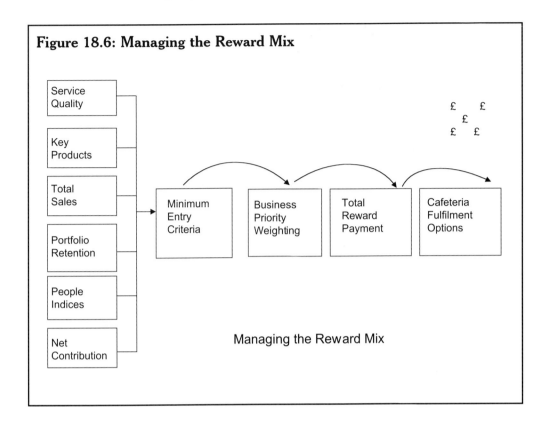

Figure 18.6: Managing the Reward Mix

Service Quality

Key Products

Total Sales

Portfolio Retention

People Indices

Net Contribution

→ Minimum Entry Criteria → Business Priority Weighting → Total Reward Payment → Cafeteria Fulfilment Options

£ £ £ £ £

Managing the Reward Mix

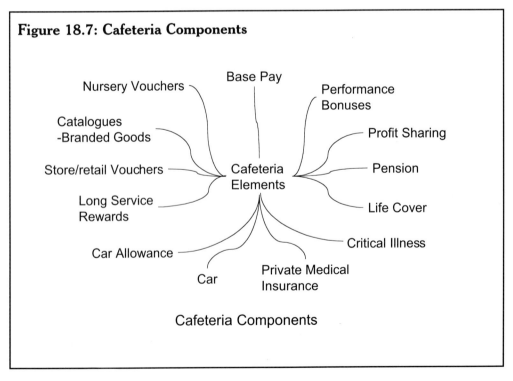

Figure 18.7: Cafeteria Components

Cafeteria Elements

- Base Pay
- Nursery Vouchers
- Performance Bonuses
- Catalogues -Branded Goods
- Profit Sharing
- Store/retail Vouchers
- Pension
- Long Service Rewards
- Life Cover
- Car Allowance
- Critical Illness
- Car
- Private Medical Insurance

Cafeteria Components

work to encourage team spirit, collective responsibility and help to break down demarcation lines. They are particularly relevant where there is a high level of interdependency among the team members in terms of achieving the group output. One of the risks of group bonus schemes is that some team members may 'coast', and this requires careful management.

There are a number of criteria for the success of an incentive scheme:

Table 18.8 Incentive Scheme Success Criteria

- It should be appropriate to the type of work and the staff employed.

- The reward should be clearly and closely linked to the effort of the individual or group.

- Individuals or groups should be able to calculate the reward they get at each level of output they are capable of achieving.

- Individuals or groups should have a reasonable level of control over their efforts and therefore their rewards.

- The scheme should operate by means of a defined and easily understood formula.

- The scheme should be properly installed and maintained.

- Provision should be made for controlling the amounts paid to ensure they are proportionate to effort.

- Provision should be made for amending the rates in defined circumstances.

Source: 'A Handbook of Personnel Management Practice', Armstrong M., Kogan Page 1993.

Strokes

In addition to money, one of the most powerful reward mechanisms is recognition. Any type of recognition, whether verbal or non-verbal, is described as 'strokes' and can be physical or non-physical.

Strokes can be positive or negative. Most people give more importance to and are more affected by negative strokes such as criticism, a pay cut or peremptory behaviour – their impact can outweigh the impact of positive strokes by a ratio of five to one – ie it takes five positive strokes to balance one negative stroke. Think about your own experience here.

Positive strokes might be a smile, a hand-written note of thanks, a pay rise, applause or a compliment from a respected peer or superior. It pays to take time to recognize and celebrate success when it occurs – otherwise it may be overtaken or soured by subsequent events. Acknowledge advancements even if the major sale may still be some way off. Do not be constrained by the environment – in this area determine your own way of working and take care to exhibit a consistent set of values and behaviour.

18.6 Sales Force Automation

Many companies are turning to sales-force automation systems. These often form part of an integrated enterprise-wide CRM system but can also operate on a stand-alone basis. These systems remain relatively rare in the corporate banking environment but they do bring a number of benefits.

Among these are:

● Control of the sales and marketing cycle.

● Once only entry of key data.

● Management of complex relationships between multiple contacts and organizations.

● Enforcement of best practices and processes across the organization.

● Creation of a comprehensive knowledge-base about customers, products and the user's marketplace.

● Easy integration of data and processes with other information systems.

● Complete and consistent visibility of all customer information across the whole business.

● Complete scalability for any number of users both connected and remote and support for a wide choice of user devices.

● Support for a global operations with multiple languages and multiple currencies.

To get a better understanding of what they can do, visit some of the Web sites such as www.siebel.com, www.poweredbyascent.com and www.eware.com.

Looking at one of the areas in a little more detail:

Account Management

This can be used to:

● view a list of accounts and information about them;

● view detailed information about an account, including the contacts, activities, and opportunities associated with the account;

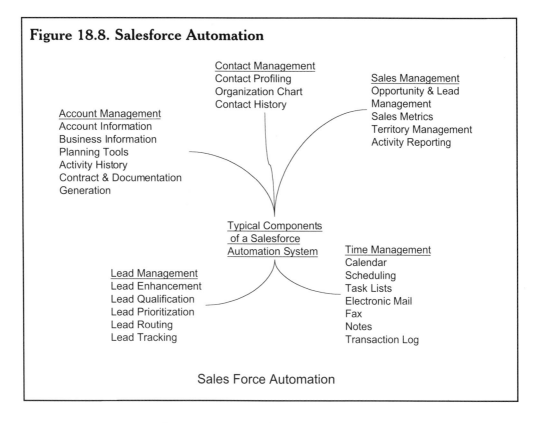

Figure 18.8. Salesforce Automation

Sales Force Automation

- create accounts and enter account information, including information about any parent or sub-accounts;

- define categories of information for accounts;

- view and edit an organization chart for an account;

- attach files created in another application to the account record;

- use charts to review important account information in a graphical format.

Activity Management

An activity is a task or event that is generally, but not always, performed for a contact, account, or an opportunity. You can track various categories of activity. Based on the type of activity you are creating or viewing, all or just a subset of the activities views will be relevant.

This can be used to:

- view a list of all activities or activities related to a particular account;

- enter new activities that are related to accounts;

- view information about an activity, including the status of the activity, priority, and associated dates (for example, when it starts and when it is due);

- enter activities that are administrative or personal;

- update activity information as the status and priority of activities changes;

- prioritize activities and assign scheduling dates;

- attach files created in another application to the record for an activity.

Opportunity Management

An opportunity is defined as a potential revenue-generating event, with a close date, and a win probability. An opportunity is typically related to one or more accounts, contacts, and activities.

Use the opportunities views to:

- view opportunity details, such as, projected close date, revenue amount, and win probability;

- view opportunity-related information about accounts, contacts, and activities;

- view a list of all opportunities in the database;

- enter information about new opportunities;

- track the status of an opportunity through the sales cycle from creation to closure;

- update information about opportunities as they move through the sales cycle;

- use opportunity organization charts to display and edit a visual profile of an opportunity's political structure and reporting hierarchies;

- track notes about opportunities;

- attach files created in another application to the record for an opportunity;

- create a personalized record of information about an opportunity by customizing your own opportunity categories view;

- add new sales cycles.

Source: Siebel Sales CD v 5.0 1999.

19
THE WAY FORWARD

19.1 Chapter Overview

In this chapter we briefly reprise the key themes, reiterate what relationship managers need to do well and finish with an holistic look at the organizational and cultural components of relationship management.

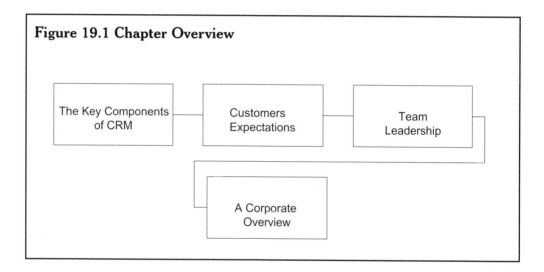

Figure 19.1 Chapter Overview

The Key Components of CRM — Customers Expectations — Team Leadership — A Corporate Overview

19.2 The Key Components of CRM

We shall assume at this stage that a customer relationship management strategy is a given – although recognizing that it is only one of a number of strategic options that a bank can choose. Its appeal is that it can offer a route to competitive differentiation. Essentially the focus on relationship management stems from a very basic economic premise that it is better to keep existing high-value customers rather than go through the lottery of recruiting new customers (Chapter 1).

Effective relationship management is about the successful integration of Processes, People and Technology (PPT). A brief overview of the technology is provided by way of background in Chapter 2. We can superimpose these PPT components over the model for the influences on strategic intent that we looked at in Chapter 3, where other models are also identified that focus the marketing activity of the bank. The need to do this in way that complies with ethical regulatory and best business practice rules surfaces in Chapter 4.

The start point is a clear understanding of the corporate capabilities and key processes in a company using the models and mindsets in Chapters 5 and 6.

Really to be customer-centric, the only way of approaching this is to look into the bank from the outside and see how it looks through the customer's eyes. This may mean 'backward engineering' many established processes so that they become customer-focused – rather in the manner of the Value Chain, again from Chapter 6. Portfolio management (Chapter 7) is a key process element that recognises corporate sales activity is based on a 'major sales' philosophy. In addition, key account planning (Chapter 8), prospecting, lead generation and sales funnel management (Chapter 9) can all be regarded as core processes that may be automated to a greater or lesser extent depending on the approach taken by your bank.

Technology can then be applied in various ways to these processes but in doing so there must be a clear of understanding of the impact it may have on the way things are done, in particular the people aspects. What will staff be expected to differently and how will measurement and reward systems be recalibrated to cause this to happen?

Figure 19.2 Key Components of Relationship Management

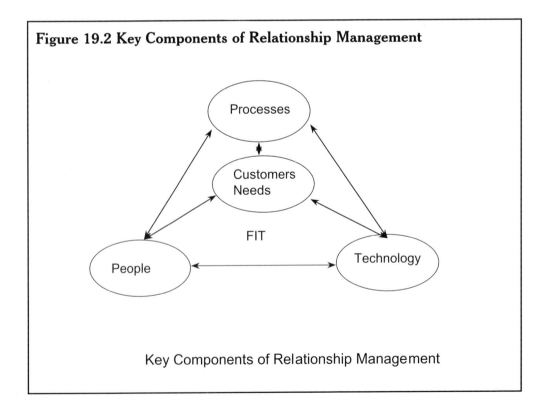

Key Components of Relationship Management

19.3 Customers' Expectations

Research consistently says that customers want their bank – which means their relationship managers – to understand them and their business and to empathize with them if they wish to achieve trusted advisor and strategic partner status.

The starting point is an understanding of the industry and the customer's capabilities (Chapter 10), the way they make decisions (Chapter 11), and the optimum communications mix to move the customer through the relationship cycle (Chapter 12). For a relationship manager, heightened self-awareness and the ability to categorize customers are key capabilities (Chapter 13), as are strong presentation and communication skills (Chapter 14).

A critical concept is that of the 'consultative' mindset introduced in Chapter 15 – trying to understand the customer's issues unencumbered at this stage by the requirements of the bank. This can be helped by a number of the models and processes introduced in the earlier chapters.

19.4 Team Leadership

In the context we are addressing, team leaders and sales managers can be viewed as synonymous. What is particularly noticeable about much of relationship banking, however, is the extent to which it relies on multiple resources and suppliers within the organization. In this context team leader is probably a more appropriate term. The range of activities pertinent to a team leader is identified in Chapters 16 to 18. Particular points of emphasize are the need for situationally appropriate leadership, a strong coaching culture, a compelling mix of tangible and intangible rewards and the 'vital few' key performance indicators that nonetheless measure performance in the round.

19.5 A Corporate Overview

If we tried to thread all these themes together the following sort of picture might emerge. This really emphasizes that in choosing a relationship management strategy the bank must view the organization as a whole and understand the issues of internal connectivity. We could use the McKinsey 7S model to surface the mix of issues. Reflect on your own bank's performance and the relative strengths and weaknesses as you consider the range of issues we have talked about.

Figure 19.3: The McKinsey 7S Framework applied to a Relationship Management Culture

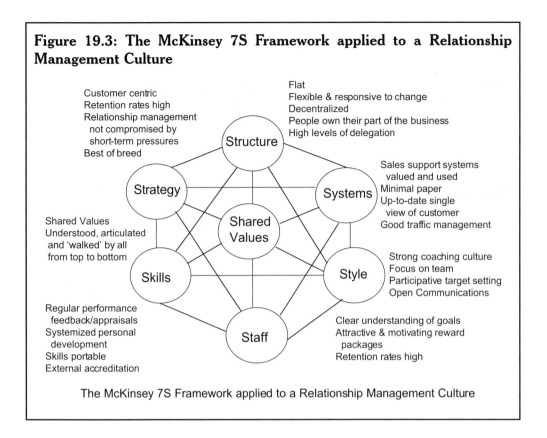

The McKinsey 7S Framework applied to a Relationship Management Culture

Appendix

KEY ACCOUNT PLAN FORMAT

1. Base Information				Date			
Customer				Facilities Review Date			
Completed by				Reviewed by			
Other Bank Relationships				Reviewed by			
Current Income Streams	Deposits	Lending	Fees	Money Transmission		Asset Finance	International Fees
	International Interest Income	Treasury	Other Specialist 1	Other Specialist 2		Other Specialist 3	Total
Description of Business – nature of business – sector/industry – size & ranking – management – no. of employees							
Key Financials	Sales	% change	Profit	% change		Total Assets	% change
	Sales Per Employee		Profit Per Employee			Variable/Fixed Costs Ratio	
	Net Profit/Sales		Net Profit/ Total Assets			Debt/Equity Ratio	
	Geographic Split (1)		Geographic Split (2)			Geographic Split (3)	
How does the company fund itself and manage risk?							

2. Customer's Business Characteristics

7 S Overview – for example - Mission & Values (comment on any recent changes) - Leadership Style - How is the company organized? - How are decisions made? - How do communications flow? - How is performance motivated, evaluated, rewarded? - Who gets ahead & how? - Structure & skills of finance function?	Shared Values (customers, colleagues, partners)	
	Strategy	
	Structure	
	Style	
	Staff	
	Systems	
	Skills	
Customer's Key Performance Indicators		
Basis of Market/ Customer Segmentation		
Customer Proposition		
Customer's Competitive Position - main competitors - source of advantage		
Industry Characteristics -size/growth/ margins		
Customer SWOT	Strengths	Weaknesses
	Opportunities	Threats
Description of Relationship - level of closeness contracting/ expanding /stable sales/progress this year		
What kind of relationship does the customer prefer and what are his expectations of the role of the bank?		

3. Key People Analysis				
Key People 1	Name			
	Position			
Personal Interests				
Social Style	Amiable	Expressive	Analytic	Driver
Key Player Analysis	Playmaker	Agent	Neutral	Enemy
Career Indicator	Performer	Rising Star	Deadwood	Queries
Current Access Level	Met Only	Possible	Easy Access	
Drivers	Personal		Business	
Personal Compelling Value Proposition				
Key People 2	Name			
	Position			
Personal Interests				
Social Style	Amiable	Expressive	Analytic	Driver
Key Player Analysis	Playmaker	Agent	Neutral	Enemy
Career Indicator	Performer	Rising Star	Deadwood	Queries
Current Access Level	Met Only	Possible	Easy Access	
Drivers	Personal		Business	
Personal Compelling Value Proposition				
Key People 3	Name			
	Position			
Personal Interests				
Social Style	Amiable	Expressive	Analytic	Driver
Key Player Analysis	Playmaker	Agent	Neutral	Enemy
Career Indicator	Performer	Rising Star	Deadwood	Queries
Current Access Level	Met Only	Possible	Easy Access	
Drivers	Personal		Business	
Personal Compelling Value Proposition				

4. The Bank's Competitive Positioning				
Current Suppliers	1	2	3	4
Products taken				
Products offered				
Level of Satisfaction				
Analysis	Strengths	Strengths	Strengths	Strengths
Our Position				
	Weaknesses	Weaknesses	Weaknesses	Weaknesses
Our Position				
Estimated Share of Wallet				
Competitor's Probable Strategy & Goals				
Risk of Defection	High	Medium	Low	
To us				
From us				

5 Analysis of Account Relationship		
SWOT Analysis	Strengths	Weaknesses
	Opportunities	Threats
Elevator Summary Speech		

6. Goals & Objectives	
Goal Statement	
Specific SMART Objectives	
1	
2	
3	
4	
5	

7. Strategy & Tactics				
Overall Strategy				
Individual Strategies				
1				
2				
3				
4				
5				
Strategy Strengths				
Strategy Weaknesses				
Tactical Action Plan	What	Who	When	Budget
1				
2				
3				
4				
5				

8. Opportunity Outlook

Event	Description	Value	When	Key Internal Specialists to be involved
1				
2				
3				
4				
5				

9. Plan Conclusions

Assumptions Made	

Risk Identified	Risk	Contingency Plan
1		
2		
3		
4		
5		

Critical Success Factors	
1	
2	
3	
4	
5	
Any Further Comments	

Source: Derived from © ProAct Business Development Ltd. 2001.

BIBLIOGRAPHY

ADAIR, J. (1968) Action Centred Leadership, Wiley, 1968.

ALESSANDRA, A. CATHCART, J. and WEXLER, P., (1988) Selling by Objectives, Prentice Hall.

ARMSTRONG, M. (1991) A Handbook of Personnel Management Practice, Kogan Page.

ARGYRIS, C. (1990) Overcoming Organizational Defenses, Prentice Hall.

BAKER, M.J, (1997) The Marketing Book, Butterworth Heineman.

BELBIN, M. (1981) Management Teams: Why they Succeed or Fail, Heineman.

BERRY, L.L. and PARASURAMAN, A. (1991) Competing through Quality, Simon & Schuster.

BREE T.P. de, (May 2002) Shareholder, Customer and People Value, Financial World.

CHEVETON, P. (2000) Key Account Management, The Route to Profitable Key Supplier Status, Kogan Page.

COOKE, P. (Jan/Feb 2001) Customer Care Means Saying 'No' Sometimes, Customer Management.

COPE, M. (1999) The Seven Cs of Consulting, Prentice Hall.

CROFT, L. (1994) Management, Bankers Workbook Series.

DIBB, S., SIMKIN L.,PRIDE W.M., FERRELL, O.C. (2001) Marketing Concepts and Strategies, Houghton Mifflin.

DOYLE, P. (2000) Value-Based Marketing, John Wiley and Sons Ltd.

EUNSON, B. (1995) Communicating with Customers, John Wiley & Sons.

FSA Handbook Release 001 01 December 2001.

FINANCIAL WORLD (May 2002) Winning through Knowledge Part II.

GREENWICH ASSOCIATES (2001) Financial Services Without Borders, How to Succeed in Professional Financial Services, John Wiley & Sons.

Hall, E.T. (1989) Understanding Cultural Differences, Intellectual Press.

HART, C.W. and JOHNSON, M.D., (Spring 1999) A framework for Developing Trust Relationships, Marketing Management.

HEIMAN. S. and SANCHEZ, D. with TULEJA, T. (1998)The New Strategic Selling, Kogan Page.

INTERNATIONAL JOURNAL OF BANK MARKETING Skills Volume 8 Issue 6, 1990, Volume 9 Number 3,1991, Volume 10 Number 1, 1992.

IRONS K., Managing Services Companies, Strategies for Success, Economic Intelligence Unit, 1994.

JAMES, D. (1999) Managing People in Organizations, CIB Publishing.

JAMES, D. (2002) Personal Development and Team Management, Financial World Publishing.

JOBBER, D. (Ed) (1997) The CIM Handbook of Selling and Sales Strategy, Butterworth Heineman

JONES, G. and GOFFEE, R. (July 2002) The Weak Shall Inherit the Earth, Financial World.

KAPLAN, R. and NORTON, D.P. (1996) The Balanced Scorecard: Translating Strategy into Action, Harvard Business School Press.

KHANDPUR. N.K., WEVERS, J. (1998) Sales Force Automation using Web Technologies, John Wiley & Sons.

KPMG, (1997) Report 'Banks: A Change of Style'.

LAWRENCE, P.A. and LEE, R.A. (1989) Insight into Management, Oxford University Press.

LEFTON, R.R. BUZZOTTA, V.R. SHERBERG, M. (1980) Improving Productivity Through People Skills, Ballinger Publishing Company.

McDONALD, M. and ROGERS B. (1998) Key Account Management, Butterworth Heinemann.

McGREGOR, G. (1966) The Human Side of Enterprise, McGraw-Hill.

MONTGOMERY, R.L.(1981) Listening made Easy, Amacom Books.

NFO FINANCIAL SERVICES, (1998) Middle Market Corporate Banking Survey.

PAYNE, A. (1993) The Essence of Services Marketing, Prentice Hall.

PORTER, M.E. (1985) Competitive Advantage, The Free Press New York.

PORTER, L.W. and LAWLER, E.E. (1968) Managerial Attitudes and Performance, Irwin-Dorsey.

Bibliography

RACKHAM, N. (1988) Account Strategy for Major Sales, Gower Publishing Co. Ltd.

RACKHAM, N. (1990) Making Major Sales, Gower Publishing Co. Ltd.

RACKHAM, N. and RUFF, R. (1991) The Management of Major Sales, Gower Publishing Co. Ltd.

RACKHAM, N. (1995) Spin Selling, Gower Publishing Co. Ltd.

SALES AND MARKETING MANAGEMENT (January 1990) The Shape of Things to Come.

SCHNEIDER, B. and BOWEN, David E. (Fall 1999) Understanding Customer Delight and Outrage, Sloan Management Review.

SENGE, P.M. *et al* (1994) The Fifth Discipline Fieldbook, Brealey Publishing.

SHARMAN, D. (1999) The Perfect Meeting, Random House Business Books.

SHEPPARD, R. (March 2002) So, you Understand Referrals, do you?, Marketing Business.

SCHULTZ, D.E., TANNENBAUM, S.I., and LAUTERBORN, R.F. (1992) Integrated Marketing Communications, NTC Business Books.

SHOSTACK G. Lynn (1987) Service Positioning through Structural Change, Journal of Marketing.

SMITH, M. (December 2001) Picking Up Good Habits, Financial World.

STREWART, R. (1967) Managers and Their Jobs, Macmillan.

TANNENBAUM, R. and SCHIMDT, W. (May-June 1973) How to choose a leadership pattern, Harvard Business Review.

TREACY, M. and WEIRSEMA, F. (1997) The Discipline of Market Leaders, Harper Collins.

TROPMAN, J.E. (1980) Effective Meetings: Improving Group Decision-Making, Sage Publications.

TUCKMAN, B.(1965) Development Sequences in Small Groups, Psychological Bulletin 63.

US BUSINESS BANKING BOARD (1993) Report: Measuring Share of Wallet.

VROOM, V.H. (1964) Work and Motivation, John Wiley & Son.

WADDINGTON, C.H. (1977) Tools for Thought, Jonathon Cape.

WATKIN, C. (July 2002) Style Leaders, Financial World.

WATKINS, C. (1999) Marketing, Sales & Customer Services, The Chartered Institute of Bankers.

WESTLAND, J.C. (1999) Global Electronic Commerce: theory and case studies, Massachusetts Institute of Technology.

YIP, G. and MONTGOMERY, D. (2001) Global CRM Challenges, Critical Marketing.

ZINELDIN, M. (1996) Bank-corporate client 'partnership' relationship: benefits and life cycle, International Journal of Bank Marketing, Vol. 14 No. 3.

INDEX

A

Access channels	24
Account team audit	159
Action plan, formulate an	248
Adoption curve, the	147
Agreement, separating understanding from	216
Amiable	177
Analytical	178
Ansoff's matrix	41
Approach	182
Assertiveness v aggression	173
Assessment centres	262

B

Balanced scorecard	28
Bank silos	73
Bank structure	225
Bank, external to the	66
Bank's competitive positioning	107
Basic account information	105
Beliefs and assumptions	185
Bespoking the product	212
Best practice	110
Blueprinting	84

Body language	180, 190
Boston matrix	40
Boundary spanning	205
Building rapport	207
trust	200
Business characteristics	106
description of	134
development	88
development strategies	93
information	133
plans, the need for	133
Buyers, bargaining power of	36
Buying decisions, types of	139

C

Career indicator	147
Cash cows	41
Categorizing plans	132
Chairperson, the	242
Change – working to make things happen	203
Chinese walls	55
Clarify – understand the real issues	202
Close – signing off with style	204
Closing	192
Coaching	249

Cold calling	120
Communicating effectively	191
Communication styles	175
mix	155
assessing different types of	156
Competitive advantage and differentiation	11
Competitor analysis	108
Competitors, locking out	153
Complaints handling	162
Confidentiality	55
Confirm – measuring the effectiveness of implementation	203
Conflicts of interest	55
Consultative mindset	200
Contact centre	24
management	24
Contact matrix, developing a	157
Contingency approaches	232
Continue – making sure the full benefits are realized	204
Controlled Functions	57
Conversation, Sustaining a	182
Core components	133
purpose	88
Corporate overview	281
Create – developing a deliverable solution	202
Credit	88
Critical success factors	240
CRM, Components of a	
CRM architecture	21
defining	17
drivers of	1
economics of	6
key components of	279
origins of integrated systems	19
Customers	88
getting it right from the start	201
data, external sources of	22
database	22
information systems	22
planning conference	158
profiling	127
satisfaction and loyalty	71

selection criteria	99
self-service	19
know your	56
choosing the right one	8

D

Data protection	57
Data, internal Sources of	24
Datamarts	24
Deal with any resistance	248
Decision-making process	140
Decision-Making Unit (DMU)	142
Delivery options	188
Designated investment business	56
Developing a dialogue	191
Difficult situations	243
Do's and don'ts	246, 250
Dogs 41	
Draft a structure	194
Driver 176	

E

E-commerce	20
Effective listening	178
EFQM excellence model	79
Empathy and trust, importance of	67
Employer, being an employer of choice	257
Ethics	53
Expectancy theory	252
Expressive	177
Eye contact	182

F

Final thoughts	192
Finalize the content	194
Financial	135
Fishbone diagram	82
Five forces analysis	35
Force field analysis	85

Index

G

Gaining agreement	212
commitment	217
Gap 1	65
Gap 2	65
Gap 3	66
Gap 4	66
Gap 5	66
Gap analysis	135
Getting the other person to keep talking	183
Global account management	100
Goals and objectives	107

H

Heterogeneity:	5

I

Income generation	89
Induction	263
Industry assessment	125
profiling	123
types	124
Inseparability	4
Intangibility	4
Interviewing	258

K

Key Account Plan Components	105
Key Player, Identifying the	145
Knowledge Management	25

L

Language	182
Lead Generation	113
Lead Sources	114
Leadership	229
Leadership Styles	230
Legacy systems	21
LePESTCo	32
Letter writing checklist	196
Levels of responsiveness	146

M

Major activities and responsibilities	88
Making sure you understand	184
Management by objectives	264
account	276
activity	277
factors	130
opportunity	278
performance	264
Managing conflict	239
the tensions	70
Market analysis	134
Marketing automation	19
financial services	4
mix	45
plan	45
strategy, building a	32
Marketplace	1
Matching expectations and perceptions	68
Matching perspective, achieving a	153
Maximum leverage, areas of	215
McKinsey 7S framework	76
Measure, what to	268
Measurement, the devil of	30
Measuring accessibility	147
Meeting objectives, setting your	207
Meetings, running effective	239
the need for	239
Middleware	21
Misunderstandings, rigorously testing for	216
Model meeting	247
Money, the role of	254
Motivation	251
through corporate organization	255

N

Need theory	251
Negotiation	213
New entrants, threat of	35

O

Objective setting	266
Offer, defining the	59
On the day	190
Opportunity outlook	107
Organize your material	194
Organizing and structuring the material	194
Outcome, reaching an	216
writing up the	244

P

Pareto analysis	82
Pay, what to	272
People	47, 134
Perishability	5
Personal qualities	167
Personal space	180
Physical cues	180
Place	47
Plan conclusions	107
Planning monitoring and control	228
Popularity stakes, winning the	233
Portfolio analysis	97
planning models	39
Positioning	44
Pre-briefing	187
Present your views	248
Presentation, structuring your	188
Presentations, making	187
Price	46
Probing	183
Process	47
Process mapping and analysis	81

Product	46
Product industries	124
Production analysis	128
Product-market match	127
Promotion	48
Psychometric tests	261

Q

Qualifying leads	117
Question marks (or problem children)	41
Questions, planning and using	216

R

Recruitment	257
Referrals	119
Relationship cycle	152
Relationship manager, role of the	87
Report production	196
Reputational risk	54
Resource management	229
Revenues, forecasting	100
Rivalry among existing firms:	35

S

Sales automation	19
effectiveness	269
making major and complex	89
manager the attributes of a	228
process, summarizing the	220
Sales force automation	19, 276
management	226
management systems	24
objectives	226
strategy	227
structure	227
Sales funnel	116
Saying no	219
yes	219

Segmentation	42
Self-assessment questionnaire	173
Self-image	172
Service and service fulfilment	19
Service industries	125
measurement	63
Service quality	63
gaps	64
factors influencing	66
people related	67
physically related	67
systems related	67
the dimensions of	159
Setting the scene	247
Share of wallet	95
Shared values	77
Shareholder value	27
Single view of customer	24
Situational analysis	32
Skills	78
assessing your own	169
conceptual	229
core	167, 245
facilitation	243
managerial	169
people	245
technical	168
thinking	168
Solution, delivering the	219
presenting the	210
Staff	78
Stars	40
Strategic imperative	3
intent	38
perspective, adopting a	30
Strategy	77
and tactics	107
Strokes	275
Structure	78
Structuring delivery	61
Style	78
Substitutes, threat of	36
Suppliers bargaining power of:	36
SWOT	36, 107
Systems	78
Systems thinking	80

T

Target market selection	39
Target setting	95
Targets and motivation	253
Team behaviour audit	238
building	236
dynamics and behaviours of	234
leadership	281
members	235
presentations	193
role of	234
working	89
Teamwork, improving	236
Telephone appointments	120
Tests cover	261
The four Cs of marketing	48
Time management	220
Training	263
effectiveness	264

U

Understand their views	248
Understanding and evaluating customer	
business plans	132
competition	33
key roles	144
needs	208
people	107
relationships	9
relationship role	165
total offer	60
what customers will pay for	63
yourself	172

V

Value chain analysis	75
equation	210
Voice	181

Working notes   194
Writing a report   193
        an article   196
        as a skill   193